Investment Policy Guidebook

FOR TRUSTEES

FIFTH EDITION

Investment Policy Guidebook FOR TRUSTEES

Eugene B. Burroughs

INTERNATIONAL FOUNDATION OF EMPLOYEE BENEFIT PLANS

The opinions expressed in this book are those of the author and contributors. The International Foundation of Employee Benefit Plans disclaims responsibility for views expressed and statements made in books published by the Foundation.

Edited by Judith A. Sankey, CEBS

Copies of this book may be obtained from:
Publications Department
International Foundation of Employee Benefit Plans
18700 West Bluemound Road
P.O. Box 69
Brookfield, Wisconsin 53008-0069
(262) 786-6710, ext. 8240

Payment must accompany order.

Call (888) 334-3327, option 4, for price information or see www.ifebp.org/bookstore

Published in 2005 by the International Foundation of Employee Benefit Plans, Inc.

Library of Congress Control Number: 2004109103
ISBN 0-89154-590-5
Printed in the United States of America

1M-7.04

Dedication

This book is dedicated to the thousands of women and men
who serve as trustees of employee benefit plans.
In most instances they serve without pay and face the potential
of becoming personally liable for their fund activities.
Because of their unselfish devotion to their task,
many other thousands will enjoy the rewards
of the successful funding of the benefit payments promised.

Table of Contents

Acknowledgments

The first and second editions of this guidebook were prepared by ad hoc committees of the International Foundation in 1976 and 1981. Henry S. Hunt, who chaired both committees, and Marc Gertner participated in writing both the first and second editions. Others who served on the first committee were John H. Blakey, Paul R. Doyle, Harrison Givens Jr., David Livingston, Thomas A. Morton, Juan B. Rael Jr. and Gilbert K. Reeves. Additional members who served on the second committee were H. J. Brownlee, Eugene B. Burroughs, Robert D. Cooper, John P. Dickey, William R. Fry, Joseph J. Gayda, Daniel S. Kampel and Albert Morrison Jr. Many trustees have benefited over the years from the willingness of these International Foundation members to share their time and expertise in this manner.

This and previous editions are not the work of one person. Many individuals, most of whom are actively involved in the educational program of the International Foundation, have directly and indirectly contributed to the publishing of this book. Making significant contributions were Gerard Arnone, Bryce Barnes, Mark Brossman, Susan Brown, Mark Caropreso, Richard Ferlauto, Marc Gertner, Ian D. Lanoff, Vince Martin, Giulio Martini, Jennifer Mink, Terrence Moloznik, Patrick Moore, Paul Patterson, Monte Tarbox, Ralph Weinberg, Jennifer Winfield, Carl Zangardi and Clare Zempel. I have extensively quoted many other individuals to reinforce points I have made and have endeavored in each instance to identify the quotation source. Finally, my wife Betty provided her usual encouragement as I dedicated the necessary time to complete the project.

I would also like to express my appreciation to INTECH and Janus Capital Group Inc. for their significant contribution of providing most of the charts and tables depicted in this book.

I am grateful to each of these individuals for their support and assistance. As with any participation in a Foundation activity, we are the richer for it!

About the Author

Eugene B. Burroughs, CFA
Fairhope, Alabama

Eugene B. Burroughs is an independent investment consultant. He also serves as an advisor to the Taft-Hartley team at INTECH. For 21 years he was director of investments, International Brotherhood of Teamsters, serving as the in-house investment coordinator for the union's operating account and two related pension funds.

Mr. Burroughs is a chartered financial analyst, a past president of the Washington Society of Investment Analysts, a former member of the board of directors of the Financial Analysts Federation (FAF) and was chair of FAF's 1985 annual conference. He received the 1991 *Pension World* Employee Benefits Man of the Year Award and has been the recipient of three presidential appointments to serve on the Advisory Committee of the Pension Benefit Guaranty Corporation.

Mr. Burroughs authored *Investment Success for the Employee Benefit Plan Fiduciary, Investment Policy Guidebook for Trustees,* third and fourth editions, and served as editor of *Trustees and Their Professional Advisors* and *Multiemployer 401(k)/Defined Contribution Plan Guide,* all published by the International Foundation.

An indication of Mr. Burroughs' commitment to the goals of the International Foundation education program is his accumulation thus far of over 500 service credits on his service participation roster. Beginning in 1976, with a presentation at a trustees institute, his contributions have been that of author, speaker, moderator, membership booster, advisory director, committee chair and committee member. He presently serves as a member of the Investment Management Committee.

About the Contributors

Gerard Arnone is currently eastern regional manager for Comerica Bank's Taft-Hartley marketplace. His responsibilities include sales and relationship management. Mr. Arnone has over 30 years' experience working with jointly administered funds. He has a breadth of experience in all phases of trust operations with a heavy concentration in relationship management. He has spoken at International Foundation educational programs.

Bryce Barnes is founder and principal of Quantel Associates, Inc., an independent investment and actuarial consulting firm in Clinton, New Jersey, and has provided consulting services to Taft-Hartley funds for more than 40 years. Services have included the development of asset allocation guidelines based on an analysis of fund liabilities, as well as the selection of investment managers. A frequent speaker, Mr. Barnes has also testified before the U.S. Department of Labor Advisory Council on Employee Welfare and Pension Benefit Plans on the subject of "Soft Dollars and Commission Recapture." He is a certified investment management analyst, a member of the Investment Management Consultants Association, a member of the Investment Consultants Advisory Panel (sponsored by the AFL-CIO Office of Investment) and a member of the American Academy of Actuaries. He received a B.A. degree from Rutgers University, where he majored in mathematics.

Mark E. Brossman is a partner in Schulte Roth & Zabel in New York City, where he heads the firm's employment and employee benefits department. He serves as counsel to numerous multiemployer pension and welfare plans with expertise in investment issues, proxy voting and shareholder activism, fiduciary liability, and tax and litigation issues. Mr. Brossman also serves as special ERISA counsel in problem situations including U.S. Department of Labor investigations and litigations, and as author, teacher and speaker in the ERISA area. He co-authored *Social Investing of Pension Funds: For Love or Money* (International Foundation, 1982) and has written for the *Employee Benefits Journal* and other publications. Mr. Brossman received a B.S. degree in industrial and labor relations from Cornell University and J.D. and LL.M. degrees from New York University School of Law. He is a frequent International Foundation author, speaker and committee member.

Susan I. Brown is an associate at Groom Law Group. She joined the firm in 2003 following a judicial clerkship and two years of private practice in the areas of employee benefits, traditional labor and employment law, and litigation. She works primarily in the areas of ERISA Title I and Title IV. Ms. Brown received her J.D. degree cum laude and Order of the Coif in 2000 from the University of Pennsylvania Law School, where she served as an editor for *The University of Pennsylvania Law Review.* She spent her last year of law study as a visiting student at Stanford University Law School. Following law school, Ms. Brown worked in the U.S. District Court for the Southern District of New York as a law clerk to the Honorable Constance Baker Motley. Ms. Brown earned her B.A. degree magna cum laude and Phi Beta Kappa from Duke University in 1993, and she received an M.A. degree in English literature from Washington University in 1996. She is admitted to practice in the District of Columbia and in New York.

Mark Caropreso is a financial consultant, portfolio manager and financial planning specialist with one of the country's largest financial services firms, where he has worked for over 11 years. He provides investment management consulting services to multiemployer and corporate benefit funds, as well as advising individual investors. Previously, Mr. Caropreso worked as a carpenter through Carpenters' Local #370. He received a B.S. degree in finance at Siena College. Mr. Caropreso is a member of Eastern Contractors Association and the International Foundation of Employee Benefit Plans.

Richard Ferlauto is the director of pension and investment policy for the American Federation of State, County and Municipal Employees (AFSCME), where he is responsible for representing public employee interests in retirement and benefit systems. Prior to joining AFSCME, he was the managing director of Proxy Voter Services, a division of Institutional Shareholder Services, which provides proxy advisory services to Taft-Hartley and public fund sponsors. Mr. Ferlauto also was a consultant with the AFL-CIO, where he helped launch the Office of Investment and its corporate governance program. He is a well-known speaker on corporate governance issues. Mr. Ferlauto worked for the Center for Policy Alternatives, a nonprofit public policy think tank, serving as policy director from 1993-1996. He has served as an expert advisor to the U.S. Department of Labor ERISA Advisory Working Group, the U.S. General Accounting Office, and the U.S. Department of Housing and Urban Development. Mr. Ferlauto is co-author of two books: *A New Housing Policy for America* (Temple University Press) and *Employer-Assisted Housing: A Benefit for the 1900s* (Bureau of National Affairs). He has also been a chief of staff in the New Jersey State Assembly and helped establish the American Affordable Housing Institute at Rutgers, the State University of New Jersey. Mr. Ferlauto is a 1978 graduate of Georgetown University.

Ian D. Lanoff entered the private practice of law in 1982 after serving for five years as administrator of pension and welfare benefit programs at the U.S. Department of Labor, where he was responsible for the development and administration of the Department's ERISA regulations and enforcement policies governing private pension and employee health and welfare plans. Previously, he served as counsel to the U.S. Senate Committee on Labor and Public Welfare and as general counsel to the United Mine Workers of America Health and Retirement funds. At Groom Law Group, Mr. Lanoff represents multiemployer pension and welfare benefit plans, public employee plans, corporate plans, institutions that provide investment advice and services to employee benefit plans, and labor unions and corporations that sponsor plans. He received his B.A. degree and Phi Beta Kappa from the University of Michigan Law School, and his LL.M. degree from Georgetown University Law School. Mr. Lanoff is listed in *The Best Lawyers in America* directory and was included in *Washingtonian* magazine's list of the best lawyers in Washington.

Giulio Martini is senior vice president and head of Quantitative and Currency Strategies–Value Equities, Bernstein Investment Research & Management, a unit of Alliance Capital Management LP. In July 2003, he was appointed to head the newly created quantitative strategies team within the value equities unit. The group is responsible for ensuring the most effective uses of Bernstein's quantitative research within the portfolio management process. Mr. Martini continues to work with international and global value clients and as the lead person shaping currency management tools and strategies. He was named chief international economist with responsibility for currency strategies and senior portfolio manager on the international and global value equities team in 1992. Prior to that, Mr. Martini had served as a senior economist concentrating on U.S. research since joining Bernstein in 1985. Previously, he conducted economic research and taught at the Institute of Employment Policy at Boston University for three years. Mr. Martini earned a B.S. degree from the University of Colorado and an M.A. degree in political economy from Boston University. He also completed all course and examination requirements for the Ph.D. program in economics at Boston University.

Jennifer Mink is a vice president and senior consultant with Investment Performance Services, LLC, an independent investment consulting firm servicing defined benefit and defined contribution plans throughout the United States. She works on all aspects of client funds including investment policy design, asset allocation strategies, performance monitoring and manager searches and is responsible for client relationships and marketing efforts in the Mid-Atlantic region. She also specializes in international equity and hedge fund of funds research and education for IPS. Prior to joining IPS, Ms. Mink served as an investment consultant with Wachovia Securities in Philadelphia, Pennsylvania, where she consulted exclusively for Taft-Hartley benefit funds. Prior to consulting, she started her career as a licensed stockbroker affiliated with AXA Advisors, LLC, where she provided a broad range of financial planning and investment services to individuals and businesses, in addition to conducting comprehensive retirement planning seminars tailored to the Taft-Hartley marketplace. Ms. Mink earned her B.S. degree from North Carolina State University and her M.B.A. degree from Rider University Graduate School of Business.

Terrence S. Moloznik is executive director of investments for the National Electrical Benefit Fund (NEBF), headquartered in Washington, D.C. In this position, he oversees the investment activities for two large retirement funds. He also coordinates the development of investment policies, guidelines and investment strategies for the board of trustees. Prior to his current position, Mr. Moloznik worked for The Bear Stearns companies as a vice president specializing in investment consulting and fiduciary services for benefit funds in the Taft-Hartley and public fund sector. Included in his 29 years of investment experience are several positions with large Taft-Hartley pension funds. Mr. Moloznik is a certified financial planner and has an M.B.A. degree, specializing in investments and marketing. He is a frequent speaker at International Foundation programs.

Patrick Moore is director of client services for Metropolitan West Asset Management LLC, a Los Angeles-based fixed income advisor with $14 billion under management. He has 17 years of experience in the institutional investment industry, across consulting and portfolio management. Since January 2000, Mr. Moore has developed and directed the client services effort at Metropolitan West. He works with the portfolio management team to communicate investment strategies, risks and performance to pension fund, endowment, hospital and mutual fund clients. Prior to joining MWAM, he spent six years at Bankers Trust in Los Angeles where his responsibilities included the delivery of comprehensive consulting services, performance measurement and analysis to Bankers Trust clientele in the South and West. Mr. Moore started his career in 1987 at Wilshire Associates, where he provided asset allocation analysis for banks, insurance companies and investment consultants across the United States, the United Kingdom and Australia. Mr. Moore holds a B.S. degree in mathematics and an M.B.A. degree, both from the University of California, Irvine. He is a member of the Association for Investment Management and Research (AIMR) and the American Statistical Association.

Paul J. Patterson, FSA, is a principal with the Seattle office of Milliman USA and has been with the company since 1970. He specializes in retirement benefits and has recently focused on the actuarial aspects of larger corporate and Taft-Hartley pension plans. In 1995, Mr. Patterson also served as Milliman's first "ambassador" to the United Kingdom, where he helped introduce the company's people and resources and U.S. way of doing business to Milliman's first European partners. He has written numerous articles for professional business journals and spoken at various professional meetings on pension-related topics. Mr. Patterson earned his B.S. degree from Gonzaga University, Spokane, and M.S. degree from the University of Washington. He holds several designations, including fellow, Society of Actuaries; enrolled actuary, ERISA; and member, American Academy of Actuaries. Mr. Patterson is a frequent International Foundation speaker and author.

Monte Tarbox, CEBS, is vice president and director of consulting standards at Independent Fiduciary Services (IFS). He has spent 13 years as an investment consultant serving multiemployer plans in the United States and Australia. Mr. Tarbox joined IFS in 2001 to fill a newly created position as director of consulting standards and to provide investment advice to pension fund trustees. He previously served for two years at the AFL-CIO Center for Working Capital in Washington, D.C. As the first executive director, he established the organization by recruiting staff, organizing conferences for trustees, conducting original research into issues of capital stewardship, publishing a newsletter and developing trustee training curriculum. Prior to his appointment at the Center for Working Capital, Mr. Tarbox spent three years in Australia as a senior investment consultant to Industry Fund Services in Melbourne, Australia. Over that period, he advised funds across a variety of industries, including construction, hospitality, education and public service. In the United States, Mr. Tarbox worked as an investment consultant at the Marco Consulting Group from 1990 to 1996. He served Taft-Hartley defined benefit, defined contribution and medical insurance funds throughout the United States covering electricians, plumbers, carpenters, bricklayers, ironworkers, teamsters and other unionized workers. Mr. Tarbox holds a B.A. degree from Carleton College and an M.B.A. degree from the University of Chicago Graduate School of Business. He obtained the Certified Employee Benefit Specialist (CEBS) designation from the International Foundation in 1995.

Jennifer S. Winfield, CFA, is senior vice president of INTECH. She joined the firm in June 1999 from Manning & Napier Advisors Inc., where she was primarily responsible for the sales and marketing effort of their consulting division. Ms. Winfield spent 11 years prior to that in sales and portfolio management for HSBC Asset Management Americas Inc. and the former Marine Midland Bank with both their domestic and international investment divisions. She holds her chartered financial analyst designation, has an M.B.A. degree in finance from Clarkson University and a B.A. degree in economics from St. Lawrence University. Ms. Winfield has 18 years of investment experience.

Carl Zangardi is vice president, investment specialist at INTECH, with emphasis in the Taft-Hartley market segment. Previously he spent 13 years as vice president of institutional sales and marketing for Prudential Asset Management, where he was responsible for the development, distribution and servicing of institutional asset management products for Taft-Hartley benefit funds. Prior to joining Prudential, Mr. Zangardi was a member of the United Food and Commercial Workers (UFCW), Steelworkers and International Brotherhood of Teamsters (IBT). He served as chairman of the IBT Local 95 Pension and Health and Welfare funds from 1983 to 1990 and as plan administrator for both funds. Mr. Zangardi hold a B.S. degree from Penn State University and an M.B.A. degree from William and Mary.

Preface

This book is written for and dedicated to trustees. It is written for the carpenter, the contractor, the printer, the association executive, the nurse; individuals who though they are very busy in their respective crafts and professions find themselves also serving as fiduciaries of employee benefit funds.

It has not been the author's intent to be either technically precise or to fully explore a particular subject. Rather, the emphasis has been on being practical and, hopefully, insightful. The book is not intended to be an investment treatise, but a reference tool addressing the "what, why and how" of preparing an investment policy statement for a multiemployer plan.

Trustees play a significant role in the benefit payment funding process, for if they collectively address their investment management responsibilities in an objective, professional manner, they may find their stewardship producing over the life of the plan the major portion of the benefit payments stream. Interest compounded, dividends reinvested, rents redeployed and realized capital gains successfully reinvested are powerful elements in the wealth enhancement process. To the degree trustees are successful in systematically adding value over time from investment operations, less of a need exists to increase employer, or employee, contributions to the plan, and potential is enhanced for increasing benefit payments for retirees who no longer contribute productively to the workplace.

The successful funding of the future pension benefit payment promise through investment operations is made possible through the exercise of prudence, the application of time-proven principles, the dedication of people conducting themselves in a professional manner and the resultant efficacy of the adopted policy and practices.

The ultimate goal of this book is to provide a guide to the various steps that are necessary for trustees to take as they finalize an investment policy statement.

Section 402(c) of ERISA permits trustees to delegate authority to manage, acquire or dispose of fund assets to one or more investment managers. Moreover, Section 405(d)(1) provides that if an investment manager has been appointed, "no trustee shall be liable for the acts or omissions of such investment manager or managers, or be under an obligation to invest or otherwise manage any asset of the plan which is subject to the management of such investment manager."

Although the ERISA language would seem to significantly reduce trustee liability for investment decisions, there are some conditions that must be met first. Delegation of investment responsibility requires that: (1) the investment manager is selected with reasonable care and (2) his activities are properly monitored.

These two conditions–careful selection and proper supervision–attach a new priority to the development of a written investment policy. In order to exercise reasonable care in the selection of a manager, trustees first must determine what they expect from their manager. They must formulate specific investment objectives with prospective managers. Obviously, the best way to avoid confusion or misunderstanding about the fund's investment objectives is to put those objectives in writing.

Similarly, if trustees wish to ensure proper supervision of their investment manager once he or she is selected, they must have a set of investment objectives and guidelines against which to measure their manager's performance. These objectives and guidelines must be communicated effectively to the investment manager so that he or she is fully aware of the basis upon which the manager's performance will be evaluated. Again, such objectives and guidelines should be written to avoid any misunderstanding or confusion.

The need for written investment policy is, of course, nothing new. It has always been advantageous for trustees to have a written policy, not only as a defense against personal liability but, equally important, as a practical approach to the rather complex business of investing large sums of money on behalf of plan participants. Even in the absence of any legal considerations, a written investment policy has a number of practical advantages:

- It creates a positive climate in which both the trustees and their manager can talk constructively about what it is they really intend to do with the fund's assets.
- It provides trustees with a rational basis for selecting investment managers who may have different management styles or philosophies.

- It avoids contradictory instructions to the investment manager by giving the manager a clearly defined set of investment goals.
- It helps trustees explain to plan participants or other interested parties why one type of investment was made rather than another.
- It leads to better trustee understanding of financial consequences of various investment alternatives and the impact of investment decisions on the actuarial soundness of the plan.

To reach our ultimate goal of finalizing the investment policy statement for our plan we must proceed in a "procedurally prudent" manner. In other words, we need to use common sense, ask the right questions of the right people, be objective as we debate around the table the pros and cons and come to a consensus as to what appears to be the best course of action over the long term for our fund. Trustees do not need to know the myriad of technical aspects of investing. Their goal should be, however, to cultivate from their storehouse of observations *insightful conclusions* that can resourcefully prepare them to enter into a meaningful dialogue on investment issues with their fellow trustees. A malady of trusteeship today is the potential to suffer from "information overload." From all the chaff that comes one's way it is difficult to identify the kernels of wheat. However, for the trustees who successfully separate out the wheat from the chaff, an investment harvest awaits them!

We will begin "where the buck stops"; you guessed it, with YOU, the trustee. Trustee preparedness will be followed by several chapters on your plan's environment, the multiemployer context, actuarial concerns, the global economic influences on your asset values and legal considerations. Risk and return in the securities markets and the investment characteristics of the various asset classes (which will become your vehicles for funding benefit payments) will provide the context within which you will consider the appropriate performance objectives for your plan.

You are now ready to consider the structure for your portfolio. Subjects such as investment operations, investment management, portfolio guidelines and asset allocation are explored for the purpose of attaining the goal: the finalizing of . . . the investment policy statement.

We will not either implicitly or explicitly recommend a "model" investment policy. In fact, to do so would negate the basic purpose for which this book was written: namely, to assist trustees and their advisors in the development of an investment policy specifically tailored to the needs of their own particular fund. Since no two Taft-Hartley funds are alike in terms of their benefit levels, liquidity needs or cash flows, no two investment policies can be expected to be alike. Appropriate investment objectives for Fund A may be totally inappropriate for Fund B. However, the decision-making process that produces an investment policy statement remains essentially the same for all funds. This *decision-making process* is the focal point of the book.

Although sample investment policies are included, they are intended as *illustrations only*. They illustrate the form and coverage that a carefully designed policy might take. The substance of such a policy, however, is a matter that trustees must decide for themselves.

It also should be emphasized that a written investment policy is not a static document. Indeed, any investment policy must be reviewed periodically to ensure that the investment objectives and guidelines are still realistic in light of changing plan factors and changing economic, social, political and legal conditions. Time and events will have their effect on the profile of the economic environment and on the investment outlook, and a fund's investment policy must be responsive to such changes.

Finally, a word about the "snippets" I will be inserting in the text. A *snippet* is a "scrap of information" that I think you will find helpful. It may be a quotable saying I have collected over time, an observation, an anecdote, even a tongue-in-cheek comment. Whatever, I hope they prove to be insightful, or humorous. Here is one to end this preface. . . .

> **Let not the motivation for developing and adopting an investment policy statement be because you are "legally required" to do so, or because it is the "prudent" thing to do, but because it is the *right thing to do* if you want to maximize the potential to achieve investment success.**

Chapter 1

The Prudent Trustee

If you are serious about the quest to become initially qualified as a *prudent trustee,* and ultimately qualified as a *prudent expert,* your first task is taking inventory of your personal investment awareness. To the degree that you are uncomfortable with investment principles and terminology, you will also to that extent be insecure in investment decision making. Such insecurity will compromise the investment program of the fund that you serve, resulting in inferior performance. Increasing your storehouse of knowledge will not only advance your comfort level in decision making but will also result in enhanced investment return.

> Knowledge, like diversification, also provides investors with protection and profit, with safety and gains . . . By acquiring skills and information, as through diversification, investors gain the performance advantage.
>
> *Brinson/Ibbotson*

More important than acquiring knowledge is *cultivating the proper attitude.* Let's take an attitude check. Do you consider yourself alert, open-minded and patient? These are all characteristics of the prudent trustee.

Being a *goal-oriented person is* also helpful. Four main goals to adopt are:

1. Multiplying your efforts by using the investment professionals that serve your fund
2. Endeavoring to maximize the return of your fund through the application of time-proven investment principles
3. Endeavoring to minimize the risk to your fund by adopting policy guidelines that will protect portfolio values and
4. Focusing on your performance objectives: do not be deterred by all the "media noise" that distracts us from our commitment to long-term goals.

> Any enterprise is built by wise planning, becomes strong through common sense and profits wonderfully by keeping abreast of the facts.
>
> *Book of Proverbs*

Above all else, the prudent trustee knows the right questions to ask. Asking insightful questions leads to solving a plan's investment riddle. Such questions as . . .

1. What are our cash flow needs?
2. What is our investment planning horizon?
3. What are our performance objectives? How much return should we seek? How much risk can we endure while seeking that return?
4. What investment vehicles are we going to authorize for use in the portfolio?
5. What type of investment managers should we seek, and whom should we choose?

In the quest to finalize the appropriate policy, dozens of questions will have to be addressed. This is where patience will have to be exercised; it is a long and arduous task to develop investment policy. This is good; the dialogue will be instructive and the game plan will become obvious as the answers come forth.

There is a difference between being a *prudent person* and qualifying as a *prudent trustee.* All of us in our personal lives recognize the wisdom of exercising sound judgment, of being cautious, discreet, circumspect and managing carefully with economy. But the adoption of the Employee Retirement Income Security Act of 1974 (ERISA) introduced the notion of *prudent expert*–a higher standard to which you will be held as a fiduciary of an employee benefit fund. It is with this higher standard in mind that we will map out a *procedurally prudent* methodology to adopting your plan's investment policy.

Although you may never attain superior investment management skills, you can gradually build upon your common sense, intuition and hard-earned "street-smarts," adding those time-proven principles of investing that will enable you to add value to your fund. Although you may not be judged to be a *prudent expert* now, that is not nearly as important as your willingness to endeavor to become one!

> I will prepare myself, and when the time comes,
> I will be ready.
>
> Abraham Lincoln

Chapter 2

Developing a Global Perspective

By *global* I mean both the BIG picture and *worldwide* in scope.

> A study of economics usually reveals that the best time to buy anything is last year.
>
> Marty Allen

When was the last time you played Monopoly? If the roll of the dice was kind to you, you amassed a fortune as you built hotels on Boardwalk and Park Place. Fortunately, the real "Monopoly Game" you are engaged in as a trustee does not depend upon chance; it is built upon rational securities markets where reward is commensurate with risk.

Unfortunately, many trustees fail to see the relationship between the political, social and economic environment and the values of the securities in their plan's portfolio. Without an appreciation for the cause and effect between the global economic environment and their portfolio, these trustees hope that their random decisions ("roll of the dice") will be favored by Lady Luck and the portfolio will prosper. Rolling the dice is no substitute for investment policy decisions that both exploit, and hedge against, the larger events that affect portfolio values.

> Perspective is the ability to see the forest *and* the trees. To see each part in its relation to the whole. Perspective is the ability to see how financial markets interrelate; to see when a trend is in reality a fad; and when the road most traveled is not necessarily the path to take. Perspective is more than applied experience. More than simply seeing more. It is driven by a vision of knowing what to look for. And supported by the confidence that comes from having the depth of talent needed to produce results. It is a view from the high ground of objectivity. Along with a healthy disregard for the impossible.
>
> *Shearson Lehman/American Express*

Impact of Inflation

In my opinion, the most significant influences on your portfolio's valuations are the level and direction of the prices charged for commodities and services, not only domestically but globally. Whether prices are stable, rising (inflation), rising but at a de-accelerating rate (disinflation) or falling (deflation) will determine whether the portfolio should be tilted toward financial assets (stocks and bonds) or toward tangible assets (real estate, oil and gas, etc.).

As a general rule, you should favor *financial assets* when:

> Invest in inflation. It's the only thing going up.
>
> *Will Rogers*

1. Inflation is stable or declining
2. Government is encouraging private sector activity
3. Economy is growing
4. Productivity is improving and
5. Consumers are saving, and investors are investing.

Conversely, you should favor *tangible assets* when:

1. Prices are rising
2. Taxes are rising
3. Government is overly regulating the private sector and
4. Consumers are not saving, and investors are not investing.

This "tilting" of the portfolio as you observe the various pricing cycles unfold is part of the *asset allocation decision,* which we will cover in detail in a later chapter. The rewards are significant for those plans that fortuitously emphasize those classes of assets that have intrinsic characteristics that are favored in the ensuing price environment, enabling the portfolio to exploit the turning point in the general level of prices.

Investment consultants and investment managers can help you learn from the past; such knowledge will help you and your fellow trustees to deploy, and redeploy, your assets to exploit these price changes. These pricing cycles are long by nature; this is not an attempt to time the shorter cycles in the securities markets and not a suggestion for frequent massive redeployment of the assets.

> Trends, like horses, are easier to ride in the direction they are already going.
>
> *John Naisbitt*

If you have selected a "balanced" manager (one who includes various asset categories in the portfolio), he or she will watch these pricing trends and reallocate the portfolio accordingly. However, if you have a mix of specialist managers (each manager supervising a different asset category), the trustees must assume responsibility for the aggregate portfolio's overall mix. An investment consultant can be helpful in this important decision.

> Inflation is like toothpaste. Once it is out, it's hard to get back in again.
>
> *Anonymous*

Cause and Effect

Since the level of general prices has such a significant impact on our economy, one of the primary tasks of the Federal Reserve is to anticipate the evolving movement of prices and adopt policies to assure continuing economic stability. The Federal Reserve "manages" the economy and promotes price stability through fiscal, monetary and lending policies. These activities can have a significant impact on the level of interest rates.

Interest rates and money supply will affect the gross domestic product. Gross domestic product will affect corporate earnings, which in turn will affect dividends. The levels, and direction, of interest rates and dividend growth will affect the values of the securities in the plan's portfolio.

There *is* a cause and effect relationship between political, social

> Things are not getting worse; things have always been this bad. Nothing is more consoling than the long perspective of history. It will perk you up no end to go back and read the works of progressives past. You will learn therein that things back then were also terrible, and what's more, they were always getting worse. This is most inspiring.
>
> *Molly Ivins*

and economic events and the investment performance of the portfolio. In response to these external influences you will have "winners" and "losers" among the portfolio holdings (hopefully, more winners, in numbers and magnitude, than losers!). To the degree that you see the connection between the economy and your portfolio's securities values, you will become increasingly more confident in your asset allocation decisions.

You and your fellow trustees are not "rolling the dice." You are learning from the past, observing the present and making informed judgments about a probable future. Such prescience will enable you and your fellow trustees to adopt policy that will prove to be successful in the future.

Chapter 3

Risk and Return

The ultimate funding goal of the investment operations is to assure that an adequate amount of dollars will be available on a timely basis to meet the accrued benefit payments. The trustees must balance their desire to enhance the values of the trust fund with a prudent regard for the protection of the accumulated principal. With their desire to control the overall risk posture of the fund, the trustees should adopt policy that will facilitate the achievement of their long-term objectives.

To assist them in this process, the trustees ordinarily retain one or more investment managers who engage in activities targeted to achieve the trustees' investment goals. Thus, it becomes the joint task of the trustees and retained managers to adopt (trustees') and implement (managers') policy that will lead to the creation of a diversified portfolio with a *risk/return posture deemed to be the most appropriate given the funding needs of the plan.*

If you are to participate in the decision regarding the appropriate risk posture for your fund, it is important to understand the risk/return characteristics of the various asset classes. There are two investment principles that are fundamental to achieving success in the investment funding process.

Exhibit 3-1

LEVEL OF RISK ASSUMED
DETERMINES LEVEL OF RETURN ACHIEVED

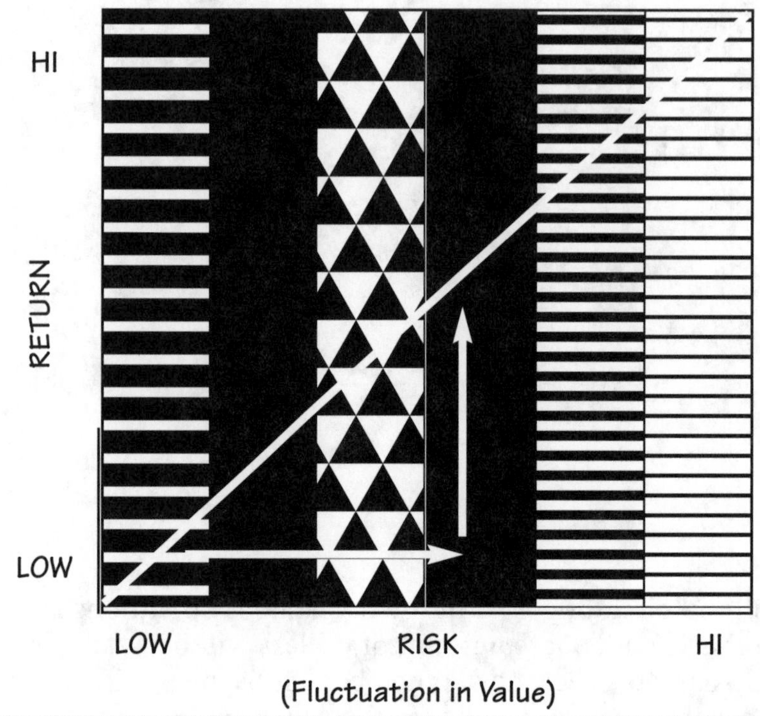

First, *risk and return are related.* The level of risk assumed will determine the level of return achieved. (See Exhibit 3-1.)

Secondly, adopting and adhering to the longest investment planning horizon permissible tends to reduce overall portfolio risk since longer holding periods increase the probability that the historically expected returns from the various asset classes will, in fact, be achieved. (See Exhibit 3-2.)

> Sometimes it's risky not to take a risk—if you walk backward you never stub your toe.
>
> *Harvey Mackay*

Exhibit 3-2

RETURN: EXPECTATIONS VS. REALIZED—
STOCKS, LONG BONDS, REAL ESTATE

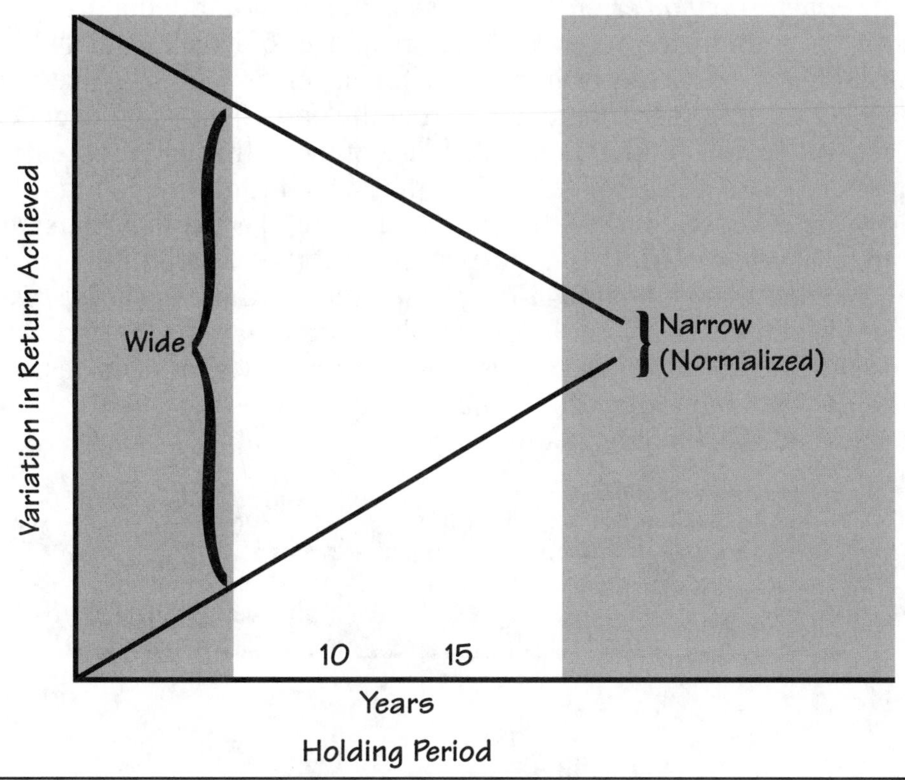

Investment Risk

Risk is a many-faceted concept. The degree of volatility (fluctuation in value) experienced during the holding period, and the uncertainty of the value at termination of the holding period, are risks that are impacted by other risks: financial risk, interest rate risk and purchasing power risk.

Financial (business) risk is the uncertainty embraced by a plan as to whether the companies in the portfolio will remain financially viable. What is the level of assurance that rents will be received, principal returned, dividends received and interest payments collected?

Interest rate (market) risk is the uncertainty that the plan embraces related to the values of the securities in the portfolio during the holding period, and market opportunity levels upon reinvestment of those securities, and the income from the securities. Market price changes in the future positively and negatively impact the value of the securities already in the portfolio.

Purchasing power (inflation) risk is the uncertainty that the plan faces in its ability to preserve the buying power of its accumulated assets. This is particularly important for a pension plan, since it is deemed socially desirable to assure that the participants and beneficiaries will be able to maintain a standard of living throughout their retirement years not too distant from that which they enjoyed in their first year of retirement. With inflation at "only" 4% over 15 years, the purchasing power of $1 is almost cut in half! (See Exhibit 3-3.)

And, if that isn't enough for you to address, there is *manager selection risk,* which is the uncertainty the trustees face as they grant to investment professionals the discretionary supervision of the assets. The decisions made by the manager over time either positively, or negatively, affect plan valuations.

> **The stock market is only distantly related to economics. It's a function of greed, apprehension, and panic, all superimposed on the business cycle.**
>
> *Raymond F. DeVoe Jr.*

Addressing Risk

To specifically address financial (business) risk, trustees can establish guidelines in their investment policy statement to assure that minimum quality standards are preserved in the portfolio construction process. To specifically address interest rate (market) risk, trustees can limit duration, dedicate/immunize, attempt market timing, use options and futures, diversify internationally or use private placements. To specifically address purchasing power (inflation) risk, trustees can purchase U.S. Treasury inflation-protected securities (TIPS), emphasize common stock, or buy real estate and other tangible assets. To specifically address manager selection risk, trustees can retain more than one manager or index all or a portion of the portfolio.

It is worth repeating: *The capital markets over the long term behave rationally; the level of risk embraced is rewarded by a commensurate level of return.* Those asset classes, such as small stocks, that

Exhibit 3-3

THE "HIDDEN" RISK: INFLATION
Loss of Purchasing Power Value of $1

Number of Years	Rate of Inflation 4%	6%	8%	10%
5	$0.82	$0.73	$0.66	$0.59
10	0.66	0.54	0.43	0.35
15	0.54	0.40	0.29	0.21
20	0.44	0.29	0.19	0.12
25	0.36	0.21	0.12	0.07
30	0.29	0.16	0.08	0.04

Source: David Blitzstein.

Exhibit 3-4

NORMAL RANGE OF REAL RETURNS FOR SELECTED ASSET CLASSES

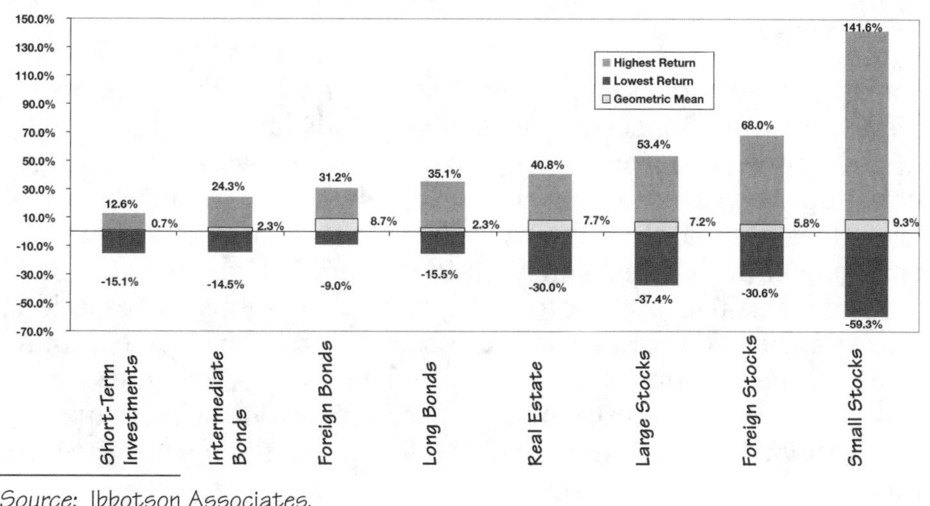

Source: Ibbotson Associates.

experience the greater amount of price volatility during the holding period have also historically produced the highest level of returns. Conversely, those assets with less relative volatility, such as Treasury bills, have produced the lowest level of returns. (See Exhibit 3-4.)

Portfolios that are more heavily weighted with variable assets (stocks, long bonds and equity real estate) are expected to achieve higher *real* rates of return over the long term than portfolios that emphasize the less variable assets, i.e., intermediate and short-term bonds and cash equivalents. However, enduring interim volatility during the holding period is a prerequisite to achieving enhanced portfolio valuations in the future.

Unrealized and Realized Losses

Enduring *changes in value* while holding securities resulting from portfolio volatility is very different from enduring *losses in value* when selling the securities. An inappropriate response (emotional?) during a painful holding period may provoke you to abort the original course of action, and sell, and perhaps *realize* a loss, that in retrospect may have been unnecessary if a "cooler head" had prevailed.

> The roller coaster ride is only dangerous if you get out of the car.
>
> *R. Charles Tschampion*

For convenience in reporting performance, investment managers break up the year into four quarterly "windows." The market, however, does not march to the calendar; we must not adopt portfolio-changing policies based solely on the terminal dates selected for reporting performance. Seek to make rational decisions, not emotional ones; toughen your resolve to increase your *staying power,* permitting an investment course of action to realize its targeted goal. Understanding the risk/return characteristics of the various classes of assets will fortify you against the error of interrupting the normal investing cycles.

Investment Planning Horizon

Time is on your side! The passage of time permits you to:

1. Compound your returns through reinvestment of income and capital gains.

> *Think long term.* Do not let transitory changes in stock prices alter your investment program. There is a lot of noise in the daily volatility of the stock market, which too often is "a tale told by an idiot, full of sound and fury, signifying nothing." (Macbeth would doubtless agree.) Stocks may remain overvalued, or undervalued, for years. Patience and consistency are valuable assets for the intelligent investor. The best rule is: STAY THE COURSE.
>
> *John Bogle*

2. Ride out the inevitable bear markets.
3. Participate in the long-term upward trend of the stock market.

Having your eyes fixated on the proper planning horizon can prevent you from aborting an investment program at the wrong time. You are *investing* plan monies, not speculating on current prices; "hitch your wagon to a star," and ride it for the long term!

Your manager(s) is responsible for the day-to-day decisions and is most probably looking at a time horizon stretching out three to five years. You, as a trustee, are looking longer term and are seeking insight as to those trends that will impact your portfolio far into the future. Identifying the true length of your fund's investment planning horizon is a primary responsibility of the trustees.

> Time marches on. Time dramatically enhances capital accumulation as the magic of compounding accelerates. At an annual return of +10%, the additional capital accumulation on a $10,000 investment is $1,000 in the first year, $2,400 by the tenth year, and $10,000 by the 25th year. At the end of 25 years the total value of the initial $10,000 investment is $108,000, nearly a tenfold increase in value. Give yourself the benefit of all the time you can possibly afford.
>
> *John Bogle*

Diversification

To protect a fund's future valuations from being overly vulnerable to the fortunes of any one asset class, trustees are encouraged to adopt policies that will lead to the construction of *diversified portfolios*. An employee benefit plan portfolio's value is the sum of its component parts. If the plan is to reach its ultimate performance objectives, these component parts must, each in its own way, make a contribution to the whole fund. No class of assets exists in isolation. Such an orderly blending of related investment components is not happenstance but must be carefully orchestrated to produce a harmonious conclusion. Thus, a cardinal rule in plan investing is DIVERSIFY, DIVERSIFY, DIVERSIFY.

> The smart rabbit has three holes.
>
> *Chinese proverb*

Every investment decision should have as its objective either the enhancement of the portfolio's return, or the reduction of risk, or both. The diversified portfolio balances financial risks and returns so that the pursuit of return goals does not entail unnecessary risk. The purpose of diversification is not merely to increase returns, but rather to achieve a desired level of return with a minimum of risk. In a later chapter we will discuss how you can allocate your assets among various classes to *exploit* the risks in the markets to your fund's *return advantage.*

> Diversify. In stocks and bonds, as in much else, there is safety in numbers. No matter how careful you are, no matter how much research you do, you can neither predict nor control the future.
>
> *Sir John Templeton*

Investment Return

Let us now consider *investment return:* the amount we receive in income during the holding period, plus, or minus, the appreciation or depreciation in value upon disposition.

Exhibit 3-5 depicts the various asset classes in the order of their risk/return profile. You will note that whereas Treasury bills have the lowest risk they also provide the lowest return. Conversely, futures contracts are the riskiest asset; also offering the *potential* for the highest return. Within the constraints of your investment planning horizon, you will be best served by permitting your manager to use as many of these asset classes in the portfolio as his or her expertise will allow.

Return and time march along together providing through the power of compounding enhanced portfolio values. *Small* differences in return, compounded year after year, significantly enhance the terminal

Exhibit 3-5

INVESTMENT OPPORTUNITIES

High Expected Return

- Futures contracts
- Gold/precious metals
- Oil drilling partnerships
- Stock index options
- Stock options (puts and calls)
- Small over-the-counter stocks
- Growth stocks
- Real estate growth partnerships
- Real estate income partnerships
- Real estate investment trusts
- Public utility common stocks
- Blue chip common stocks
- Zero coupon bonds
- Convertible bonds
- Bbb corporate bonds
- Bond unit trusts
- Aaa corporate bonds
- Long-term municipal bonds
- Ginnie Maes
- U.S. government bonds
- Annuities
- Bank certificates of deposit
- U.S. Treasury notes
- Short-term municipal bonds
- Money market mutual funds
- Bank money market accounts
- U.S. Treasury bills

Low Expected Return

High Risk

Low Risk

Source: The Complete Investor: Instruments, Markets and Methods, Geoffrey A. Hirt and Stanley B. Block. 1987 Business One Irwin, page 446.

value of the more profitable assets. The longer the funds are left invested, the greater impact compounding will have on the terminal value.

Do you need any further encouragement to maximize the amount of common stock in your portfolio (if your planning horizon permits it) than seeing the compounding effect of having invested in stock over the long term, as reflected in Exhibit 3-6?

In Exhibit 3-7, note how the annual returns from the S&P 500 Common Stock Index have fluctuated from year to year. But look at the ten-year (Exhibit 3-8), and 20-year (Exhibit 3-9) returns. Holding stocks for ten years almost eliminates the possibility of experiencing a down period (one period at −.09%). Holding stocks for 20-year holding periods in the past eliminated all negative returns and resulted in a lowest period return of +3.1%. One cannot be positively assured that the past will repeat itself, but observing the past is a better schoolmaster than speculating that the future will have a different risk/return profile. The lesson here? Exercise *patience* when investing in the variable assets, and you will be rewarded with higher returns.

> Nothing ventured, nothing gained. It pays to take reasonable interim risks in the search for higher long-term rates of return. The magic of compounding accelerates sharply with even modest increases in annual rate of return. While an investment of $10,000 earning an annual return of +10% grows to a value of $108,000 over 25 years, at +12% the final value is $170,000. The difference of $62,000 is more than six times the initial investment itself.
>
> *John Bogle*

Exhibit 3-6

WEALTH INDICES OF INVESTMENTS IN THE U.S. CAPITAL MARKETS 1926-2003 (Year-End 1925=$1)

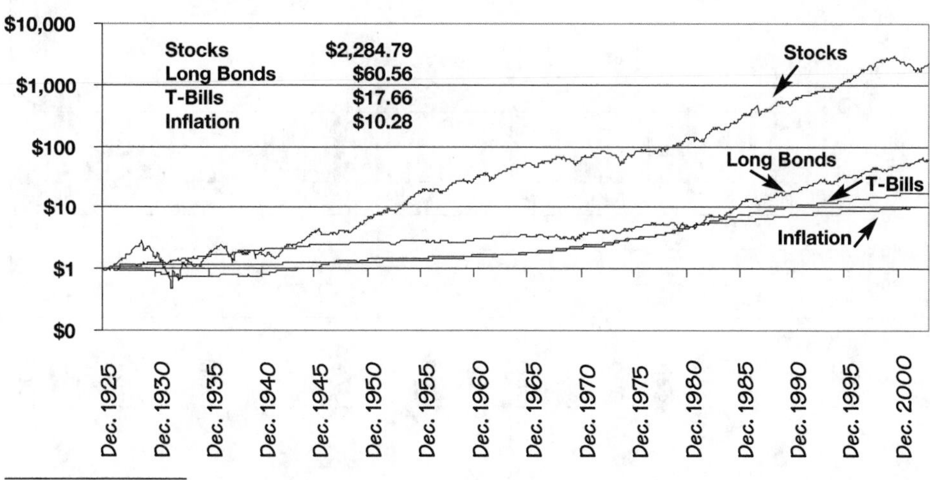

Source: Ibbotson Associates.

Exhibit 3-7

VOLATILITY OF RETURNS—ANNUAL RETURNS

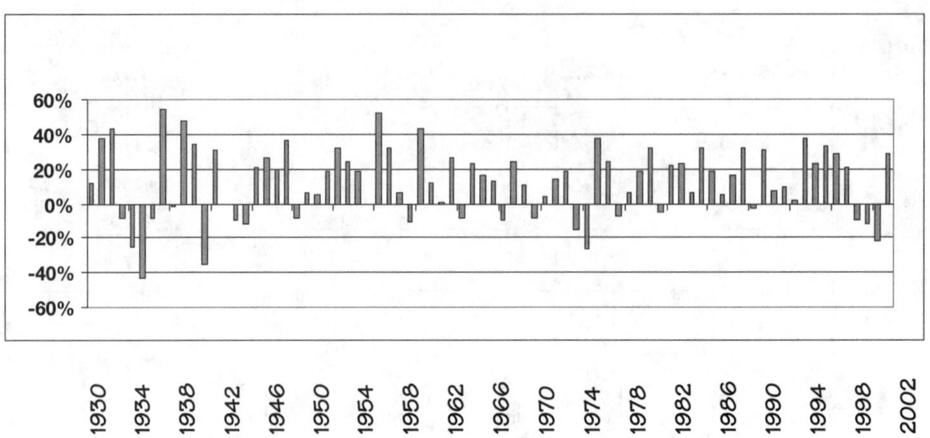

◆ INTERMEDIATE GOVERNMENT BONDS

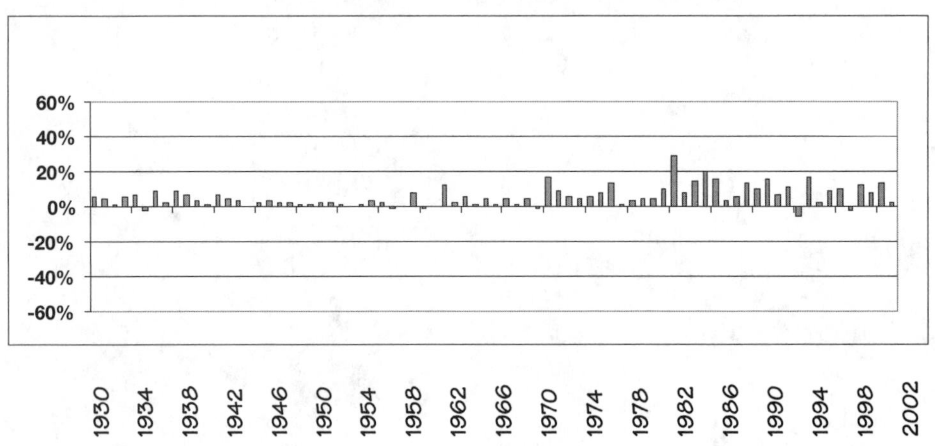

◆ T-BILLS

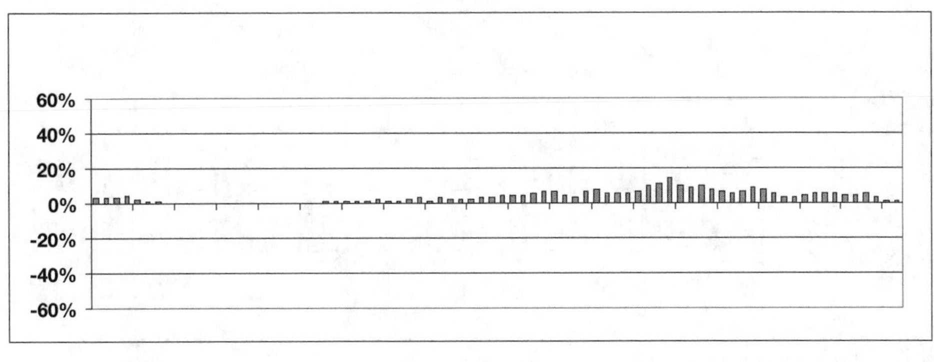

Source: Ibbotson Associates.

Exhibit 3-8

VOLATILITY OF RETURNS— 10-YEAR ANNUALIZED RETURNS

◆ STOCKS

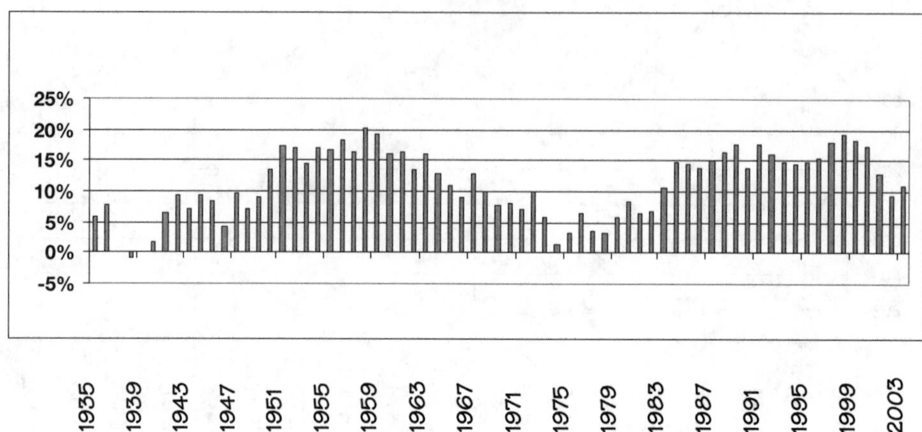

◆ INTERMEDIATE GOVERNMENT BONDS

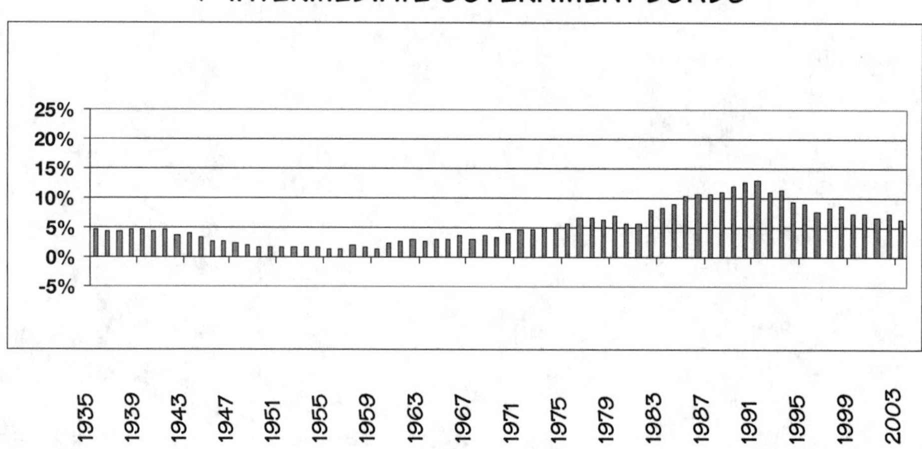

◆ T-BILLS

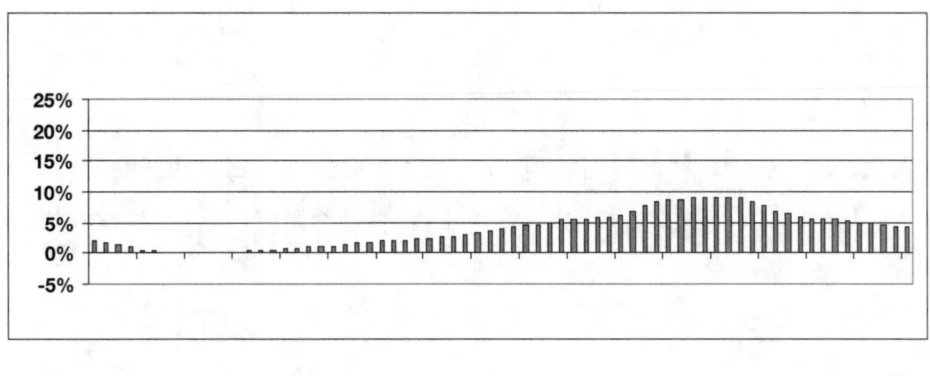

Source: Ibbotson Associates.

Exhibit 3-9

20-YEAR ANNUALIZED RETURNS

◆ STOCKS

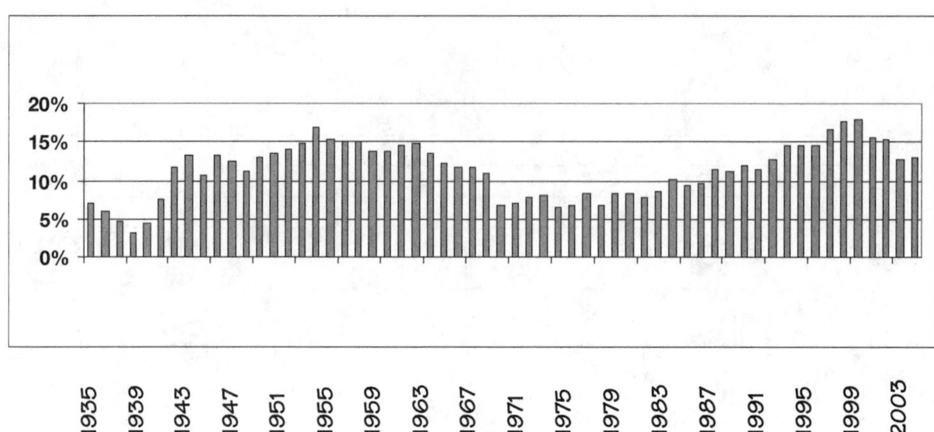

◆ INTERMEDIATE GOVERNMENT BONDS

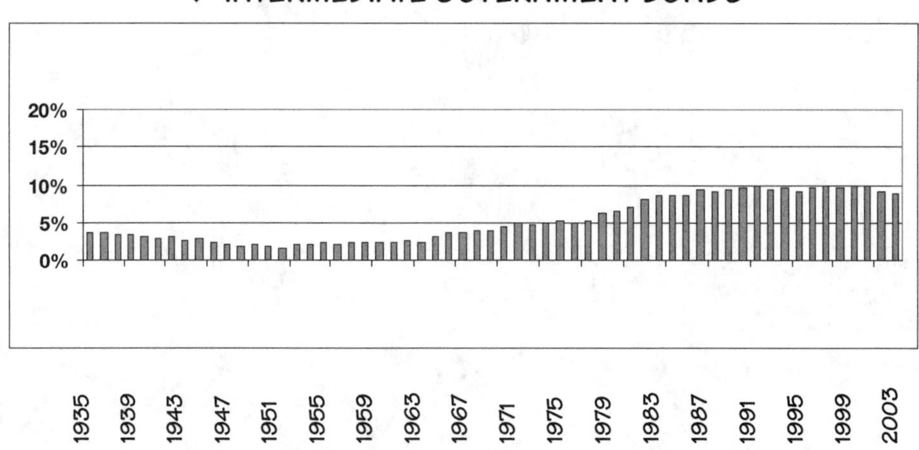

◆ T-BILLS

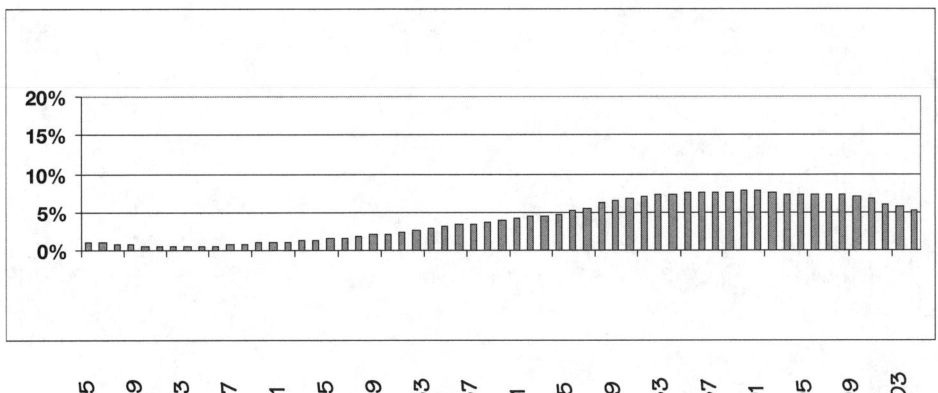

Source: Ibbotson Associates.

Chapter 4

Investment Performance Measurement

Contributed by Patrick Moore
Metropolitan West Asset Management

Introduction

In the presentation of investment performance to plan trustees, rarely, if ever, does the question arise, "How is that return *calculated?*" It's an important point to make because typically, any primer on investment performance measurement would take you through a technical whirlwind of algorithms and statistics including various return and risk measures. While it is certainly helpful to possess some understanding of the computations for these metrics, the development and adoption of standards by professional organizations such as the Association for Investment Management and Research (AIMR) (to be renamed the CFA Institute) and the Investment Management Consulting Association (IMCA) have standardized their reporting so as to rightfully emphasize analysis as opposed to calculation. The development and automation of standardized reporting means that the data can be analyzed with confidence, with little fear of computational error. As a result, this chapter can focus on the framework for such an analytic approach and leaves the arithmetic for another place.

Any performance measurement process has at its root the notion of measurability relative to some benchmark. Much as sports teams' performances are measured with short-term metrics such as game outcomes and longer term metrics such as the standings of wins and losses, investment performance can be evaluated on short- and long-term bases. And, like sports, short-term setbacks, i.e., the occasional loss, do not mean that long-term success is out of reach.

Just as the sports fan does not need to be a professional athlete to be able to tell whether or not her or his team is doing well, the trustee assessing investment performance does not need to be an investment professional (despite what many might like you to believe) to critically evaluate performance. The key to performance evaluation is knowing (1) the investment objective, (2) the appropriate measures (scores and standings) and (3) the benchmarks (opponents) in the process.

The Analytic Framework

An investment program is not unlike any other process in which objectives are set forth and procedures are established for periodic monitoring and requisite adjustment. As with any goal-oriented process, a periodic assessment is necessary to (1) ensure that the objectives of the program are on target to be met and (2) determine the necessity for midcourse reformulation of goals.

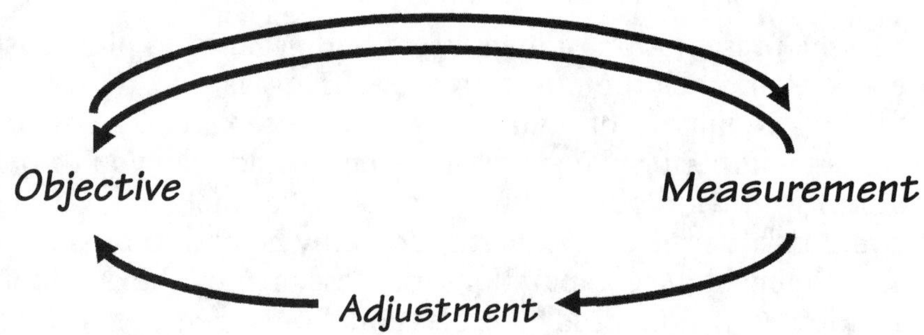

In this continuous cycle, linking the measurement to the objective is the trustee's domain. Of most importance to trustees is the ability to ask the right questions:

- ◆ What are my returns? What are the components of that return?
- ◆ Why does my manager have different numbers than my performance measurement vendor?
- ◆ How do those returns compare to:
  –Spending needs?

–Index benchmarks?
–Other funds/managers?

- How do we act on this information?
- Are managers adding value where they profess expertise and presumably on the basis for which they were hired?

Rate of Return Basics

With investments, the ultimate goal is universally stated in terms of rates of return, and the key metric is the *total* rate of return. The *total rate of return* is simply the sum of the portfolio's (1) change in market value over the period and (2) income (in the form of dividends, coupon payments, rents or interest) divided by the beginning market value.

If the market value falls by an amount that exceeds the income generated during the period, the rate of return will be negative. While this simple return calculation can be complicated by contributions or withdrawals, as a trustee, you should assume that your vendors are adequately equipped to handle cash flows to the portfolio and make adjustments to the calculation as needed.

A Brief Aside on Computational Consistency

While the computation of rates of return has been standardized, there still seems to be no resolution to the occasional performance inconsistencies that arise between investment manager and performance vendor, whether that vendor is a custodial bank or an independent consultant. The reason for the discrepancy is straightforward and comes about despite the good intentions of both manager and vendor. Because the main inputs to the periodic rate of return computation are beginning and ending market values, any disparity between those market values by source may cause computed performance to diverge by source. Most frequently, the difference in market value is explained by how alternate pricing sources value the securities in the portfolio. Why does this occur? Because not all the holdings in your portfolios are exchange traded on a daily basis, like stocks, but instead are traded over the counter more infrequently. As a result, the prices of certain holdings, notably fixed income and real estate, could very well have *estimated* prices on performance measurement dates, which are typically the end of each month or quarter. And, needless to say, different pricing sources will have different prices.

Is this a big deal? Certainly, vast differences in reported prices compromise confidence in at least one of the sources, and efforts should be made to reconcile broad discrepancies. For small differences, we can agree to disagree. The important issue for trustees to know is that, whether large or small, *these discrepancies will be eliminated* at the time of sale because the only price that matters, in the end, is the one that a buyer agrees to pay. Extending the sports parallel from above, for example, it doesn't matter to the outcome of a baseball game if different opinions arise on whether or not a runner got on base via a hit or an error. What matters to the game is whether or not the runner *scores.*

Comparing the Results

Once the rate of return is calculated, the most logical question is "How did we do?" The answer to that depends. Here we introduce the notion of absolute and relative returns. *Absolute return* is an *objective* term and simply means the calculated total rate of return, or the raw return. Recalling our introduction, we would call this *your* scoring output. *Relative return* is a more *subjective* term and refers to performance as it relates to some benchmark or investment alternative, e.g., other managers. In the terms of our introduction, we would call this the score of the game, or your score against some opponent. The reason relative return is more subjective is that, many times, players like to shift opponents in the middle of the game, likely to ones not performing as well.

An example from the late 1990s might best illustrate the point. Through the end of 1999, broad equity market benchmarks such as the Standard & Poor's 500 Equity Index had enjoyed terrific returns, exceeding 20% annually over the preceding three- and five-year measurement periods. Now, if you had a manager that achieved, say, 17% annually over the same time frames, you'd have to admit that *absolute* performance was pretty good, in fact, outstanding. However, since you could have invested in the S&P 500 and achieved better annual returns, you'd likely be disappointed in your *relative* return. (In fact, conservative estimates showed that 75% of active equity managers underperformed the S&P 500 for the five-year period ended December 31, 1999.) Complicating the evaluation of relative return is the ability to compare the performance of your manager with nearly every firm managing client portfolios–It's never too hard to find a higher performer somewhere! At the same time, consultants, managers and sponsors look for ways to explain why their particular performance lagged the benchmarks.

So, what's a trustee to do? A key prescriptive is to always remember a portfolio's objective laid out in the investment policy. This includes not only the overall portfolio's objective, but the objectives for individual manager assignments as well.

For pension plans, a minimum rate of return target is often specified as some real rate of return plus an assumption for inflation. Typically, this is aligned with the actuarial interest rate at which prospective plan benefits are discounted. You will notice that this is more or less an *absolute* rate of return target. If the plan consistently earns a higher rate of return than the actuarial interest rate, then it allows for benefit improvements or, alternatively, reductions in contributions by the sponsor. While the actuarial rate of return represents a minimum target, a more practical performance objective is the outperformance of some benchmark tied to market proxies representative of your asset allocation. For example, if an overall portfolio has a target asset allocation of 60% stocks and 40% bonds, it makes sense to evaluate the performance against a benchmark that blends the returns of two benchmarks: a stock benchmark (60%) and a bond benchmark (40%).

At the individual manager level, target returns are specified invariably as market benchmarks, i.e., *relative* rates of return. Since market benchmarks represent a rate of return that sponsors could obtain (through index managers) at extremely low cost (and getting lower all the time), there's little reason to settle for anything less. As an example, the S&P 500 return can be bought by investors of even middling portfolio sizes for 0.05% to 0.10% of assets under management.

In addition to the ability to obtain index performance at a nominal cost, there's always the option of hiring other managers at the same cost as an existing active manager. When relative performance is measured among various managers of the same asset class, for example, equity managers, or the same investment style within an asset class, for example, short maturity bond managers, a common technique is *universe comparison.* In its most basic form, a universe will consist of the compilation of periodic and cumulative returns of a particular asset class or style, and the rank ordering of those returns. The rank ordering will be scaled from "1" to "100," known as percentiles, with the top performer earning the "1" ranking. The 50th percentile, or median, is the return level at which half the returns are better and half are worse. If a universe is created based on a manager's professed expertise, it is not unreasonable for trustees to expect a manager to be among the top 50% of managers in that universe over *all* measurement periods.

Taking Action (Or Not)

With investment performance computed no less than quarterly, it means that at least four times per year, based on the results, you might feel the urge to take action as it relates to your asset allocation or your managers. As it should, analysis should always lead to options on the taking of action. Certainly one of these options (and always the path of least resistance) is to take no action. More difficult, however, is changing directions, whether it means increasing equity allocation or terminating a persistent underperformer. Any credible analytic process demands occasional, albeit not spurious, action. Otherwise, there may be no point to it.

The key is a well-designed investment policy, implemented dispassionately. By using the investment policy as the touchstone to the process, a constant reminder of performance objectives exists. Usually, the objectives are given adequate time to unfold, typically market cycle-oriented periods of three to seven years. Most often, this patience exists only on paper. When strategies are undertaken, sometimes decision makers expect immediate gratification. While it's not unreasonable to demand performance from your portfolio, part of the rationale for diversification is the expectation that your investments will not move in lockstep. Some will be up, others may be up further, while others may lag. As a trustee, you should have confidence in the process by which your asset allocation was developed rather than in an ability for past performance to dictate future performance. What's worse is to let emotion drive the decision-making process.

Conditions in the fixed income market in 2002 and 2003 punctuate this last point. In mid-2002, investor fears grew into what arguably could be called a panic as a result of an accumulation of unwelcome events: a bear market among equities unseen since the late 1930s, a recession and subsequently sluggish economic recovery, heightened geopolitical fears and corporate governance failures. Driven by a *flight to quality* (tendency of investors to sell risky investments and transfer them to the relative safety of cash and bonds), corporate bonds experienced equitylike price volatility and terrible short-term performance. Managers that held corporate bonds, especially those bonds affected by the uncharacteristically extreme price swings, found their performance diverge dramatically from their benchmarks for a 100-day period in the summer of 2002. Many investors, irrationally thinking that corporate bonds would continue to suffer indefinitely, opted to lock in losses for the "safer" confines of the Treasury bond market. Managers with diversified investments across the fixed income sectors, including corporate bonds, found themselves replaced by managers that had fared relatively well in the flight to quality. Such an emotional, rather than measured, response was costly, as over the next 15 months corporate bonds outperformed Treasury bonds by more than nine percentage points. On a $100 million portfolio, that represents in excess of $9 million!

In baseball, where seasons last 162 games, it's extremely rare to find an ultimate World Series winner that went through the regular schedule without at least one five- or six-game losing streak. Imagine, if on the heels of such a bad spell, wholesale trades took place, or minor leaguers were brought up to play out the season. Is it likely that the goal of reaching and winning the World Series would have been reached? Hardly. Likewise, investment decisions should be driven by a focus on long-term objectives. Reduced pension funding costs or improved participant benefits can be likened to winning a Super Bowl.

That, however, does not mean that critical short-term evaluation cannot take place. With respect to your portfolio managers, the constant questions in front of them should be "Where do you profess to add value?," "How will you demonstrate this?" and "How frequently?" In fact, the investment policy should incorporate a manager's responses to these in the form of an addendum and hold them to it. Any manager that asserts expertise and proves unwilling or unable to support that assertion quantitatively does not deserve to be managing your money. Even without a formal attachment to the investment policy, these are fair questions that deserve attention.

Conclusion

- Pure computation of investment performance does not give the complete picture of how well a portfolio is performing.
- The goal of an investment program should be to relate the measurement process to the objective-setting process so that the portfolio and managers are constantly evaluated under consistent standards.
- Performance measurement becomes meaningful when it is compared with portfolios that adhere to similar guidelines (as created by benchmarks or other investment portfolios).
- By asking the right questions (and making sure that those questions are adequately addressed), trustees can base their decision making on a more systematic process rather than on capricious intuition.

Importantly, the role of trustee is more coach than fan, underscoring the need to adhere to a process of measured and well-informed decision making. More often than not, in sports as well as in investing, sound decisions lead to victory. And isn't that what we're ultimately after, whether the goal is winning a championship or overcoming an unfunded liability?

Chapter 5

The Investment Return Assumption

Contributed by Paul J. Patterson
Milliman USA

Pension Funding Basics

The funding framework of a defined benefit pension plan involves many elements. The investment return assumption used by the plan's actuary has a key role in the way the plan's benefits are designed and delivered. This investment return assumption is in turn influenced by the way the plan's assets are invested.

Over the entire lifetime of the plan the fundamental actuarial mathematics are actually very simple. Contributions plus investment earnings must equal benefits paid plus expenses. The role of the investment return assumption (or interest assumption as it is often called) is to make this equation work when the timing of the payments can differ by many years. The investment return assumption is a measure of the time value of money.

The difference in timing between contributions and benefit payments is what creates the pension fund because contributions made today must be saved and invested to pay retirement benefits in the future. The investment return assumption is used to balance the plan's resources (invested assets plus future income) with its future benefit commitments.

The Actuarial Model

Within the fundamental pension equation (contributions plus investment earnings equal benefits plus expenses) the trustees of a plan have direct control over the benefits. The pension plan is kept in balance (solvent) by the trustees' decisions about the amount and timing of future benefit payments. The plan's actuary helps the trustees in this endeavor.

Actuaries use their expertise in mathematics and computers to develop complex models that simulate the future of a pension plan. Using actuarial assumptions about when people retire, how long they live and a variety of other factors, they predict when and how much will be needed over the future of the plan in order to pay the promised benefits.

In the actuarial model, the investment return assumption helps balance the projected future benefit needs with the invested assets and future income (contributions and investment earnings). In effect, the investment return assumption serves as a fulcrum in the model as the trustees set the future benefit levels to keep the plan in actuarial balance. When the investment return assumption is higher, more income is anticipated from the invested assets so larger benefits appear to be affordable. And of course, the converse is true.

The investment return assumption operates over time. A dollar of benefits today is worth much more than a dollar of benefits ten years from now. Why? Because the dollar paid out today is no longer available to the trust. A dollar saved for ten years, on the other hand, earns investment return. At 7%, for example, it would be worth almost two dollars ten years from now.

The actuarial model and its investment return assumption are budgeting tools that allow longer term benefit planning. They allow the trustees to make decisions about the amounts of benefits affordable by the plan and about distributing these benefits between generations of participants.

It is important to understand that the actuarial model is just that—a model. In reality, the investment return is a result of the fund's investment process, something distinct from the actuarial model. In the long run, the amount of benefits affordable by the plan is not driven by the investment return assumption; it is driven by the actual investment returns.

Understanding the Power of Investment Return

The investment return assumption has a powerful effect on the size of a plan's projected benefit liabilities. Why? Because a pension plan is a long-term undertaking and lifetime pension benefits are paid out over long periods of time. The long-term nature of the liabilities reflects the power of compounding.

A commonly accepted rule of thumb is that a 1% improvement in the actual rate of return during the lifetime of the plan will allow the plan to afford benefits that are 15% to 20% higher! Keep in mind that the higher asset values and the higher benefits they produce are a result of superior investment returns, however, not of the assumption used by the actuary.

It is important to distinguish between the assumed investment return and the actual investment return. The assumed return is an educated guess about actual future returns. Whenever the fund earns more than the assumption, the plan experiences a gain; a loss occurs when the actual return falls short. If more gains than losses occur over a period of years, something must be changed (usually benefits) to bring the plan back into financial balance.

Today's actuarial models take advantage of ever-increasing computer power. They can be used to examine the sensitivity of a plan's benefits and solvency to the investment returns and to the investment return assumption. These tools allow trustees to understand the effects of realizing investment return different from the rate assumed, and to understand the potential benefit implications of their investment decisions.

Laws and Regulations

Federal pension laws require the plan's enrolled actuary to select the investment return assumption based on his or her best estimate. Actuarial standards of practice specify the methods by which actuaries do this. In general, the standards indicate that the investment return assumption consists of several elements: the risk-free rate of return, the inflation component and the risk premium associated with the relative risk of the fund's investments.

The assumed rate of investment return is also guided by the recent history of actual rates of return on a plan's investments. Having noted this, it must also be noted that the assumed rate operates only on future expectations. The actuarial model is required to take into consideration the current value of a fund's assets and by implication, all investment gains or losses to date. The assumed rate of return should be a long-term measure of anticipated returns over both up cycles and down cycles. Its selection should not be overly influenced by inordinately high or low returns in recent periods.

Taken together, the laws and regulations lead the actuary to a range of acceptable investment return assumptions–the "best estimate range." Should the assumed return be set near the high, or low end of this range? The answer to this question may have benefit and funding policy implications.

Policy Issues

Suppose the best estimate range of possible investment return assumptions is 7% to 8%. What rate should be selected for a particular pension plan? The decision of the actuary is affected by a number of factors including the composition of the investment portfolio and the relative maturity of the plan and its industry. Trustee input is also important.

One general policy issue involved in determining where the assumption should fall in the range of possible assumptions can be characterized as "more now versus more later." An assumption at the high end of the range allows the plan to credit larger benefits now at the risk of having to reduce accruals later if the performance fails to achieve the assumption. At the lower end of the range, smaller benefits would be credited now, but with the greater likelihood of increases later on.

Most Taft-Hartley plans end up with an assumed rate of investment return nearer the lower end of the best estimate range because the trustees are more comfortable making the decision about how to improve benefits than about how to cut them.

Pension plans sponsored by companies are better positioned to use a higher investment return assumption. If a company's plan fails to earn the assumed return it can increase its contribution to make up the shortfall. A Taft-Hartley board of trustees seldom has this luxury.

Investment policy also affects the selection of the investment return assumption. A well-managed portfolio with 50% or more allocated to equity investments, for example, has an expected return that is higher than one invested primarily in fixed income instruments. The plan's actuary will take the fund's investment profile into consideration when selecting the assumed rate of return.

Conclusion

The assumed rate of investment return has an important role in helping the pension plan trustees and its advisors set the proper balance between the plan's resources and its benefit commitments. Trustees should make sure they understand the role of the assumption in this process, and in particular they should examine the implications of earning more or less than the amount assumed. With this information the trustees can understand the risk associated with asset returns that differ from the investment return assumption.

In the long run, benefits are driven by the actual investment return. The assumed rate of return is only a tool to help deliver these benefits over time. Keeping this in mind, the fund should strive for the best possible return on its investments and not simply be satisfied to earn the actuarial assumption.

Chapter 6

Legal Considerations in the Investment of Plan Assets

Contributed by Mark E. Brossman
Schulte Roth & Zabel

Trustees of benefit funds are legally responsible for the "prudent" investment of fund assets. This aspect of a trustee's job may be the most important. If the fund's investments are successful, the bargaining parties will have increased flexibility, benefits can be improved, and/or contributions can be reduced. If, on the other hand, the investment results are poor, promised benefits (pension or health and welfare) may become difficult to provide, and difficult choices concerning benefit reductions may have to be made. Further, a trustee's personal liability for a breach of his or her fiduciary duties is the greatest with respect to investment issues because the dollars at stake are so high.

ERISA's Fiduciary Duties

Section 404 of ERISA sets forth the basic responsibilities of a "fiduciary" as follows:

> A fiduciary shall discharge his duties with respect to a plan *solely in the interest* of the participants and the beneficiaries and–
>
> A. For the *exclusive purpose* of:

i. Providing benefits to participants and their beneficiaries and

ii. Defraying reasonable expenses of administering the plan.

B. With the care, skill, *prudence* and diligence under the circumstances then prevailing that a prudent man acting in a like capacity and familiar with such matters would use in the conduct of an enterprise of a like character and with like aims;

C. By *diversifying the investments* of the plan so as to minimize the risk of large losses, unless under the circumstances it is clearly prudent not to do so, . . .

D. *In accordance with the documents* and instruments governing the plan insofar as such documents and instruments are consistent with the provisions of this title.

Prudent Expert

The above statutory requirements have been described as a *prudent expert rule.* If you are responsible for the investment of millions (perhaps billions) of dollars, you will not be judged on how you invest your own personal portfolio. Instead, your decisions will be compared against the investment decisions of other large institutional investors, e.g., other Taft-Hartley funds, college endowments, government funds, corporate funds, etc. Without doubt, large sophisticated institutions utilize professionals to advise them and to manage their investment assets. Your decisions will be judged by a very high standard indeed.

Investment Consultant

The courts have recognized that plan fiduciaries cannot be expert in all phases of employee benefit plans. Investments are very complicated. Accordingly, retain an investment consultant. Trustees have an affirmative obligation to seek the advice and counsel of independent experts when their own ability is insufficient under the circumstances. The consultant's job is to work with the trustees to answer their questions about different asset classes and to develop an asset allocation model. The consultant's advice should set forth the benefits and risk of a particular investment decision in a form that is comprehensible, and should provide sufficient analysis and grounds for making informed decisions.

One of the hallmarks of prudence under ERISA is whether the fiduciary undertook a thorough and complete investigation before embarking on a particular course of investment action. Once the trustees have agreed on the asset allocation, the investment consultant can work with the trustees to locate qualified professional investment managers with expertise in a specific asset class, e.g., large-cap growth.

The investment advisor has one other very important duty. The advisor must provide comparative data to the trustees concerning investment performance. For example, if a fund employs an investment manager who achieved a return of 10% in a given year, this result is in many ways irrelevant. While 10% may seem great, if comparable investment managers utilizing the same investment strategy, e.g., small-cap growth, achieved a 25% return, the manager's performance may have been quite poor. In contrast, a fixed income manager's return of 1% in a year may be outstanding if comparable managers had a negative return.

Duty to Promulgate Investment Guidelines

Under ERISA, investments must be diversified so as to minimize the risk of large losses. Trustees are responsible for setting the overall investment policy including proper diversification. It is recommended that trustees, working with an investment consultant, develop written investment guidelines. There are a myriad of factors to consider when promulgating investment guidelines including:

- ◆ The nature and size of the plan
- ◆ Whether the particular investment is reasonably designed, as part of the portfolio, to further the purposes of the plan, taking into consideration the risk of loss and the opportunity for gain (or other return) associated with the investment
- ◆ The composition of the portfolio with regard to diversification
- ◆ The liquidity and current return of the portfolio relative to the anticipated cash flow requirements of the plan
- ◆ The projected return of the portfolio relative to the funding objectives of the plan.

Guidelines should include:

- ◆ The rate of return sought through management of the plan assets
- ◆ The level of acceptable risk tolerance and diversification latitude
- ◆ A clearly defined delineation of investment restrictions
- ◆ The scope of the investment manager's discretion to acquire and maintain particular forms of assets and to determine the amounts of each type of asset
- ◆ The time frame for measuring performance

- ◆ The procedures to be used in monitoring and evaluating the performance of the investment manager.

Such guidelines assure overall diversification of the portfolio and provide specific direction to investment managers.

Duty to Prudently Select Investment Managers

Retain professional investment managers to invest your fund's assets. ERISA permits the delegation of investment duties to an "investment manager." Under Section 3(38) of ERISA, the following entities may be an investment manager under ERISA, provided that the entity has acknowledged in writing that it is a fiduciary with respect to the plan:

(i) An investment adviser registered under the Investment Advisers Act of 1940, as amended (the "Advisers Act") (in certain circumstances, an investment advisor registered under the laws of a State may qualify as an investment advisor);

(ii) A bank, as defined in the Advisers Act; or

(iii) An insurance company qualified under the laws of more than one State to manage, acquire or dispose of plan assets.

As a trustee of an employee benefit plan, you will be approached by many investment professionals seeking to invest plan assets. Your decision should not be swayed by who wines and dines you the best or takes you golfing, but by the investment manager's experience and ability with the investment style identified for the position in question. In order to prudently select an investment manager you should obtain information including the following:

- ◆ A history of the investment manager's experience in the investment management business, including the total amount of assets under its control
- ◆ A statement of the investment manager's investment approach or philosophy
- ◆ The number of pension plan accounts and other accounts under the investment manager's management and their total current fair market value
- ◆ A detailed schedule of investment management fees
- ◆ A description of the investment manager's current staffing and details as to the general experience and educational qualifications of the individuals who would be primarily responsible for the plan's account

- A tabulation of time-weighted annual rates of total investment return
- The existence of any current or past litigation
- Whether the firm, or any of its principals, has ever undergone bankruptcy, or similar proceedings; has had its registration or license revoked or activities restricted; has ever been sued by a client or the SEC; or has ever been denied fiduciary liability or fidelity insurance
- Financial information relating to the investment manager
- The investment manager's policy with respect to the voting of proxies
- A description of the investment manager's business structure, principal owners and affiliates.

A comprehensive investment management agreement must be executed. While the contents are subject to negotiation, at a minimum the contract should provide representations that the investment manager is an investment manager within the meaning of Section 3(38) of ERISA and is a fiduciary (within the meaning of Section 3(21)(A) of ERISA) with respect to the plan's assets under investment. In addition, the manager must obtain a bond in accordance with Section 412 of ERISA and should maintain fiduciary liability insurance in an amount determined by the plan fiduciaries to be sufficient under the circumstances. Finally, the manager should agree to attend meetings of the board of trustees; obtain "best execution" of all trades; and indemnify the trustees from any damages arising from their breach.

Ongoing Duty to Monitor

Trustees have a duty to monitor the investments made by, and the overall performance of, the investment manager(s). The investment consultant should provide comparative analysis to assist you in evaluating investment results. In addition, trustees should review reports provided by the investment manager; ascertain compliance with the investment guidelines; and meet with the manager from time to time to review performance and the market environment. If a manager underperforms for an appropriate period of time, he or she should be fired. In addition, the asset allocation and investment guidelines should be reviewed periodically. Market conditions change and it may not be prudent to "stay the course."

Proxy Voting Guidelines and Shareholder Activism

The U.S. Department of Labor has held that voting proxies is an element of a trustee's fiduciary responsibility. Many funds have delegated proxy voting to the investment manager. Other funds have promulgated proxy voting guidelines and require investment managers to vote the proxies in accordance with their guidelines. Still others delegate proxy voting to a company specializing in such tasks. Whatever option is adopted, the proxy voting policy should be included in the statement of investment policy.

The DOL has gone further and has encouraged plan fiduciaries to include activities intended to influence the corporations in which a plan owns stock. The DOL has stated that this type of shareholder activism is consistent with ERISA if the policy is based on the reasonable expectation that the value of the plan's investment in the corporation will be enhanced. Accordingly, some funds have engaged in shareholder activism, including the submission of shareholder proposals on a variety of corporate governance and social issues.

Fiduciary Liability

ERISA imposes personal liability on plan fiduciaries who, by breaching their fiduciary duties, cause plans for which they are responsible to incur losses. Section 409 of ERISA provides that a fiduciary who breaches any of the responsibilities, obligations or duties imposed upon him or her as a fiduciary shall be subject to certain penalties, including personal liability to reimburse the plan for any losses resulting from each breach; the possible imposition by the DOL of an additional 20% penalty on the amount involved; responsibility for restoring to the plan any profits made through the use of plan assets; and being subject to such other equitable or remedial relief as a court may deem appropriate.

In order to determine liability, courts have adopted a "but for" approach to assessing money damages for breaches of fiduciary duty. Liability is imposed on the amount that would restore the plan to the position it would have been in "but for" the breach. Hence, even if an improper decision results in a positive return, damages will nevertheless be assessed if a prudent decision would have resulted in an even greater return.

Co-Fiduciary Liability

Section 405(a) of ERISA provides that a plan fiduciary shall be liable for a breach of fiduciary responsibility of another fiduciary with respect to the same plan if he or she:

(i) Participates knowingly in, or knowingly undertakes to

conceal, an act or omission of such other fiduciary, knowing such act or omission to be a breach of fiduciary responsibility;

(ii) By failing to fulfill his or her own fiduciary responsibilities, has enabled the other fiduciary to commit such breach; or

(iii) Has knowledge of a breach by such other fiduciary and fails to make reasonable efforts under the circumstances to remedy the breach.

As a result, a fiduciary cannot escape liability by remaining silent or failing to act. In fact, every fiduciary must exercise prudence to prevent his or her co-fiduciaries from committing a breach of fiduciary responsibility and must jointly manage and control plan assets unless specific duties have been allocated among them.

Fiduciary Duties Unique to Defined Contributions Plans

Section 404(c) of ERISA provides rules for relieving a fiduciary of liability for investment decisions that are "passed through" to plan participants in certain individual account plans, such as money purchase pension plans, profit-sharing plans and 401(k) plans. Under Section 404(c) of ERISA, if a plan provides for individual accounts and permits a participant or beneficiary to exercise control over the assets in his or her account, and that participant or beneficiary actually exercises such control, then he or she will not be deemed a fiduciary by reason of such exercise and any person who is otherwise a plan fiduciary will not be liable for any loss resulting from the participant's or beneficiary's exercise of control over his or her account.

DOL regulations contain requirements in order to derive the benefit of Section 404(c). The regulations provide that:

(i) A plan must provide a participant or beneficiary the opportunity to exercise independent control over the assets in his or her account;

(ii) A plan must offer an opportunity to select, from a broad range of investment alternatives, the manner in which such assets will be invested; and

(iii) A participant or beneficiary must, in fact, exercise such control with respect to the investment of those assets.

Detailed rules and regulations have been adopted dealing with such issues as the types and numbers of investment choices, time periods to change investment choices, information to be provided to participants and beneficiaries, etc.

Soft Dollar Arrangements

"Soft dollar" arrangements often involve a situation where (i) an investment manager of a plan enters into an agreement with a broker whereby the investment manager will direct a certain percentage of its securities transactions to the broker for a commission in return for additional goods or services from the broker, e.g., research; and (ii) where the plan directs the investment manager to execute securities transactions through a brokerage affiliate of the investment consultant in order to receive consulting services with soft dollars. Soft dollar arrangements may run afoul of the fiduciary rules under ERISA because such arrangements may benefit a third party (the broker) or a fiduciary (the investment manager or consultant) instead of the plan and its participants and beneficiaries.

Section 28(e) of the Securities Exchange Act of 1934 provides a safe harbor to investment managers who use commissions generated from the accounts they advise to obtain research and brokerage services. The SEC has warned that the soft dollar practice may be detrimental to plan participants since the higher commissions are passed on to participants. An SEC report cites instances where, instead of receiving research products and services, some investment managers used soft dollars to pay for their own cellular phone services, personal travel, theater tickets, marketing and interior design, and construction expenses. We recommend that contracts with consultants and investment managers require disclosure of all soft dollar arrangements.

Conclusion

Some investments fail. The fact that a particular course of action resulted in a loss is not per se indicative of a lack of prudence. If trustees have carefully and knowledgeably, with the advice of experts, developed an overall investment policy; retained expert investment managers to effectuate their policy; and monitored performance, they will not be liable if some segment of the market drops. Investing is serious. Take it seriously.

Chapter 7

Characteristics of the Asset Classes

An understanding of the differing characteristics of the various asset classes is the first step in developing a portfolio of assets, the aggregate characteristics of which are the most appropriate given the funding objectives of the plan.

Just as you and I have differing personalities, so do bonds, stocks, real estate and the other asset classes. They differ as to degree of:

- ◆ Marketability
- ◆ Stability
- ◆ Liquidity
- ◆ Preservation of purchasing power
- ◆ Growth in value and
- ◆ Current income.

No one asset class, or security, can provide each of these characteristics. In fact, all asset classes are lacking in their ability to provide *all* of these attributes. Thus it is important to understand the differences when deciding which asset classes to authorize for use in the portfolio by the manager and how much of each asset class may be included in the portfolio.

Let us define the various investment characteristics:

- ◆ *Marketability*–the ease with which a security can be bought or sold; listed securities generally have the greatest marketability.

- *Stability*–principal does not fluctuate in value, or if it does, it fluctuates very modestly over time. The opposite of a *stable* asset is a *volatile* asset.
- *Liquidity*–assets with this attribute can be converted to cash without loss in principal value; a *liquid* asset is one that is both highly marketable and stable in value.
- *Preservation of purchasing power*–a characteristic of those assets whose growth in value, plus income, when combined (total return), exceeds the inflation rate. Enables the portfolio to remain competitive with the increasing costs of goods and services.
- *Growth in value*–an asset whose aggregate value increases over time as the result of market appreciation or income reinvested.
- *Current income*–that portion of the return that is received in interest payments, dividends, rents, etc.

Characteristics of the Asset Classes

- *Bonds* generally provide marketability and current income. They are weak in providing stability, liquidity, preservation of purchasing power and growth in value.
- *Stocks* provide marketability (listed stocks), preservation of purchasing power (especially growth stocks) and growth in value. Conversely, they can be unstable, at times illiquid and weak in providing income.
- *Real estate* is strong in providing preservation of purchasing power, current income and growth in value. However, do not look at all for real estate to provide marketability, stability in value or liquidity.
- *Money market instruments* are very strong in providing marketability, stability and liquidity. (Is it any wonder, then, that health and welfare funds favor the use of money market instruments?)

The investment manager is responsible for understanding and evaluating the characteristics of the *individual* securities he or she places in the portfolio. The trustees, however, authorize the classes of assets and therefore must be *acquainted with the attributes of each class.* Building the plan's diversified portfolio involves the selection from among a wide menu of alternatives those classes whose inherent characteristics combine to achieve a collective appropriateness as to quality, return potential and related volatility.

Chapter 8

Bonds

> *Gentlemen prefer bonds.*
>
> *Andrew Mellon*

Bonds have traditionally been the asset class most preferred by trustees in their quest to assure success in the benefit payments funding process. Stocks have always been relegated to minority positions in jointly trusteed plans.

A *bond* is a debt security issued by the government, government agencies, municipalities or corporations. Unlike the stockholder who has an ownership interest in the corporation, a bond purchaser is lending money to the issuer. In return, the purchaser of the bond has a contractual right to receive the principal on the maturity date and periodic interest payments (usually twice a year) from the bond issuer. The reinvestment of these periodic, stated interest payments, known as *coupon* payments, can result in a substantial accumulation over time.

Alternatively, many debt instruments contain no coupon payments. These instruments, known as *pure discount* or *zero coupon* instruments, promise to pay the face amount at maturity and are sold for less than the promised future payment.

Bonds issued by corporations are either *secured* or *unsecured*. A *secured* bond is backed by the assets or property of the issuing corporation. Under a *mortgage bond,* for example, the lender's (bondholder's) investment is backed by the property of the issuing corporation. If the corporation fails to pay the coupon payments or fails to return the principal upon maturity, the bondholder may acquire the underlying property.

An *unsecured* bond is not backed by any assets but, rather, by the general credit of the issuer. An unsecured corporate bond is known as a *debenture*. The owner of a debenture has a subordinate claim to corporation assets in the event of liquidation.

Other types of bonds are *convertible bonds*, which can be exchanged for common stock by bondholders; *income bonds*, which require the issuing company to pay interest only when earned; and *tax-exempt bonds*, which pay interest that is not subject to federal, state and/or local income tax.

Several organizations have developed bond rating systems that assess the credit worthiness of a bond issuer in regard to a specific bond issue. The ratings are based on the likelihood of default, the nature of the obligation and the relative position of the obligation in the event of bankruptcy or reorganization. Standard & Poor's Corporation, for example, has developed the following corporate and municipal bond rating system:

- AAA–Extremely strong capacity to pay interest and repay principal
- AA –Very strong capacity to pay interest and repay principal
- A –Strong capacity to pay interest and repay principal, although susceptible to adverse economic conditions
- BBB –Adequate capacity to pay interest and principal
- BB, B, CCC, CC (speculative issues) –Uncertain payment of interest and repayment of principal
- C –Income bonds on which no interest is being paid
- D –Payments currently in arrears.

Junk bonds refer to bonds with a speculative credit rating (BB or lower). The high yields available on junk bonds are due to the greater risk of default on interest and principal repayment.

These "high yield" bonds have become so popular that one consulting firm argues that they should be a separate asset class, based upon their distinct return, risk and correlation statistics.

The federal government also issues debt obligations. The Treasury Department sells *bills, notes* and *bonds,* which are backed by the faith and credit of the government and are exempt from state and local taxes. *Treasury bills* (or T-bills, as they are often called) have maturities of one year or less and require a minimum investment of $10,000. *Treasury notes* have maturities ranging from one to ten years, and *Treasury bonds* have maturities of ten years or more. Both notes and bonds can be purchased for as little as $1,000.

A relatively new debt obligation of the federal government is the U.S. *Treasury inflation-protected security (TIPS)* account. TIPS provide two cash flows: coupon payments and principal accruals. The coupon payments are made semiannually, at the bond's fixed rate. This rate includes no inflation premium. Inflation risk is accounted for on behalf of the buyer by the Treasury adjusting the principal to reflect changes in the consumer price index (CPI). An investor does not receive the actual accruals until the bond matures, but they affect the coupon payments, which are calculated on the current principal amount, as it is adjusted over time for the changes in the CPI. As long as the bonds are held to maturity, they will beat inflation.

One way for trustees to gain an inflation hedge is to designate TIPS as a distinct and separate asset class. A TIPS account can then be funded whenever portfolio constraints require rebalancing, but the trustees are reluctant for whatever reasons to further fund stocks, traditional bonds or real estate. Thus, with a history of periodically funding a TIPS account, the trustees would have the satisfaction that action had been taken to prepare in advance for the inevitable RTM (reversion to the mean) move in general prices and the resulting negative impact on the real value of the financial assets in the portfolio.

Bond managers have developed a number of strategies and products to effectively control the risk in bond portfolios and otherwise constructively exploit this asset class. If a bond is purchased and held to maturity, one need only be concerned primarily with changes in the financial fortunes of the company or the industry it is in. However, most bond portfolios are actively traded in a market that fluctuates in price and so a primary concern is *interest rate risk.*

If you buy a bond at par (100% of face value) and hold it until maturity, you can redeem it at par, receiving 100% of face value. Unfortunately, during the holding period there are many factors that influence the market price of the bond you hold, and since the plan's auditors require that your bond must be *marked to market* your bond investment will fluctuate in value, over time.

As prevailing interest rates rise, the prices of outstanding bonds fall. Likewise, when rates fall, bond prices rise. The longer the time before a bond matures, the greater the effect that rate changes have

Exhibit 8-1

$1,000 BOND WITH AN 8% COUPON RATE

Years to Maturity	Price if Interest Rates Drop to 6%	Price if Interest Rates Rise to 10%
3	$1,054	$949
5	$1,085	$923
10	$1,149	$875
20	$1,231	$828

Source: *Selecting Investments for Your Retirement Account*, Fifth Edition, Richard D. Glass and Stan Marshall. Investment Horizons, Inc. ©2000, page 27.

on price. (See Exhibit 8-1.) Why? Because a bond is a *fixed income* security and you are promised a fixed level of interest over the life of the bond; the only way the bond you hold can stay competitive to the currently marketed newly issued bonds, if interest rates should rise, is for its yield to increase, i.e., the principal value of the bond is discounted downward in the secondary market.

Yield to Maturity

Yield to maturity is the yield, or return, provided by a bond to its maturity date; determined by a mathematical process, usually requiring the use of a "basis book." For example, a 5% bond pays $5 a year interest on each $100 par value. Let's assume interest rates rise and the price of the bond drops to $95. To figure its current yield, divide $5 by $95–the market price of the bond–and you get 5.26%. Assume that the same bond is due to mature in five years. On the maturity date, the issuer is pledged to pay $100 for the bond that can be bought now for $95. In other words, the bond is selling at a discount of 5% below par value. To figure *yield to maturity,* a simple and approximate method is to divide 5% by the five years to maturity, which equals 1% pro rata yearly. Add that 1% to the 5.26% current yield, and the yield to maturity is roughly 6.26%.

$$\frac{5\%\text{ (discount)}}{5\text{ (yrs. to maturity)}} = 1\%\text{ pro rata, plus } 5.26\%\text{ (current yield)} = 6.26\%\text{ (yield to maturity)}$$

Bond Duration

In addition to the concept of yield, you should also be aware of a favored risk measurement of bond managers, *duration. Duration* is the measure of the price change of a bond to a change in its yield to maturity. It summarizes in a single number, the characteristics that cause bond prices to change in response to a change in interest rates. Duration is more precise than maturity because it takes into consideration the amount of the coupon, how frequently you get paid and the price of the bond. The price of a bond with a duration of three years will rise approximately 3% for each 1% decrease in its yield to maturity. That price will decrease 3% for each 1% increase in the bond's yield. If you know the weighted average duration of your bond portfolio you will have a feel for the impact that a change in the level of interest rates will have on the portfolio's market value.

Interest Rates

Nothing has a more immediate impact on the value of your bond and stock portfolios than changes in the level of interest rates.

> I used to think if there was reincarnation, I wanted to come back as the president, or the pope, or a .400 baseball hitter. But now I want to come back as the bond market. You can intimidate everybody.
>
> *James Carville*

The factors that influence the changes in interest rates are:

- The outlook for inflation
- Federal Reserve policy
- Supply and demand for credit
- Global influences and
- Investor's immediate past experiences.

Anticipating these changes, a portfolio manager can make active bets on interest rate movements while also engaging in sector swaps, etc.; can forgo (or limit) interest rate anticipation moves while still actively trading the portfolio with arbitrage moves; or can immunize or dedicate the portfolio and forgo shorter term upside potential (or limit downside risk) through a wholly passive approach. These strategies can be implemented using government, corporates, utilities or mortgage-backed securities and derivative instruments.

Why would a trustee include bonds as a part of the plan's funding mechanism? First, the plan (the lender) has a *preferred claim* on the income and assets of the issuer (the borrower). The lender has a *contractual right* to return of stated principal and to receive the periodic stated interest payments. From these rights springs a plan's expectation of receiving and cultivating a steady stream of cash flow. It is the *periodic reinvestment* of this stream that permits a plan to exploit the principle of the "power of compounding interest." In just 20 years, $100 growing at 7% (i.e., 4% inflation +3% "rent" for loaning money) results in an accumulation of $386. The tax-exempt status of the plan increases all the more the efficacy of compounding interest.

The success of a bond investment depends upon whether the financial accumulation from ownership compares favorably to the original expectations at purchase. If a plan's objective is to produce a real rate of return, the income stream from the bond should exceed the loss due to inflation in purchasing power of the principal. Unfortunately, this is only one of the risks faced in bond investment. Others are credit (default) risk (if the issuer goes bankrupt), interest rate risk (if bonds must be sold below the price paid), call risk (if the issuer calls in the bond in a lower interest rate environment) and reinvestment risk (if comparable, creditworthy bonds are paying a lower rate of interest when principal or coupons are being reinvested).

Bond risk can be controlled. Besides the use of interest rate futures, there are many portfolio management techniques that can provide comfort to the trustees. *Inflation risk* can be reduced by buying bonds only when the real spread (interest rates minus probable inflation) is at a premium. Correctly assessing when a premium spread is available takes a combination of astute historical perspective, forecasting ability and luck! The phenomenon of lagging return premiums probably exists because bond buyers, having previously erred in their forecasting of inflation's rise, demand high rates long after inflation has subsided in intensity.

Credit risk can be controlled through the exercise of superior credit analysis and adequate quality threshold guidelines. *Interest rate risk* can be reduced by keeping maturities short, dollar-cost-averaging purchases, and adopting the various immunization and dedication strategies.

Partitioning out the retired lives and purchasing bonds dedicated to meet these benefit payments as they fall due has become a popular planning technique, particularly during periods of high interest rates. In some cases, the potential this technique offers for withdrawal liabilities reduction (or elimination) to the multiemployer plans has been sufficient to justify the trustees implementing such a risk-reduction strategy. To manage *call risk,* one must simply "read the fine print." *Reinvestment risk* can be eliminated by purchasing zero coupon bonds or laddering (equally spacing maturities) the bond portfolio.

The attributes of the successful bond manager and the manager's role in implementing the trustees' bond policy guidelines are discussed in Chapter 24.

Chapter
9

Common Stock

The characteristic that most attracts the employee benefit plan investor to common stock is its ability to add *real* value to a portfolio. Since one of the long-range goals for many employee benefit plans is to pay benefits in inflation-adjusted dollars, then the choice of common stock has proven to be a productive funding facility.

> Remember, my son, that any man who is a bear on the future of this country will go broke.
>
> J.P. Morgan

Stock evidences ownership of a corporation represented by shares. Pension funds are interested in owning stock for several reasons, including capital appreciation, dividends and voting rights. When the price of a stock increases above its purchase price, the stock has experienced *capital appreciation.* A stock's price may increase when the underlying company is economically successful and when there is demand for the stock in the market. When the stock's price increases, the investor may either sell the stock at a profit or hold it, hoping it will continue to appreciate.

Stocks are either *common* or *preferred. Common stockholders* participate in the earnings of a corporation through dividends.

Corporations are not required to pay dividends and the dividend amount is discretionary. Still, many expend these funds to reward stockholders and to enhance the corporate image.

Another less tangible stockholder right is participation in the management of the corporation through voting. As owners of the corporation, stockholders elect the directors and decide other corporate issues through the voting process. A stockholder can attend the corporation's annual meeting or other special meetings to vote the shares or can give written authorization to someone else to vote the shares. This is called a *proxy*. (See Chapter 19 for the trustees' responsibilities regarding the voting of proxies.) In the event of a liquidation, common stock owners also have a claim upon the corporation's remaining assets after all debts have been paid.

Preferred stockholders have the same ownership interest as common stockholders but ordinarily do not have voting rights. Owners of preferred stock have a *superior* claim to dividends over common stock owners. If dividends are declared by the issuing corporation, preferred stockholders will receive their dividends first, and only then will the remaining earnings pass through to the common stockholders. Also, unlike dividends on common stock, preferred stock dividends usually are fixed by the corporation and are cumulative. When a corporation liquidates, preferred stockholders also have a superior claim over common stockholders to any remaining assets.

Descriptive names have developed in the market to describe groups of stocks sharing similar characteristics. *Blue chip* stocks are high-grade stocks from leading companies that have a long history of earnings. *Cyclical* stocks are from companies whose earnings shift with business cycles. Industries generally regarded as cyclical include steel, cement, paper, machinery, airlines, railroads and automobiles. *Defensive* stocks are stable stocks that perform well during periods of uncertainty or recessions. Utilities, food and drug companies, and gold mining companies are considered to be defensive stocks. *Interest-sensitive* stocks relate to companies whose production is closely associated with interest rates. Examples are building and construction companies, banks and life insurance companies.

Growth Versus Value Stocks

Many investment managers confine their selection universe to either *growth* or *value* stocks. A *growth* stock is a stock of a corporation whose earnings have increased consistently over a number of years and shows every indication of considerable further expansion.

Most growth stocks provide a relatively *low* dividend yield; many pay no dividend at all. They are primarily attractive for price appreciation potential, especially from a long-range standpoint. Growth companies have characteristics that include the following:

1. A young and aggressive management team
2. Strong emphasis on research and development
3. A favorable record of sales and earnings
4. A line of essential products that seems destined to increase in popularity over the years, while new ones are constantly introduced.

On the other hand, *value* stocks pay a relatively *high* dividend yield and generally have the following additional characteristics:

1. Low price/earnings ratio
2. Price is less than book value
3. Low price to cash flow.

Depending upon the aggregate demand of investors, growth and value stocks can outperform or underperform one another, from time to time. (See Exhibit 9-1.)

Exhibit 9-1

GROWTH STOCKS VS. VALUE STOCKS
December 31, 1978 = 100

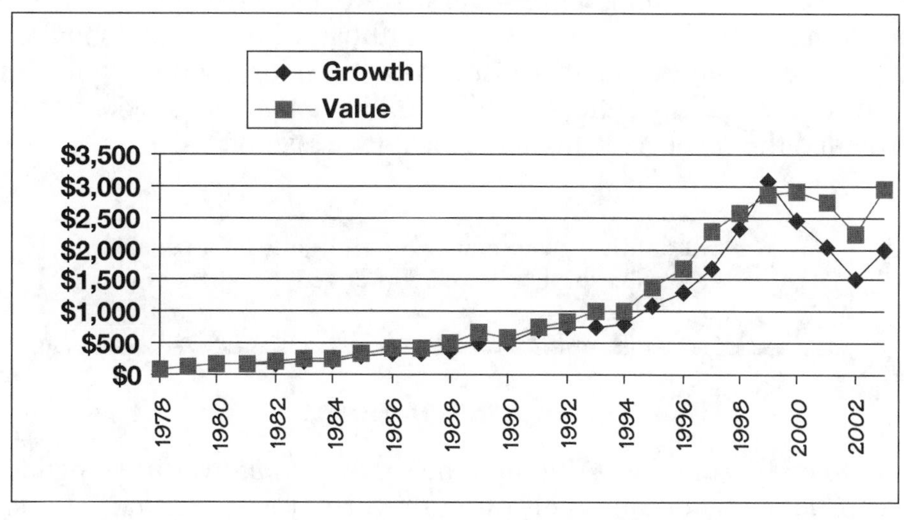

Source: Ibbotson Associates.

Exhibit 9-2

AVERAGE ANNUAL TOTAL RETURN
S&P 500 vs. Ibbotson Small Co. Index

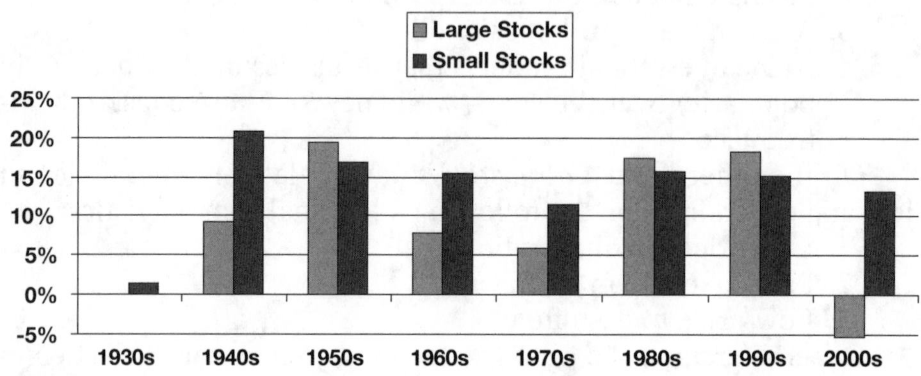

Source: Ibbotson Associates.

Small Cap (Capitalization) Stocks

Over the *very long term,* small cap stocks have significantly outperformed large cap stocks. However, those who invest in small cap stocks must exercise patience; there have been long periods where the additional volatility suffered while holding small cap stocks has not provided the "expected" higher return. (See Exhibit 9-2.)

> Small stocks are outperforming big stocks in every region of the world. This is exactly what God intended.
>
> *Rex Sinquefield*

A Market of Stocks

Keep this in mind: Although the stock *market* over the long term has produced a double-digit rate of return, it is still a market comprised of *individual stocks,* each of which has its own characteristics: growth, value, large cap, small cap, etc., and as we go through the

Exhibit 9-3

GROWTH IN EARNINGS, DIVIDENDS AND PRINCIPAL VALUE
Standard & Poor's 500 Index

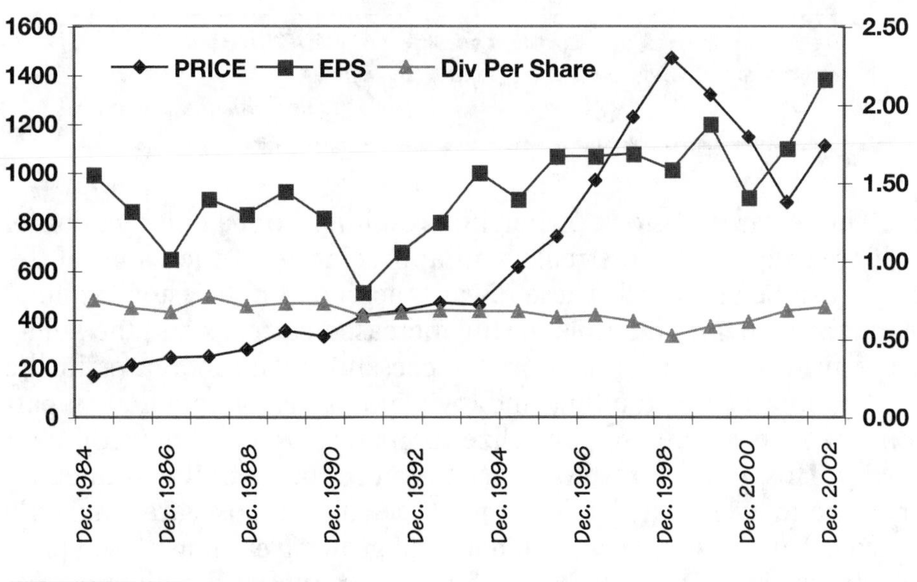

Source: Ibbotson Associates.

shorter cycles, the stocks in your portfolio may very well diverge from the broader market and from other portfolios. Therefore, it is incumbent upon you to know the sector of the market and the capitalization sizes your manager has chosen to concentrate in, in order to know *why* your portfolio is diverging in return from the broader market. Absent this insight, you may fire the manager at the wrong time! Both the manager and your fund will end up losers.

Earnings Drive Share Prices

The driving forces behind stock prices are the companies' earnings. (See Exhibit 9-3 for the relationship, over time, between earnings, dividends and stock values.) Complementing earnings and dividends in their impact on stock prices are investor confidence, the business outlook and the level of interest rates. Even though earnings and dividends may be increasing nicely in an expanding environment, stock prices can be negatively impacted from rising interest rates; investors discount the anticipated flow of dividends by using the *current* level of rates and may choose to buy the higher yielding bonds instead of stocks. As Exhibit 9-3 reflects, there is a "cause and effect" between earnings, dividends and stock prices, but it is certainly not a smooth progression over time.

> Do not be fearful or negative too often. For 100 years optimists have carried the day in U.S. stocks.
>
> *Sir John Templeton*

The rewards of stock ownership, resulting from a combination of an increasing dividend stream and appreciation in the value of the shares, can be unlimited. These rewards accrue from investors' willingness to pay a higher multiple for the increased earnings and the ability of the firm to "manage its store" successfully. The increases in the price/earnings (P/E) multiple and dividend payout stream flow in part from the firm's ability to capitalize on its research and development activity. This, in turn, fosters consumer acceptance of its products or services and eventually leads to increased sales. If costs are efficiently controlled, increasing sales should lead to growing earning power, profitable reinvestment opportunities for the earnings and, ultimately, increased confidence shown by the investment community in the firm's ability to manage its affairs successfully in the future. Investors, reflecting their increased confidence in the future fortunes of the firm, will increase their activity in accumulating the stock, which, in turn, will bid up the price/earnings multiple. Thus, the P/E multiple becomes a measure of the attractiveness of a particular security versus all other available securities as determined by the investing public.

> The worst crime against working people is a company which fails to operate at a profit.
>
> *Samuel Gompers*

Reading the Stock Quotations Pages

As a trustee you are most concerned with the contribution the common stock portion of your portfolio will make to the funding needs of your plan, less concerned with the fortunes of any one stock in the portfolio; and you should not at all be distracted from your long-term objectives by the daily fluctuations of the individual stocks. Having said that though, we should at least know how to read the stock quotations found daily in the newspapers; your manager, and particularly the securities traders who execute the buy and sell decisions made by the manager, follow these quotes constantly.

Let's look at the common stock of General Motors:

As Quoted

(1)	52 weeks Hi	55.55
(2)	52 weeks Lo	32.84
(3)	Stk	GenMotor
(4)	Sym	GM
(5)	Div	0.50
(6)	Yld %	4.3%
(7)	PE	9.21
(8)	Vol 100s	23520
(9)	Hi	47.18
(10)	Lo	46.07
(11)	Close	46.57
(12)	Net Chg	−0.43

Explanations

(1) (2)	Highest and lowest prices of the stock, for the last 52 weeks.
(3) (4)	Stock name and symbol.
(5)	Estimate of the annual dividend per share. If you owned 100 shares of GM, you would receive a $200 check for the cash dividend.
(6)	If you bought GM at yesterday's close (46.57), and you receive in cash dividends over the next year (0.50) you will have a yield of 4.3% on your investment.
(7)	PE is an abbreviation for *Price/Earnings Ratio.* How many times earnings is GM selling for? At this time GM is selling for 9.21 times earnings. The P/E ratio reflects the confidence investors have that a company well into the future will continue to successfully "grow its earnings." The higher the number, the further into the future are investors discounting the company's current earnings.
(8)	Sales of shares, in hundreds, the previous day. Almost 2.4 million shares of GM traded!
(9)(10)(11)	GM's highest, lowest and closing price for the previous day.
(12)	Reflects net change of stock's closing price from the day before to yesterday's close.

The attributes of the successful common stock manager and the manager's role in implementing the trustees' common stock policy guidelines are discussed in Chapter 24.

Chapter 10

Real Estate

Real estate assets comprise the world's oldest and largest investment market. Even though land and improvements have been a favored asset class for wealthy, private investors, only in the past three decades has real estate come to be an accepted investment for pension funds. Because of their objectives to produce growth in value and a real rate of return over time, there is a place for real estate in the pension plan portfolio, particularly for the larger plans.

> The best investment is land, because they ain't making any more of it.
>
> *Will Rogers*

The term *real estate investments* refers to an entire market, which is comprised of a multitude of different types of properties, ownership positions, structures and vehicles. The common characteristic binding them together to form a market is that all are investment interests in real property. When debt options also are counted, the magnitude of the marketplace is immense.

While real estate investments have many characteristics in common with stocks and bonds, they do not share an efficient market mechanism. To the contrary, the real estate market is an inefficient marketplace. There is no central collection point where a consensus of opinions on value is recorded. Rather, it is a marketplace of private, individual transactions. The value of a particular property depends essentially upon the decision of the buyer and seller, who will value the property through their privately negotiated transaction.

The class of *equity real estate* is added to a portfolio within the context of a pension plan's objectives to (a) exploit its long-term time horizon, (b) hedge against the possibility that higher inflationary periods may reappear (repeat of 1976-81 environment), (c) add a third asset class that offers the potential to produce *real* rates of return in *all* price environments and (d) produce a smoothing of portfolio returns because of the noncovariance of its returns with stocks and bonds.

Like common stock, equity real estate has the potential to add significant real value over time. Its hybrid nature of being both financial (leases) and tangible (bricks and mortar) in character enables its owner to hedge effectively against either a low or high inflation scenario. Overage rents, net net leases, expense escalation clauses, equity equivalent loans, etc., all result in the investor being assured that his or her principal will stay competitive with inflation. The hybrid nature of convertible participating mortgages enables the pension fund sponsor to hedge against an unknown future.

As the purchasing power of money decreases, the value of tangible assets often increases by a like amount, provided that their utility value remains unchanged. This utility characteristic of nonmonetary assets has long been recognized in economic theory. However, inflation hedging is not automatic. Nonmonetary assets, such as real estate, possess only the *potential* to provide a hedge against inflation. The realization of this potential is a function of many factors and is not without risk.

There are two primary components of the total return from real estate assets: income and appreciation. When valuing a real estate investment, only these two factors should be considered in arriving at the economic value of a property. A third value component often attributed to real estate is the *tax shelter component.* Any value attributable to this element is for a particular investor rather than to the property and is not a direct factor for pension funds.

Different types of real estate investments offer different mixes of yield. The yield from unimproved land, for instance, comes solely from appreciation. Other real estate investments, like commercial buildings, provide income. In general, the more the return is weighted toward appreciation, the greater the risk tends to be and vice versa.

The value of all real estate is a function of its use potential, and not just its actual current use. The key questions with regard to any piece of real estate are "What is the best use of this property?" and "What will someone pay to use it in that manner?" The value of real estate assets changes as their use changes. Agricultural land becomes more valuable when it can be used for residential purposes. Residential land becomes more valuable when it can be used commercially.

The main implication of this concept that land value changes as its use changes is that when there is more certainty (less risk) involved in assessing the worth of a real estate asset the closer it comes to the point of being utilized for its best use. The further into the future is its highest and best use, the less certainty (the more risk) is involved. Thus, raw land investment, which relies on future residential housing for achieving the investment objectives, is generally more risky than new fully leased office buildings.

The new office building is at its highest and best use (while the raw land is not) and, therefore, the uncertainties associated with projecting future events are minimized. Conversely, the rewards associated with the raw land investment may be several times greater than those associated with office buildings. The point is this: One must understand the risk associated with a specific investment vehicle in order to evaluate the appropriateness of such an investment for a particular portfolio.

In order to understand the value of real estate investments, one must understand how they generate income. For example, the income stream from an office building is dependent on how much rent tenants will pay to utilize their space. The price of a residential land subdivision is dependent on how much a home builder will pay for a lot to build a house. The value the home builder will pay for the lot is dependent upon how much a buyer will pay for the house. The value of an agricultural parcel is dependent on how much a farmer will pay to grow crops, which, in turn, is dependent on how much the crops can bring in the marketplace.

Real estate assets progress through a series of use changes, sometimes called the *life cycle*. Understanding the present stage of that cycle is necessary for assessing the risk properly. (See Exhibit 10-1.)

Leverage

No real estate discussion is complete without mentioning leverage. Using borrowed money increases (leverages) the return potential

Exhibit 10-1

LAND AND IMPROVEMENT LIFE CYCLE

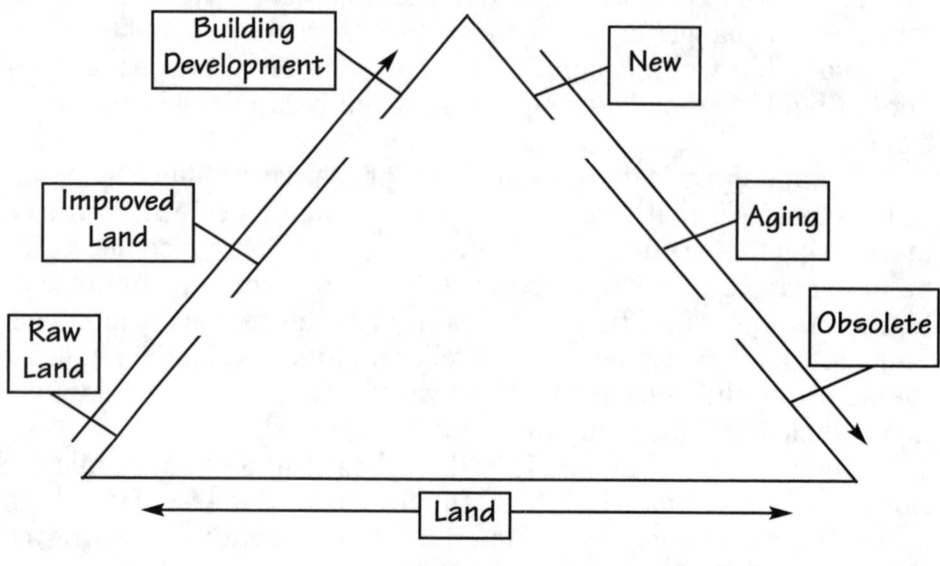

of equity capital. Real estate has been the favorite medium of leveraged investors because real estate is a tangible nonmonetary asset with a high collateralization value. Historically, lenders have been willing to accept real estate assets as security for loans. Such loans have also been made primarily on a nonrecourse basis so the investor's risk is limited to the investment in the property.

Leverage can provide many benefits to an investor, but it can also have serious consequences. Leverage may create a disproportionate increase in the return on equity as compared to the return on total price, e.g., if the return on cost increases 1%, the return on equity may increase 1.5%. The reverse also holds true; leverage may also create disproportionate losses of capital.

Leverage may change a rather conservative investment into a very risky one by increasing the operating breakeven point of a building. A building purchased on an all-cash basis may be able to break even at a 30% occupancy level; whereas, a leveraged building with a fixed amount of debt service requires a higher breakeven occupancy level. The higher the required occupancy rate, the greater the risk of negative cash flows. Notwithstanding this danger, leverage is a useful portfolio management tool–if employed properly.

Mortgages

Whereas equity real estate investments represent *ownership* of the asset, mortgage investments are *claims* against an asset and its stream of income. These instruments are loans to the owner of a property who pledges the property as collateral for securing the loan. Thus, the mortgagor's position is that of a debtor, just as in any other loan transaction.

Mortgages may be made during all phases of the life cycle, e.g.,

- Land loans
- Land improvement loans
- Construction loans
- Tenant improvement loans
- Bridge loans
- Long-term first mortgage loans
- Second mortgage loans.

Yields, loan-to-value ratios and underwriting criteria obviously vary greatly, depending on the specific set of circumstances and the nature of the borrower. A unique characteristic of most forms of real estate loans is they are placed on a nonrecourse basis, i.e., the lender agrees to look solely to the property in the event of default. This feature has obvious benefits for the borrower, but it also highlights the lender's opinion of the inherent value of real estate assets. At the same time, it places a heavy burden on the lender to value the property appropriately.

Loans that are made on a direct property-by-property basis, looking only to the borrower and property for recovery, are called *conventional loans.* Those debts are by far the most typical loan form in the commercial sector of the market.

Loans that carry a guarantee of a governmental agency or private insurer are termed *insured loans.* As such, they have an added degree of security because the lender has recourse against the insurer as well as the property. These loans are most prevalent in the residential markets. Because of the insured feature, generally they have lower yields than conventional loans. On the other hand, they are more liquid because there are active secondary markets for insured loans.

Due to the negative impact of inflation on long-term, fixed interest rate mortgages, a number of hybrid debt/equity structures have been devised to afford lenders some degree of inflation protection. All of these structures provide for increased yield in the event that inflation increases by sharing in the underlying value of the real estate asset. The following discussion illustrates some of the means by which this sharing is accomplished.

Participating mortgages: This structure is utilized in the commercial sector and is applicable only to income-producing assets. Such loans are structured to pay the lender a fixed interest rate (usually below the market rate for a fixed rate loan) plus participation in any increase in gross (or net) revenues for the property. Some participating loans also share in any capital gains achieved when a property is sold.

Variable rate mortgages: This form is employed mainly with non-income-producing properties such as single family houses. Since there is no income stream in which to participate, lenders peg increases in yield to another index such as the CPI, GDP deflator or Treasury bills. If the selected index increases, the interest rate also increases. Normally, these loans have a maximum allowable rate of increase (a cap) to enhance their acceptance by borrowers.

Trustees may participate in mortgage investments through commingled funds, similar to those available for equity real estate investing.

Real estate is known as a *lumpy* asset; it comes in large economic units. Thus, for all but the very few, very large Taft-Hartley plans, trustees' access to the funding opportunities of real estate is gained through *investing in commingled accounts.* In Chapter 24 we will discuss the characteristics of the successful real estate manager and what vehicles are available to facilitate your ownership of this asset class.

Chapter 11

Other Asset Classes

In addition to bonds, common stock and real estate, there are a number of other classes that have been authorized by trustees for inclusion within plan portfolios. All of them cannot be included in this book, but we will include discussions of money market instruments, guaranteed investment contracts (GICs) and private placements.

Money Market Instruments

A *money market instrument* is a short-term debt security (generally with a maturity of less than one year) that is both highly marketable and highly liquid. Pension plans invest in these instruments to receive interest payments on cash holdings rather than let money remain idle. Health and welfare plans and other funds with short-term planning horizons often confine their entire portfolio to money market instruments. Money market instruments include Treasury bills, U.S. government agency issues, certificates of deposit and commercial paper.

The following is a review of the most frequently used short-term investment instruments:

◆ *Repurchase agreements* are evidence of the sale of securities together with a related agreement to repurchase the same securities at some future time for a set price.

- *Commercial paper notes* are unsecured promissory notes of specific maturities and principal amounts supported by the general credit of the issuing business corporations.
- *Eurodollar time deposits* are interest-bearing deposits of specific amounts and maturities at a foreign financial or savings institution, including overseas branches of U.S. banks.
- *Eurodollar certificates of deposit* evidence time deposits of U.S. dollars in U.S. bank branches or foreign banks located outside the United States. They specify principal amount, rate of interest and maturity.
- *U.S. Treasury bills* are noninterest-bearing discount securities issued by the U.S. Treasury in order to finance a portion of the national debt.
- *Bankers acceptances* are drafts or bills of exchange accepted by banks or trust companies, with the accepting institution thereby assuming primary liability for payment in full of principal and interest at maturity.
- *Negotiable certificates of deposit* evidence time deposits with commercial banks at specific rates of interest for specific periods of time and in stated principal amounts.
- *Federal National Mortgage Association (FNMA) discount notes* are noninterest-bearing securities issued for the purpose of financing, in part, the secondary mortgage market operations of FNMA, a government-sponsored corporation.
- *Farm Credit Banks consolidated systemwide discount notes* are noninterest-bearing discount securities issued by the Farm Credit System, an independent federal agency, to finance its interim credit needs.
- *Federal Home Loan consolidated discount notes* are noninterest-bearing discount securities issued by the Federal Home Loan Banks in order to support short-term credit operations on behalf of the savings industry. The difference between the discounted purchasing price and par at maturity reflects the interest received.
- *"Yankee" certificates of deposit* are evidence of time deposits issued by the U.S. branches of foreign banks.
- *Bank short-term investment funds* are commercial bank common trust funds invested in money market instruments.
- *Bank master notes* are variable rate notes of corporate issuers

held by commercial trust departments for participation by trust department customers.

- *Money market mutual funds* are commingled funds invested exclusively in short-term instruments.
- *World Bank discount notes* are noninterest-bearing notes issued by the World Bank.
- *Interamerican Development Bank (IADB) discount notes* are noninterest-bearing discount notes issued by the IADB.

This listing is augmented periodically by corporations and agencies that seek short-term financing from the market.

It is important to keep in mind that money market accounts (even those managed by *banks*) are *not* bank accounts; thus they are not insured by the Federal Deposit Insurance Corporation (FDIC), and there is credit risk.

Guaranteed Investment Contracts

A *guaranteed investment contract* (GIC) is a deposit arrangement with an insurance company. Basically, the investor deposits money with the insurance company over a specified period of time (either one lump sum or a series of payments). On the maturity date, the insurance company repays the total amount deposited, along with the interest guaranteed to the investor, in a lump sum or a series of payments. Unlike stocks or bonds, GICs are not marketable securities.

GICs are investment instruments that imply an absolute guarantee of principal and a predetermined rate of interest to be credited over the investment's life. Although insurers imply unconditionally guaranteed protection for the principal value and interest rate of the GIC, the guarantee is only as good as the insurer's claims-paying ability. A GIC owner becomes a policyholder of the insurer, which in most states provides a senior lien over the general creditors of the insurer.

There was a time when trust funds could "blindly" rely upon the publicly available quality ratings of the insurance companies as determined by the rating agencies (Best, S&P, Moody's, etc.); not anymore. The DOL has stated that trustees should go beyond the published ratings and must make an independent evaluation of the financial stability of the issuer and the default risk of the underlying investments. This more exacting environment has caused most Taft-Hartley plans to forsake buying GICs on their own, opting instead to retain a GIC investment manager.

Guaranteed investment contracts consist of two types: *individual* and *pooled* contracts. *Individual* contracts are single contracts between one investor and one issuer. Individual contracts are sometimes sold for millions of dollars per contract to keep administrative costs down and, therefore, are out of range for many small investors.

Alternatively, *pooled* funds are more accessible to smaller investors. Pooled funds combine assets of several smaller investors to purchase larger contracts. Pooled funds can be either *open-ended* or *closed-end*. An *open-ended pool* is a continuous fund that investors may enter or leave by contract. A *closed-end pool is* designed for a specific group of investors who commit in advance.

Competitive products have arisen, namely, *bank investment contracts* (BICs) and *savings and loan investment contracts* (SLICs), and the more recently introduced *synthetic GICs*.

GICs and their "near cousins" can be a useful component of an overall funding strategy for retirement benefits. They can be used to immunize all or a portion of retirees' benefits and, in the asset allocation process, they can be used as an alternative to, or a complement to, a bond portfolio.

Private Placements

A *private placement* is a security not registered with the SEC that is sold on a confidential basis to a limited number of sophisticated investors who usually intend to hold the security to maturity.

Private securities include:

- Senior notes
- Securitized assets
- Subordinated notes
- Preferred stock
- Common stock.

A substantial amount of all debt securities issued annually in America is placed privately through direct sales to large institutional lenders.

There are advantages to both the issuer and the purchaser of private placements. The issuer saves considerable expense by virtue of bypassing the SEC's screening procedures and is able to offer such securities at a higher yield to the investor. Additionally, purchasers of private placements generally are large buyers, which enables issuers to service debt at lower cost than public issues.

Buyers of private placements may be able to negotiate an issue's maturity date, call features, sinking fund requirements, etc., thus providing an opportunity to purchase securities tailor-made for cash flow and liquidity requirements. During periods of capital shortages, the buyer frequently is able to negotiate "equity kickers" in the form of warrants, conversions to common stock, etc., which provide the chance for considerably higher rates of return than just the coupon rate. However, when considering private placements, buyers should recognize their limited marketability in comparison to publicly issued securities.

A small portion of a plan invested in a private placement commingled fund can:

1. Eliminate the "trading activities" risk of active bond management and maximize return potential through the internal compounding effect of the more passive private placement account.
2. Avoid full rate sensitivity to the marketable securities markets.
3. Provide increased return from exploiting the credit risk of the individual positions through the commingled accounts' diversification.

Commingled private placement accounts, supervised by qualified investment managers, have produced returns in excess of long-term corporates, long-term Treasuries and the Lehman Government/Corporate Bond Index.

Chapter 12

Mutual Funds

Mutual funds are investment companies that use their capital to invest in the securities of other companies. The two major types of mutual funds–*open end* and *closed end*–are described below. Open-end funds comprise the greater part of the industry and have attracted most of the employee benefit plan monies.

Open-End Funds

Open-end funds stand ready to sell shares to new investors and to redeem shares from participants on an ongoing basis. Shares are bought and sold at the so-called net asset value (NAV), plus sales load if applicable. The net asset value of an open-end mutual fund is computed daily and is determined by dividing the total market value of the securities held in the fund by the total number of shares of that fund held by shareholders. For example, an open-end mutual fund valued at $75,735,000 and having 20,250,000 shares outstanding would have a net asset value of $3.74 on that day.

The major advantage of investing in an open-end fund versus a closed-end fund is "purchasing and selling liquidity," at net asset value. In other words, the investor has an unrestricted opportunity to buy or to sell at the net asset value.

Closed-End Funds

A specific initial underwriting creates the fund and from that point no new shares are created, nor are existing shares redeemed. Shares of closed-end mutual funds trade like any other security; the price may *not* be equal to the net asset value of the fund at that time. For example, on a particular day, when the net asset value of a closed-end mutual fund is $20, shares might trade at prices higher or lower than $20.

The advantage of a closed-end fund is that the fund cannot be "diluted" with a heavy influx of new cash (new shares created) or "drained" by an unexpected withdrawal of capital (redemption). This gives both the mutual fund manager and the shareholders comfort that pursuit of the investment objectives will not be compromised by sudden and unexpected influxes or withdrawals of capital.

Load Versus No-Load Funds

One distinction between closed-end and open-end funds is that many open-end funds charge a sales fee. In the case of a so-called load fund, the offering price for shares is equal to the net asset value plus a sales charge. When a sales charge is made upon deposit it is known as a *front-end* load charge. To discourage withdrawals, some funds charge a fee upon withdrawal; this is known as *back-end* loading. There are also *low-load* funds with, for instance, 3% sales charges. When establishing positions of institutional size, the sales charge of load funds declines proportionately at prescribed breakpoints, generally reaching a 1% sales load for purchases of $1 million or more. There is no initial sales charge on a no-load fund; the shares are sold at their net asset value.

Benefits of Mutual Funds

Mutual funds offer trustees diversification, flexibility, liquidity, a means of specialization and, in some instances, cost efficiencies. In addition, the mutual fund industry is regulated by the Investment Company Act of 1940, which states that a mutual fund must set forth clearly in its prospectus its investment objectives and must adhere to those objectives until the prospectus is amended. A report of its holdings and performance experience is updated and reported quarterly.

Diversification

By owning shares of mutual funds, investors purchase a representative participation in a broad range of industries and/or companies. Diversification can be accomplished within specific investment objectives–for example, large growth companies or specific industries. The number of equity issues owned by a particular mutual fund and, thus, the degree of diversification, can vary between fewer than 50 securities to hundreds of securities, depending on the style of the management company.

Since a variety of mutual funds is available, the objectives of many trust funds can be accomplished by blending various fund types, although choosing the proper blend requires some sophistication. Many mutual fund management companies manage several funds with different stated investment objectives and risk/return characteristics. These funds managed by the same company are referred to as a *family of funds.*

Flexibility

Since most mutual funds stand ready to redeem their shares at the net asset value, timely moves can be executed quickly and efficiently. Reallocating assets can be easily accommodated by moving from one fund to another. Additionally, new capital contributions can be invested within a day's time. Third, in contrast to the delays associated with severing ties with a poorly performing independent investment manager, investments in mutual funds can be liquidated and reinvested elsewhere within 24 hours.

Cost Efficiencies

With no-load mutual funds, each dollar contributed represents a dollar of invested assets. With load funds, a contributed dollar represents a range of $0.93 to $0.99 of invested assets. Acquisition costs for new capital contributions, if invested in load funds, can be reduced via cumulative purchase privileges.

Expense charges vary considerably from one fund to another; the lower the better to permit more dollars for investment to be compounded over time. There is no need to employ custodial and portfolio recordkeeping services when using mutual funds, because such services are provided by the mutual funds themselves.

Mutual Funds for Large Plans

Large pension plans can use mutual funds to achieve specific, or highly specialized investment objectives, such as emerging growth companies, international, energy and precious metals. Because the trustees may wish to invest only a small portion of the plan's assets in a given investment category, mutual funds offer the benefits of diversification within each.

Mutual Funds for Small Plans

A particular benefit to the small pension plan in using mutual funds is the ability to create the kind of "multimanager" investment system commonly used by large plan sponsors. This program can be accomplished either by utilizing an investment advisory firm, whose responsibilities include fund selection and asset allocation, or by investing through one mutual fund management company, allocating among its *family of funds.*

Chapter 13

Hedge Funds

Contributed by Jennifer Mink
Investment Performance Services, LLC

Although hedge fund investing had been utilized by private investors since 1949, it was not until the 1980s that hedge funds gained notoriety in the "mainstream" investment world, and it took until the turbulent market volatility of the 1990s for hedge funds to capture the attention of institutional investors. Today, hedge funds represent the fastest growing and most talked about investment vehicles in the investment arena. The attractive feature of hedge funds is that they are professionally managed assets that have a low correlation with traditional asset classes such as stocks and bonds. This low correlation creates significant risk/return benefits in a portfolio through diversification by reducing the expected volatility of returns without compromising the overall portfolio expected returns. The primary objective of a hedge fund is to produce a positive absolute return while preserving capital, which makes them an attractive addition to benefit plan portfolios.

In simplest form, the term *hedge fund* refers to an investment structure and not an investment approach. A hedge fund is a privately organized, pooled investment vehicle that seeks to capitalize on market inefficiencies while neutralizing the overall direction of the capital markets and interest rates. They invest primarily in publicly traded securities and derivatives, but utilize techniques and instruments that are unavailable to traditional investment managers. It is the skill (stock picking) of the manager that is the primary factor in the returns generated by a hedge fund, not the general direction of the market, as with traditional investment management. Because of this, hedge funds are often referred to as active, skill-based strategies while traditional asset management is considered a passive, market-based approach to money management.

To understand the basic techniques that characterize hedge funds, one should be familiar with the terminology used to describe the different ways securities can be bought or sold. A traditional investment approach consists of a "long" position in a security, which simply means owning a security. When an investor thinks a security will increase in price over time they purchase the security and are considered to be *long* the position. If the price goes up the position can be sold for a profit; however, if the market and underlying securities are depreciating in value, there is no value added by owning the position and losses may be incurred. A nontraditional investment consists of "shorting" securities, which involves selling a security that you do not own with the expectation that the price of the security will decrease over time. *Short selling* is the practice of borrowing a stock on collateral from a brokerage company and immediately selling it on the market *(shorting)* with the intention of buying it back later at a lower price and returning it to the broker. A profit is made when the return from the position exceeds the cost of borrowing.

The goal of a hedge fund is to *hedge* against market gravity, or fluctuations up and down. "Hedging" attempts to decrease exposure to chance and volatility by purchasing a long position and a short position in similar stocks to offset the effect any changes in the overall level of the equity market will have on the long purchase. Generally, in a hedge fund, only positions about which the manager has conviction will be held or sold short. Managers are long (own) undervalued stocks and short (sell) overvalued stocks. That portion of a portfolio in which long positions are matched by equal dollar amounts of short positions is considered to be "within the hedge," while that portion of a portfolio not hedged by an offsetting position is considered to be exposed to market risk or to have "market exposure." Net market exposure of a portfolio can be calculated as:

$$\text{Net Market Exposure (\%)} = \frac{\text{Gross Long} - \text{Gross Short}}{\text{Capital}}$$

Many hedge fund investors may think this style of alternative investing "is Greek, to me" and to some extent that is true. Investment return generated purely by manager skill and not attributable to the overall performance of the capital markets is referred to as *alpha*. Another Greek term, *beta*, describes the sensitivity of an investment to broad market movements. In theory, investing in hedge funds is about getting alpha without getting beta. For comparison purposes, investing in traditional long-only investment funds mixes alpha and beta while investing in index funds is all about beta. The distinction between alpha and beta is becoming more important to benefit funds in portfolio evaluation.

Hedge Fund Strategies

The alpha generated by a hedge fund will vary depending on the hedge fund strategy utilized because there are many different hedge fund strategies that have distinct characteristics and varied expected returns. The three broad categories of hedge fund strategies include event driven, relative value and long/short equity. Bear in mind that each broad strategy has numerous underlying substrategies.

Event Driven

Managers of event-driven strategies invest in situations with the expectation that a near-term event will act as a catalyst changing the market's perception of a company, thereby increasing or decreasing the value of its debt or equity. These extraordinary corporate events include, but are not limited to, bankruptcies, financial restructurings, mergers, acquisitions and spin-off of a division or subsidiary. Two common event-driven strategies include distressed debt and merger arbitrage, representing 15% of hedge funds and about 32% of hedge fund capital invested.

Distressed Debt. Distressed debt managers invest in securities of companies that are experiencing financial or operational difficulties. They purchase the bank debt or high yield of a distressed entity pre-bankruptcy at a discount, anticipating either a successful reorganization or the recognition of value by other investors and a recovery in bond pricing. Managers may sell the stock or other instruments within the capital structure as a hedge.

Merger Arbitrage. Merger arbitrage managers invest in companies that are being acquired or are involved in a merger or acquisition. They only invest in announced deals and do not try to anticipate possible mergers. When a merger or acquisition is announced, the price being offered for the company being acquired is generally higher than the current trading price of that company's stock. Therefore, if a manager expects a merger to occur, it will purchase the stock of the target company and short the stock of the acquiring entity as a hedge. However, if the manager expects the merger to fall through, it will short the stock of the target company and purchase shares of the acquiring company.

Relative Value

Relative value managers seek to profit from the mispricing of related securities. This strategy utilizes quantitative and qualitative analysis to identify securities or spreads between securities that deviate from their fair value and/or historical norms. Common relative value strategies include convertible arbitrage, fixed income arbitrage and global macro.

Convertible Arbitrage. The term *arbitrage* describes the simultaneous purchase and sale of a security or a pair of similar securities to profit from a pricing discrepancy. Convertible arbitrage strategies represent about 20% of hedge funds and 20% of total hedge fund capital invested and involve the use of convertible bonds. *Convertible bonds* are bonds that can be converted into a fixed number of shares of the same company's stock. They are hybrid securities that have features of both a bond and a stock. Generally, the price of the convertible bond will decline less than the underlying stock in a falling equity market and mirror the increase in the stock price in a rising market. Convertible arbitrage managers construct long portfolios of convertible bonds and hedge these positions by selling short the underlying stock of each bond. Profits are generated by identifying pricing disparities between convertible bonds and their underlying stock.

Fixed Income Arbitrage. Fixed income arbitrage represents about 7% of hedge funds and 6% of total hedge fund capital invested. Managers take offsetting long and short positions in related fixed income securities whose values are mathematically or historically interrelated but are believed to be temporarily dislocated. Profits are generated when the skewed relationship between the securities returns to the expected range.

Global Macro. Global macro represents 7% of hedge funds and 13% of total hedge fund capital invested. Managers of this strategy employ a top-down global approach to investing, which concentrates on forecasting how global macroeconomic and political situations affect the valuations of financial instruments. Managers generate profits by identifying extreme price-to-value disparities in stock markets, interest rates, commodities, foreign exchange rates or other financial instruments and make leveraged bets on the price movements they anticipate in these markets.

Long/Short Equity

Long/short characterizes the original hedge fund concept and represents 55% of hedge funds and 45% of total hedge fund capital invested. Managers invest long and sell short in equity securities. Portfolios can be long biased, neutral or short biased. Managers have the ability to shift from value to growth and from small to medium to large capitalization stocks. The focus of the portfolios can be regional, such as long/short U.S. or European equity, or sector-specific, such as long/short technology, etc. Returns on these strategies depend on the manager's skill at picking stocks, both long and short.

Risk

The ability to identify and understand risk characteristics is one of the most important aspects of investing in hedge funds, and one should distinguish between portfolio market and nonmarket-related risk factors. Since hedge funds are private entities, they are exempt from being registered with the Securities and Exchange Commission (SEC). Because funds are not typically registered, and are often small shops with few employees, little or no information about them is made available to the public. Lack of information, coupled with the fact that there is no entry barrier for a hedge fund manager to set up shop; and considering the incentive and fee structure employed by hedge funds compared with traditional asset management, operational or business risk becomes a factor when hiring a manager. To mitigate this risk, extensive due diligence is required before hiring a manager is even considered. This process includes evaluation of the business model, systems analysis, on-site manager visits and background checks on key personnel including educational credentials, work experience, civil or criminal prosecution or litigation and personal references. An analysis of financial records of the firm and personnel is also initiated including bankruptcies, divorce and financial statements.

Another type of risk to be considered is fraud. Unfortunately fraud exists but it is not limited to the hedge fund industry. Many investors, including pension funds, experienced the implosion of firms such as Enron and Worldcom and the recent mutual fund pricing and trading scandals of many reputable Wall Street investment firms.

Although catching all fraud may be impossible, the due diligence on hedge funds, when conducted thoroughly, is a continuous process and methodical attempt to mitigate fraud.

Finally, there is market-related risk. The returns of hedge fund strategies do not depend on the gravity of the markets; however, market-related factors such as prices, correlations, credit spreads and sector or style tilts can "move against" a strategy and cause losses or more significantly trigger a manager "blowup."

Hedge Fund of Funds

A common way to mitigate the risk of a manager blowup or the exposure of investing in a single hedge fund strategy is by investing in a hedge fund of funds. A *fund of funds* is a fund that mixes and matches hedge funds, spreading the investments among many different funds and/or strategies. A fund of funds simplifies the process of choosing hedge funds, blending together funds to meet a range of investor risk/return objectives while spreading the risks over a variety of funds. This blending of different strategies and asset classes aims to deliver a more consistent return than investing in any of the individual funds separately.

A fund of hedge funds is a diversified portfolio of hedge funds constructed by a fund of funds manager. Most often the underlying funds have low correlation to one another or are uncorrelated. They are widely diversified and can be strategy-specific with numerous underlying managers executing variations of a similar strategy, such as relative value, or may be multistrategy funds that consist of managers employing many different strategies such as relative value, convertible arbitrage and long/short. Fund of funds can also have a focus on a specific sector or geographical region. The fund of funds approach has been the preferred investment form for many pension funds.

Manager Selection

Selecting and monitoring hedge fund managers is complex and is probably the single most important aspect of the investing process. When selecting a fund of funds manager, it is important to ensure they have quantitative as well as qualitative processes in place. Fund of funds managers have to have the knowledge, insight and experience of understanding the manager's "edge" in a strategy, the trading strategies employed, the risk exposure at the manager level and also the fund of funds level, and how each manager correlates to one another.

The process of manager selection, portfolio construction, risk monitoring and portfolio rebalancing by a fund of funds manager is an ongoing process. All fund of funds managers are not created equal and a poorly chosen portfolio of hedge funds can produce disappointing results.

Fund of Funds Pros and Cons

Every investment decision can be broken down into balancing the advantages and disadvantages. Portfolio diversification is probably the biggest advantage for institutional investors to invest in fund of funds. The fund of funds manager aims to deliver more stable returns under most market conditions through portfolio construction. By spreading the risk among many managers, the effects of a single manager blowup are significantly reduced.

Second, the analysis of hedge funds is a highly detailed and labor-intensive process. Collecting the information can be difficult and the overall due diligence is never-ending. It is estimated that there are roughly 7,000 hedge funds available and manager analysis is not one sided; it includes both hiring and firing. Given the opaqueness of the industry, someone from within the industry, such as a fund of funds manager, would probably have a competitive advantage in garnering information from managers and understanding its meaning than someone outside of the industry.

Finally, fund of funds are providers of access to managers and capacity. As the industry continues to grow, existing managers with a competitive edge and proven track record are making access to their funds more restrictive, while new managers continue to enter the marketplace. Fund of funds managers know how and where to find the talent and often have longstanding relationships with established managers or strong reputations within the industry that allow access to managers "closed" to new investors.

The main disadvantage to hedge fund and/or fund of funds investing would be cost. Unlike traditional managers that charge a management fee, hedge fund managers charge a management fee and also participate in the profits of the fund and receive a performance fee of typically up to 20%. Many hedge fund managers have their personal money invested in their funds, and the industry standard of performance fees/incentive fees is a common feature that lures many talented managers into the hedge fund arena. Some funds set standards for receiving performance fees such as high-water marks or hurdle rates. High-water marks specify that a manager only receives a performance fee when the portfolio value exceeds the value of its previous high. A high-water mark policy prevents a manager from taking a "bonus" for good performance in a given period without first recovering any earlier absolute losses. Hurdle rates specify the return above which a hedge fund manager begins taking incentive fees.

With fund of funds, fees are charged twice. The underlying hedge fund managers collect their management and performance fees, and then the fund of funds manager collects additional management and performance fees. Many fund of funds have begun to charge a flat management fee (although higher than the norm) and waive the performance fee, although that is not the industry standard. When evaluating fund returns, it is important to assess all performance data on a net-of-fees basis and to relate the fee structure to the value added by the fund of funds manager. It is also imperative to ask about "hidden" costs such as administrative fees that may affect returns.

Liquidity in a fund of funds can be a drawback for some benefit funds. Most fund of funds have a minimum one-year lockup on invested capital; however, quarterly withdrawals/redemptions may be made with advance notification thereafter with no penalties. Finally, there is the issue of hedge fund holdings transparency. Transparency is probably the hottest topic for institutional investors today since hedge funds traditionally do not provide information about their holdings, not even to their own investors. From the manager's perspective, there is incentive *not* to reveal the fund's positions for two reasons. First, the market can trade against the manager if the position is revealed to the market (i.e., shorts). Second, most managers believe they have an edge relative to the market and are making money by doing something the market does not know about or doing it better than the market does. Many fund of funds managers have substantial access to the underlying positions, or at least have enough information to understand the exposure and risk involved. Registration by fund of funds is becoming more common these days and with fund of funds managers taking on a fiduciary role, access to investment information is increasing.

Leverage

An important area to consider when evaluating a hedge fund investment and risk is the use of leverage. *Leverage* involves borrowing money to increase the amount invested in a certain position. Managers use leverage when they believe the return from the position will exceed the cost of the borrowed funds. Sometimes managers use leverage to enable them to take on a new position without having to liquidate existing positions. Although leverage can be beneficial, it can both magnify the risk of a strategy as well as create risk by giving the lender power over the disposition of the investment portfolio. Another by-product of leverage is unrelated business taxable income (UBTI). UBTI is generated from the profits resulting from the leveraged portion of the investment portfolio and is taxable to the investor, including U.S. tax-exempt pension funds.

Domicile

Funds domiciled in the United States are referred to as *onshore funds*. Many onshore fund of funds are registered in the state of Delaware. Some of the advantages of registering in Delaware include:

- No minimum capital is required to form a Delaware corporation.
- There is no corporate income tax on companies formed in Delaware.
- Corporate records can be kept anywhere in the world.
- Ownership of a Delaware corporation is strictly confidential.
- It is inexpensive.

However, a large majority of funds are domiciled outside of the United States in renowned tax havens such as Bermuda, the British Virgin Islands and the Cayman Islands. These funds are referred to as *offshore funds* and offer many tax benefits to U.S. and non-U.S. investors, including U.S. tax-exempt investors trying to avoid UBTI.

Benchmarks

Plan sponsors and fiduciaries in the traditional asset management industry normally require that performance be measured against a benchmark (relative return). Most hedge fund managers consider their strategies absolute return strategies, rather than relative return, and therefore no benchmarks are used. The return goal is defined in absolute terms and, if anything, measured against the risk-free rate or cash.

It is important to remember that different hedge fund strategies have different expected returns, volatilities and correlations characteristics. Some funds may serve as a "risk reducer" in a portfolio and target returns similar to fixed income with a goal of T-bills + 5%, while others serve as a "return enhancer" with higher correlations to equities and target returns of S&P 500 + 3%. Also, remember that each manager has a nuance or edge that defines how he or she achieves return, which would make benchmarking difficult since it would be nearly impossible to replicate what the manager is doing. There are some hedge fund benchmarks available, but industry experts agree that they are not truly representative of specific strategies and may include severe survivor bias (only "good" funds reporting returns). This may change with time as the industry becomes more institutionalized.

Conclusion

As the hedge fund industry continues to evolve, it is slowly becoming more regulated. The SEC is taking a more active role in oversight and many fund of funds are now becoming registered. The increased interest in hedge fund investing by institutional funds is also causing more fund managers to accept a fiduciary role in the management of assets, while structuring their funds to be compliant with ERISA's plan asset rule and the Department of Labor guidelines.

As a trustee, the most important aspect of your job is the legal responsibility or fiduciary duty as defined by ERISA for the "prudent" investment of fund assets. Section 404(c) of ERISA's fiduciary duties (statutory requirements) sets forth that a fiduciary has the basic responsibility to *diversify the investments of the plan so as to minimize the risk of large losses, unless under the circumstances it is clearly not prudent to do so.* In a portfolio context, risk is reduced by increasing the allocation of less risky asset classes or introducing assets with low or negative correlation to the core of the portfolio. Many hedge fund strategies achieve high risk-adjusted returns with low correlations to traditional asset classes, and fund of funds help minimize the risk of large losses by diversifying the risk of individual hedge funds. A case can clearly be made for the inclusion of hedge fund of funds in benefit plan portfolios.

Chapter 14

Derivatives

If your investment manager brings up the subject of *derivatives*, don't throw up your hands in frustration; the use of futures and options by your manager adds additional portfolio tools to control risk, maintain liquidity, minimize costs and/or enhance return. Price changes in the futures markets essentially mirror the cash market (options and futures prices are *derived* from their connected, underlying securities); positions can be taken at lower transactions costs and without disturbing the underlying portfolio positions.

Derivatives can now be issued based on currencies, commodities, government or corporate debt, home mortgages, stocks, interest rates, etc., etc., or even combinations of the above! You do not need to understand all the nuances of these complicated instruments, but before you enter into a course of action involving the use of derivative instruments you do need to understand the contribution such a course of action could make to your plan's overall risk posture.

Since derivative instruments can provide financial solutions to many of your manager's portfolio challenges, the trustees need to be open to the manager's recommendations for their use in the portfolio. It is incumbent upon the manager to prove to you both as to *why* they should be used and to demonstrate to you his or her *expertise* in this area.

Futures Contracts

A *futures contract* is a commitment to buy or sell a standardized quantity of a particular item for a specific future settlement date at a currently agreed-upon price. Futures contracts are traded on designated futures exchanges regulated by the Commodity Futures Trading Commission (CFTC) and are subject to daily settlement procedures. For employee benefit plans the "item" for which a commitment is made to buy or sell is usually not wheat or corn, but T-bills, T-bonds, GNMAs or some other financial instrument.

Futures contracts permit portfolio managers to hedge against price risk in the underlying instrument. For instance, your common stock manager may feel that, although a cyclical correction in the stock market appears imminent, the manager may not want to disturb the individual security positions. By selling stock index futures (futures contracts based on a broad market index) he or she could reduce the portfolio's exposure to the broad general market while retaining the individual positions.

Option Contracts

Stock option contracts can provide a combination of important investment characteristics that can improve a manager's ability to meet the objective of the portfolio. These advantages include return enhancement and risk reduction. The use of options in employee benefit plans has been limited primarily to writing so-called covered calls against stocks held already in the portfolio.

Calls permit the buyer of the contract to buy stock at a specified quote (strike price) on or before the specified expiration date. For granting this privilege, the seller of the call receives a "premium" from the buyer.

The primary result of an option transaction is to reallocate the risk in common stock ownership. The buyer pays a premium, which represents the expected risk of loss, as well as the interest cost of holding the underlying stock. For this fee, the buyer obtains the opportunity to gain the upside price potential in the stock. Conversely, the seller of the call receives a premium, which cushions the downside risk to some degree, but also limits the seller's potential for gain during the contract period. Unlike futures, option contracts can expire without a transaction occurring.

Historically, option contracts have not been used extensively by employee benefit plans. However, the inclusion of option contracts in their portfolios may permit plans in search of higher returns to utilize greater proportions of common stock as a class than they might have without the cushioning effect provided by options. Also, the pension fund can transfer short-term market risk to those who are willing to speculate on shorter term movements. The success of such hedging activity is dependent upon the insight of the particular investment manager.

Futures and options are complex instruments; leverage is used thereby increasing the magnitude of risk in any transaction, and often these markets can be illiquid. Such characteristics encourage trustees to *proceed cautiously* when authorizing their use in the portfolio. Safeguards established often include:

1. Authorizing only those managers who have in the past demonstrated skill in their use
2. Permitting their use for hedging purposes (as opposed to speculating on future prices) only
3. Establishing quantitative limits to control the impact the derivatives' positions may have on future portfolio values
4. Precise guidelines to avoid misunderstanding between trustee boards and their investment managers regarding the new derivative "exotics." (An "inverse floater" is not a government security!)

Authorizing your manager to use derivatives can provide your portfolio with a competitive advantage. Of course, like any other portfolio management decision, insightful judgment is required to produce value-adding results.

Chapter 15

Indexing

What is an *index fund?* It is a commingled account, or mutual fund, comprised of securities the characteristics of which will replicate (or substantially replicate) a designated securities index. The index fund passively provides only the return of the index, unlike active management, which seeks to provide a return superior to a reference index, or benchmark. Of course, active management often provides a return *less* than the benchmark, hence the reason for the continuing interest in index funds.

Why Indexing?

Indexing is a viable alternative to actively managed accounts for the following reasons:

1. It lowers investment management fees.
2. It provides high liquidity.
3. It has provided strong relative performance when compared to active management.
4. It lowers transactions and commissions costs.
5. It provides broad diversification.
6. It increases certainty that the return received will be commensurate with the risk taken.

7. It is not affected by personnel changes at the investment management firm.

Although a number of active managers have demonstrated their ability over the long term to add value above a benchmark index, it is difficult for the trustees to determine which managers will continue to do so in the future. Since a number of studies have confirmed that the market's actions tend to overwhelm any impact from the sector and company commitments of the managers, allocating a portion of a pension fund to an index fund(s) improves the risk/return posture of the overall portfolio.

Indexing exploits the randomness of stock prices; indexing and randomness skip along together over time oblivious to shorter cyclical revaluations, choosing instead to capture longer term value enhancements.

> *The powerful magnetism of the mean.* In the world of investing, the mean is a powerful magnet that pulls financial market returns toward it, causing returns to deteriorate after they exceed historical norms by substantial margins and to improve after they fall short. The mean is also the powerful magnet that pulls the returns achieved by portfolio managers toward it, causing a fund's return to move, over time, ever closer to the average returns achieved by other funds. Regression to the mean is a manifestation of the immutable law of averages that prevails, sooner or later, in the financial jungle.
>
> *John Bogle*

Common Stock Indexing

Some trustees have concluded that an index fund makes sense in that part of the market which is "most efficiently priced," i.e., the large capitalization stocks. They feel that small and international stocks are not as efficiently priced and can be exploited for value by insightful managers.

There are dozens of index investing alternatives available in the marketplace. Domestic stock index accounts include the following:

1. Broad market–passive index
    - S&P 500–Represents 72% U.S. Equity Capitalization
    - Russell 3000–Represents 88% U.S. Equity Capitalization
    - Wilshire 5000

2. Style-oriented–passive index
   - Large cap growth: Russell 1000 (earnings growth)
   - Value: Russell 1000 (price driven)
   - S&P midcap (400 medium capitalization stocks)
   - Small cap: Russell 2000, Wilshire "Next 1750"
3. Enhanced indexing
   - Index futures arbitrage
   - Trading strategies
   - Derivatives-based strategies
   - Mathematical strategies
4. Guaranteed index funds.

One of the reasons the S&P 500 has been such a formidable competitor is that since World War II bull markets have been longer in duration, and greater in intensity, than bear markets, and the index has the advantage of being fully invested at the beginning of bull markets. (See Exhibit 15-1.) Most managers have some cash equivalents in their portfolios at all times; often a *lot* of cash when things are the most gloomy. Any cash penalizes them during the initial, of-

Exhibit 15-1

LONG-TERM TREND IN STOCK PRICES—
S&P 500 INDEX CHANGE IN VALUE
(1949-2003)

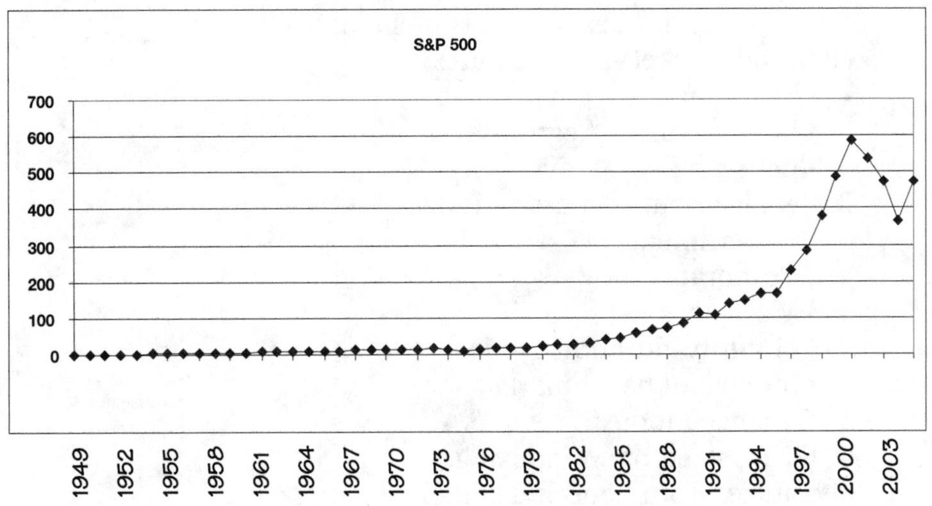

Source: Ibbotson Associates.

ten dramatic, market rises. Cash does help in bear markets, of course, but the damage to portfolio returns from bear markets tends to pale over time when compared to the larger returns achieved in the bull markets.

In addition to being there when the market starts its bull market rise, the index funds' positions are cheaper to maintain. It has been estimated that from savings realized in management fees, transaction costs and commissions, stock index funds can have as much as a 90 basis points (9/10 of 1%) advantage over actively managed accounts, and bond index funds can have as much as a 40 basis points advantage. Compounded over time, this expense savings is significant to large portfolios in dollar growth.

Bond Indexing

While indexing stock monies has become very popular, trustees have been slow to similarly invest their bond monies. Their reluctance to do so has apparently been intuitively correct because research conducted by Ennis, Knupp & Associates has concluded that "flaws in existing fixed income benchmarks prevent index funds from providing portfolios with desirable investment characteristics, and fixed income market inefficiencies create additional opportunities for active managers to add value." Also, bond managers have of their own volition controlled the volatility risk in the portfolios by providing structured strategies such as laddered, dedicated and immunized portfolios.

Domestic bond index accounts include:

1. Broad market–passive index
   - Salomon Bros. BIG
   - Lehman Bros. Aggregate
   - Lehman Bros. Govt./Corp.
2. Sector-oriented–passive index
   - Governments
   - Corporates
   - Mortgages
   - Maturity/duration groups
   - Individual benchmarks
3. Enhanced indexing
4. Guaranteed bond indexing.

Advantages from bond indexing include:

- ◆ Relatively low-cost way to invest in bonds and
- ◆ Assurance that you will do as well as the "bond market."

International Indexing

Some boards have chosen to begin their global/international investment programs by participating in an international index fund. One of the most popular international equity indexes is the Morgan Stanley EAFE Index (MSCI EAFE). It was developed in 1969 with the unique feature of being statistically adjusted to allow comparison between the stock markets of different countries and across industries. The MSCI EAFE (Europe, Australia, Far East) Index reflects the relative market capitalizations of the 20 largest non-North American equity markets. Each country's contribution toward the total EAFE Index represents a sample of companies listed in that country and reflects the relative weighting by industry capitalization of that country's equity market. An international index fund may be particularly favored by a Taft-Hartley plan that prefers not to invest directly into individual companies that are located outside of the United States.

> A thousand to ten thousand money managers all look about equally good or bad. Each expects to do 3% better than the mob. Each has put together a convincing story. After the fact, hardly ten out of ten thousand perform . . . It may be the better part of wisdom to forsake a search for needles that are so small in haystacks that are so very large.
>
> *Paul Samuelson (1989)*

Enhanced Indexing

You should also be aware of a new generation of index funds that are called *enhanced index funds.* If you can be assured that your investment will "substantially replicate" the return of a chosen index, you may be willing to take a modest amount of "manager induced" risk, which provides the potential to enhance the portfolio's return above the benchmark return. By embracing enhanced indexing, trustees hold the manager to a "short leash," permitting him or her to apply a proprietary strategy seeking a controlled, modest, return advantage over a "plain vanilla" index fund.

Many trustees dismiss the indexing alternative as a commitment to mediocrity. Those who have concluded thusly have the formidable challenge of creating an astute investment manager selection process that discovers managers who are successful in adding value above the market alternative. It can be done, but many funds have failed to do so and have been relegated to the unenviable position of changing managers every three to five years. This can be a very expensive way of conducting fund affairs.

Although some concluded 35 years ago that indexing as a funding vehicle would not stand the test of time, indexing has only proven itself a formidable competitor to active management strategies.

Chapter 16

Structured Equity–Enhanced Indexing

Contributed by Jennifer Winfield and Carl Zangardi
INTECH

Evolution of Common Stock Management

For decades investors were willing to merely "buy and hold" common stock. During the "performance era" of the 1960s, investors began to "manipulate" their portfolios in the attempt to trade up to increased values. Due to the increasing cost of trading and lack of success in producing superior returns, investors by the end of the decade became disenchanted with this "go-go" approach and began to take notice of the academic communities' increasing interest in index funds.

For many years passively invested index funds were held in disrepute by many investors; early on, critics labeled them "unpatriotic" and indicated that investors in these funds were acting imprudently and settling for mediocrity. However, as indexing became increasingly competitive to active management, investors began to passively invest more and more of their monies; equity indexing grew from approximately $480 billion in 1995 to approximately $1.7 trillion in 2003 (*Pension & Investments,* March 22, 2004). Partially fueling this increased interest in index funds was the performance of the S&P 500 Index over much of the 1980s and 1990s; during that period the S&P 500 Index was typically in the top half to top quartile of domestic equity active manager databases, outperforming an overwhelming majority of active managers.

In the 1980s the stock market, as measured by the S&P 500, returned 17% per year on average. In the decade of the 1990s the stock market returned 18% per year. In an environment in which you could achieve 17% to 18% per year without having to incur active management fees, what was the incentive to attempt to identify a manager who may add an additional 1% or 2%, net of fees? With most plans having actuarial assumptions in the 7% to 9% range, indexing a portfolio allowed trustees to achieve returns far in excess of their actuarial assumptions, with no added risk. In addition, indexing was a cheaper option for the trustees and eliminated the potential of their having selected a manager that subsequently significantly underperformed the market.

As we begin the new millennium, however, it appears that the return potential of domestic stocks may have changed dramatically. Instead of attaining high double-digit returns in this decade, stocks may provide only nominal single-digit returns. Even with the S&P 500's remarkable 28% return in 2003 factored in, the first four years of this decade have seen the market average a return of −5.34%. If the stock market achieves an average of 12.51% per year on the S&P 500 for the next six years of the decade, the entire ten-year period will have achieved average annual returns of only 5% per year. With most plans having adopted actuarial assumptions typically significantly above 5%, there is the potential for a continuing benefits funding crisis.

In such an environment, if one can with relatively high levels of probability and consistency achieve an additional 1% to 2% net of fees, the results can make a dramatic impact on the funding status of a plan. The probability that a structured product provider can demonstrate this kind of consistent and repeatable excess return generation is evidenced by the *information ratio* (which academically is defined as the excess return divided by the standard deviation of the excess return). Structured product providers typically have information ratios above .80 and often approaching 1.0; in the investment industry, an information ratio of .50 or above is considered very favorable. (The information ratio measures the amount of variability or risk in the excess return that the manager has been able to produce, and high information ratios suggest that a manager has a high level of probability of outperforming the index on a sustainable basis.)

Because of their tight risk controls, high information ratios and consistent competitive rates of return, plan sponsors and their consultants are increasingly turning to structured equity products in their search for alpha (risk-adjusted excess returns). In an environment in which the market/benchmark portfolio produces a 5% to 6% return, an enhanced index product (or similarly structured product) offers the potential of achieving a 7% to 8% return. With the added advantage of relatively lower fees than traditional active management, these strategies are a logical extension of an index portfolio already in place. Without significantly increasing the risk profile, the plan enhances its probability for higher returns.

What Is Structured Equity?

Investment processes that employ tight risk controls typically characterize *structured equity portfolio management.* A successfully managed portfolio would have the following attributes:

- Limited fluctuations in the value of the portfolio (as measured by the standard deviation of returns)
- Limited divergence of the return of the portfolio from the return of the referenced benchmark (tracking error)
- A higher risk-adjusted return when compared to its benchmark (positive alpha)
- Statistical evidence that there is a high probability of continuing consistent and repeatable superior risk-adjusted return (as measured by the information ratio).

Types of Structured Equity Portfolios

There are a variety of processes that managers can employ with limited risk in their quest to add value above the returns of the benchmark index. The portfolio management processes of all of the differing strategies result in the individual positions in the portfolio diverging from the individual positions in the referenced benchmark portfolio. These types of strategies typically fall into two broad categories; first, those that result in all-long portfolios (fully invested stock portfolios, no use of derivatives) and are achieved using any number of methods, which include traditional fundamental research, quantitative screens or mathematically applied processes. The other broad category is typically the synthetic strategies, which employ derivatives positions and broadly encompass index arbitrage-related strategies and index futures with enhanced cash management.

With such variety in approach it is obvious that all structured products are not created equal. As with the evaluation of all proposed strategies the trustees need to perform carefully their due diligence in the selection process. The portfolio management process, the appropriateness of the chosen benchmark, the past performance, and the professionalism and personal integrity of the supervising principals must be assessed.

Potential Contribution to Portfolio

Whereas in the past trustees may have adopted a barbell approach, i.e., passive index funds complemented with active management, consideration is now being given to expanding the equity asset mix to include one, or more, structured equity products. It is posited that such an addition, or additions, would result in a smoother pattern of risk and return over time. As previously mentioned, structured products (or what is often referred to as *enhanced indexing)* typically provide net-of-fee returns of 1% to 2% above the benchmark index over the long term. In an environment where plan sponsors are increasingly searching for alpha (risk-adjusted excess returns), this may be more important than ever.

Although a projected increase of 1% to 2% net of fee returns may sound like a nominal amount, the enhancement to the portfolio from compounding small amounts over time can be quite dramatic. Exhibit 16-1 reflects the power of compounding; $100 million compounding at 8% for 30 years results in an accumulation of approximately $1.1 billion for benefits; whereas this amount compounding at 10% results in an accumulation of $1.7 billion, a considerable difference. Structured equity products provide additional benefits; their excess return patterns tend to be noncorrelated with traditional active management. In a multimanager lineup or in conjunction with other structured product providers, the combination of the strategies typically results in a favorable risk/reward profile for the overall plan. Also, since the various structured products tend to be noncorrelated with one another, more trustees are considering adding more than one structured product to their equity portfolio.

Concluding Thoughts

Trustees should consider the following when contemplating adding a structured equity product to their equity portfolio:

- ◆ These strategies are a logical extension of an index portfolio that may already be in place, and tend to be noncorrelated to the return/risk profile of the traditional managers already in place. Thus, when added to an existing mix of index and active managers, the disciplined structure of these portfolios can pro-

Exhibit 16-1

MODERATE, CONSISTENTLY DELIVERED ALPHA
CAN GO A LONG WAY
Hypothetical Growth of $100 Million
for 30 Years at 8%, 9% and 10%

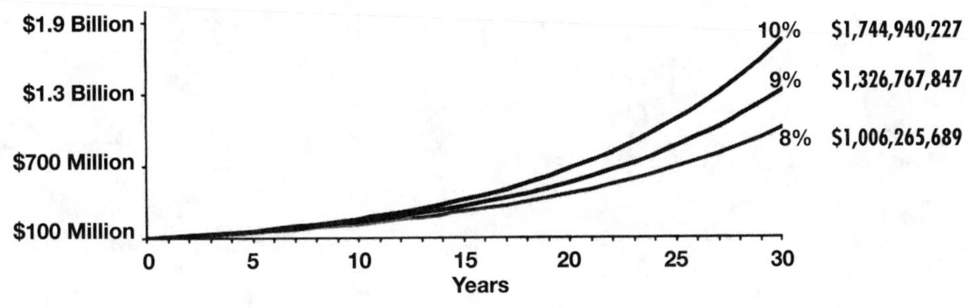

vide the potential for additional return *and* reduce overall risk in the portfolio.

- The potential to add a small increment in return to what may prove to be modest returns going forward would contribute significantly to the funding of benefits over time.
- The track records of the managers offering these products are now long enough to be validated as to their potential to add value.
- The generally higher relative information ratios of these products increase one's confidence in the probability of their continuing to produce consistent and repeatable superior risk-adjusted returns.
- In general, the fees on these products are lower than the fees charged for traditional management.

Chapter 17

International Equities

Contributed by Giulio Martini
Bernstein Investment Research & Management
A Unit of Alliance Capital Management LP

Over the last decade, investments by U.S. pension plans in foreign equities have grown meaningfully. Public funds and corporate pension plans now invest more than 10% of their assets in foreign stock markets.

Some plans have yet to take this step, however. With the world's largest stock market so close at hand, it may seem unnecessary to cross borders to invest assets. Moreover, Taft-Hartley plans, in particular, are concerned about making foreign investments that may undermine the U.S. workers they represent.

Plans that confine themselves to U.S. borders are missing important advantages that can come with overseas investing, including a broader scope of opportunities and the potential for risk reduction. In addition, it has become far easier for Taft-Hartley plans to make such investments without compromising their underlying principles.

Overseas Markets Offer Opportunity

In terms of opportunity, U.S. dominance of the global capital markets has been shrinking over the past several decades. Commanding roughly two-thirds of all stock investments worldwide in 1970, the United States today accounts for just more than half. (See Exhibit 17-1.) In other words, there are almost as many potential investments out-

Exhibit 17-1

OPPORTUNITY OUTSIDE UNITED STATES

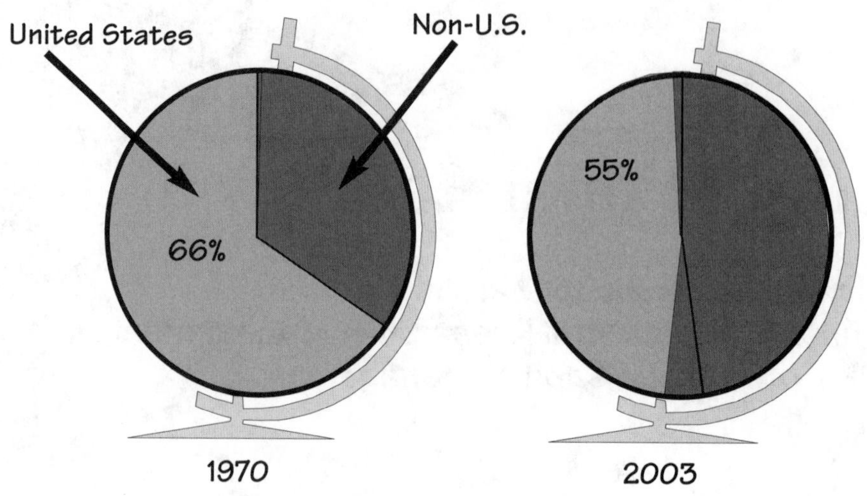

1970 figures based on MSCI World at 31 January 1970.
2003 figures based on MSCI World at 31 December 2003.
Source: Morgan Stanley Capital International (MSCI) and Bernstein.

side the United States as within. The proportion is far higher in many key industries. For example, at the end of 2003, 55% of the market value for publicly traded banking companies was based outside the United States, 66% for telecommunications companies and 73% for listed real estate companies. Restricting investment horizons can leave out some of the most compelling opportunities for reward.

In addition to offering opportunities, stock markets outside the United States can be expected to provide comparable returns over the long run. Looking over the past 20 years, for example, the best annual returns were split evenly. The United States won in ten of those years, and the other ten went to the developed markets outside the United States, as represented by Morgan Stanley Capital International's EAFE index, a commonly used barometer of performance for non-U.S. markets. (EAFE stands for the Europe, Australasia and Far East index of 20 major stock markets weighted by capitalization and currencies unhedged in U.S. dollars.) (See Exhibit 17-2.) It is true that the U.S. market's performance was particularly rewarding in the second half of the 1990s. However, the developed markets outside the United

Exhibit 17-2

BEST RETURNS VARY

Total Returns

	S&P 500 Index	MSCI EAFE Index
1984	6.3%	**7.4%**
1985	31.7	**56.2**
1986	18.7	**69.4**
1987	5.3	**24.6**
1988	16.6	**28.3**
1989	**31.7**	10.5
1990	**−3.1**	−23.4
1991	**30.5**	12.1
1992	**7.6**	−12.2
1993	10.1	**32.6**
1994	1.3	**7.8**
1995	**37.6**	11.2
1996	**23.0**	6.0
1997	**33.4**	1.8
1998	**28.6**	20.0
1999	21.0	**27.0**
2000	**−9.1**	−14.2
2001	**−11.9**	−21.4
2002	−22.1	**−15.9**
2003	28.7	**38.6**

U.S. stocks are represented by the S&P 500 index and non-U.S. developed markets by the Morgan Stanley Capital International (MSCI) EAFE index, with countries weighted according to market capitalization and currencies unhedged.
Source: MSCI, Standard & Poor's and Bernstein.

States had many strong years over the preceding decade and have outperformed the United States over the last two years. Leadership among markets is always in flux, and there is no evidence to suggest any change in that regard.

Diversification Helps Smooth Returns

These differences in the ebbs and flows of various markets' returns are important: They provide the diversification that makes investing in both the U.S. and overseas markets less risky than investing in the United States alone. (See Exhibit 17-3.) Higher portfolio volatil-

Exhibit 17-3

MIXING U.S. AND FOREIGN STOCKS REDUCES RISK

Volatility of U.S./Foreign Stock Mixes, 1970-2003

Observed Volatility

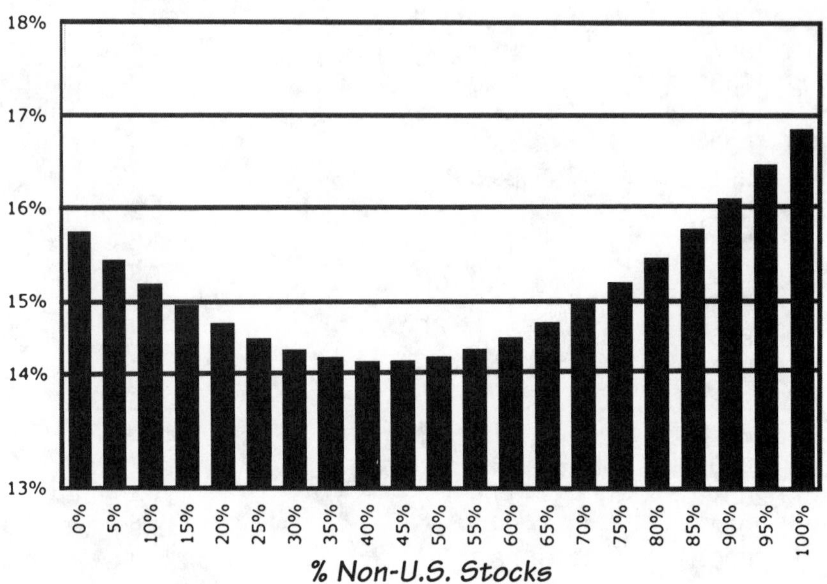

---

*Non-U.S. stocks are represented by the MSCI Europe, Australasia and Far East index, with countries weighted according to market capitalization and currencies unhedged.
Source: MSCI, Standard & Poor's and Bernstein.

ity means greater investment risk. Examining the volatility of various combinations of U.S. and major foreign market stocks over the past 30 years shows that portfolios consisting of 100% U.S. stocks, on the far left of the exhibit, are less volatile than portfolios holding 100% EAFE stocks, shown on the far right. However, portfolios containing around 40% foreign stocks bring risk down still further relative to U.S. stocks alone. Importantly, the risk-reduction benefits start right away: Even a 5-10% allocation to foreign stocks reduces risk compared to a portfolio holding U.S. stocks only.

Reducing portfolio volatility can have a very real effect on enhancing overall returns. Consider three hypothetical portfolios with a $1 investment over two years. (See Exhibit 17-4.) One that loses 10% in the first year and gains 30% the next is worth $1.17. A second that

Exhibit 17-4

VOLATILITY REDUCES RETURN OVER TIME

	Portfolio		
	A	B	C
Initial Investment	$1.00	$1.00	$1.00
First-Year Return	(10)%	0%	10%
Second-Year Return	30%	20%	10%
Average Annual Return	10%	10%	10%
Closing Value	**$1.17**	**$1.20**	**$1.21**

Source: Bernstein.

holds steady one year and then grows 20% is worth $1.20. A third that gains 10% in each of the two years is worth $1.21. All three average a 10% annual return, but they provide different amounts of money at the end. This illustrates, on a small scale, how steadier growth allows compounding to do its work more forcefully. The pattern of how performance is achieved can dramatically impact the ultimate results.

Is Globalization Reducing Diversification?

This is where diversification comes in: Different performance patterns from one country to the next help to lessen a portfolio's overall volatility. However, there are concerns that diversification benefits may be diminished as markets become more global. It is true that markets have reacted similarly to short-term global events such as the 1970s oil crisis or the Gulf War in the early 1990s. The same type of reaction was seen a few years ago with the explosion of the Internet, which made investors worldwide enamored of technology and telecom stocks. But once such events subside, investment markets tend to again be driven by underlying fundamentals of a local nature, including economic growth, corporate profit cycles, inflation and interest rates. Evidence continues to show that these factors behave largely independently from one market to the next.

Also at work is fundamental divergence in market composition. For example, as of 2003, the U.S. stock market had relatively high rep-

Exhibit 17-5

FOREIGN MARKETS OFFER DIFFERENT MIX

Percent of Market Capitalization

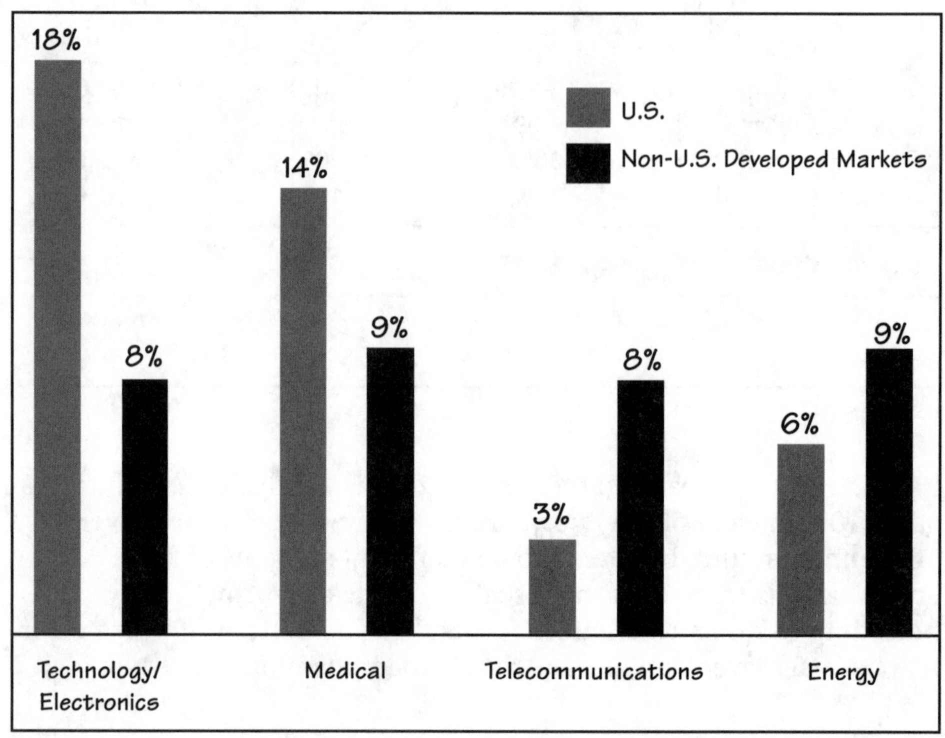

As of 31 December 2003
Source: MSCI and Bernstein.

resentation in technology and health care, while telecom and energy companies were more important in EAFE countries. (See Exhibit 17-5.) This is important because particular industries go through global boom or bust cycles. Even as one industry's stocks soar and another's declines all around the world, market-by-market exposures to these cycles will vary, and so will returns. This is another reason to believe that markets will continue behaving independently to a significant degree.

Aren't U.S. Multinationals or ADRs Diversifying for U.S. Investors?

Some have come to believe that plans can achieve needed diversification by investing solely in U.S. multinational corporations that

Exhibit 17-6

U.S. MULTINATIONALS DON'T DIVERSIFY PORTFOLIOS
Correlations With U.S. Stock Market—1975-2003

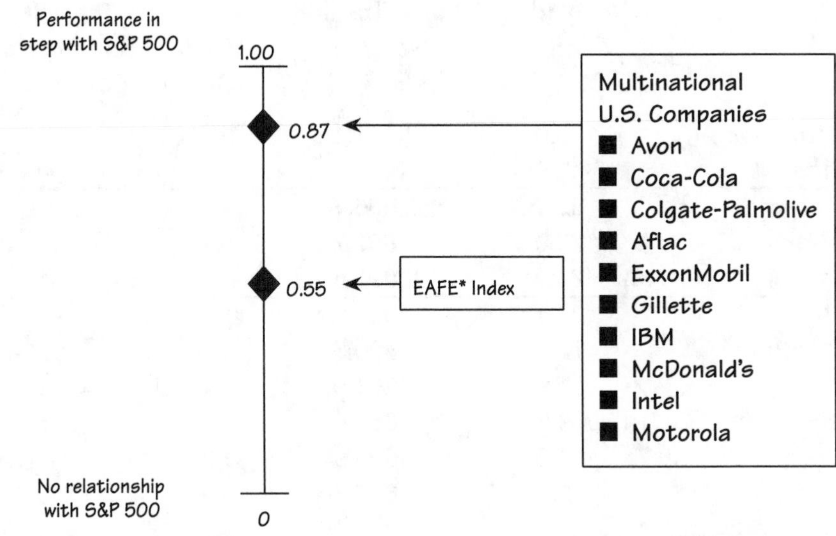

*MSCI's EAFE, with countries weighted according to market capitalization and currencies unhedged.
Source: WorldScope, MSCI, S&P and Bernstein.

source profits all around the globe. If they're doing business in Brazil and Germany, for example, aren't the companies exposed to the same business fluctuations as companies based in these countries? Research into return patterns suggests that they are not.

Measuring the similarity of returns over the past quarter-century between the S&P 500 stock index and the EAFE index reveals a 0.55 correlation, which indicates that these markets are meaningfully diversifying. (A correlation of 1.00 means they move in lockstep, while a correlation of zero indicates no similarity in behavior; anything below 0.7 is considered different enough to be diversifying.) By contrast, there has been greater similarity over the same period between the S&P 500 and a portfolio of ten longstanding U.S. companies considered among the country's most global: Aflac, Avon, Coca-Cola, Colgate-Palmolive, ExxonMobil, Gillette, IBM, McDonald's, Intel and Motorola. Here, the correlation was 0.87–well above the range thought to offer diversification benefits. (See Exhibit 17-6.) While these companies do business all around the world, their securities be-

Exhibit 17-7

ADR-ONLY STRATEGY LIMITS OPPORTUNITY

2003 Trading Breakdown

Country	ADR Trading Volume (U.S. $ Bil.)	Local Trading Volume (U.S. $ Bil.)	ADR % of Total	Number of Companies
United Kingdom	120.0	2,721.1	5.3%	88
Finland	53.9	194.9	35.7	4
France	**32.7**	**935.7**	**4.4**	**27**
Germany	**25.9**	**862.7**	**4.7**	**17**
Japan	**24.9**	**2,093.6**	**2.7**	**31**
Australia	23.1	306.3	11.6	21
Switzerland	12.6	400.5	2.9	12
Sweden	11.9	291.9	7.2	9
Netherlands	9.8	658.4	4.7	15
Spain	4.3	506.9	1.3	7
Italy	2.7	617.7	0.9	10

Source: Bank of New York, FactSet and Bernstein.

have like U.S. stocks–subject to the same business cycle and other influences that drive the U.S. market in total. Holding U.S. multinational corporations is much less effective as a diversifier of risk than owning foreign stocks.

American Depository Receipts–or ADRs–might seem to offer the best of both worlds. They trade on U.S. exchanges in U.S. dollars just like U.S. stocks, and meet the same financial-disclosure requirements that U.S. companies do, but they represent shares in foreign companies. For U.S. investors, this can make buying stock in Nokia of Finland or Sony of Japan no different from buying Coca-Cola or Johnson & Johnson; yet investors gain direct exposure to foreign companies. With ADRs, however, opportunity is severely limited. For most countries, only a relatively few companies are available to U.S. investors through ADRs. (See Exhibit 17-7.) With Japan, for example, only 31 out of the broad stock market's 3,700 listed companies offered ADRs as of 2003. For France, only 27 of its 1,000 listed companies were offering U.S. ADRs. Such small numbers of available stocks make it difficult to build a well-diversified portfolio of international companies. Moreover, trading volume in ADRs is only a small fraction of that available on these countries' domestic exchanges–below 5% in the case of Japan, France, Switzerland and Germany, making it difficult to trade portfolios efficiently. In all, availability of investments through ADRs offers far too little selection to provide the diversification needed to make international investing beneficial.

Complying With AFL-CIO Foreign-Investing Guidelines

Clearly, there can be meaningful advantages to investing outside U.S. borders. But many employee retirement plans have been reluctant to do so for fear of compromising underlying principles and labor standards. The AFL-CIO, however, provides guidance to help plans sidestep such pitfalls. Its Country Watch List, for example, provides a list of countries to be avoided because of violations of core labor standards. *Core labor standards* include the right to organize and bargain collectively, the right of association, and the right to be free of competition from child or prison labor, among others. Virtually all of the major developed investment markets guarantee such rights, and so they are all eligible for union investment in line with the AFL-CIO guidelines.

The AFL-CIO's guidelines also help assess specific investments within eligible markets by suggesting that plans screen for economic, social or environmental impact; investigate adherence to employment, health and safety, labor and environmental standards; and assess whether investment will displace American products or employment. In very broad terms, these guidelines tend to produce an emphasis on domestic-based businesses, such as utilities, banks and services, and widespread avoidance of manufacturing companies that compete on a global basis, such as autos, steel and chemicals.

The guidelines make it possible for union plans and their managers to invest internationally without fear of compromising the interests of the members they represent. It should be very feasible for the manager of a separately managed international stock account to tailor investment guidelines to meet these objectives. Labor-friendly investing is less widely available through commingled vehicles (such as mutual funds), which are typically geared for the goals of a broader cross section of the investing public. But even here, select commingled vehicles do exist that are specifically designed for the labor-union constituency with this group's concerns in mind. Moreover, our research indicates that portfolios adhering to AFL-CIO guidelines can be very competitive in terms of return and risk with other "unrestricted" portfolios. The benefits of international investing for employee plans are quite compelling, and they are becoming ever easier to achieve.

Chapter 18

Economically Targeted Investing

Contributed by Monte Tarbox
Independent Fiduciary Services, Inc.

Introduction

All investments have multiple impacts. They have financial impacts on the investor by generating investment returns, hopefully positive, sometimes negative and almost always unpredictable. They have business impacts on the party that arranges, brokers, sells or manages the investment. They have regulatory and reporting impacts. Depending on the mix of investments, they may influence a pension fund's liabilities by altering the actuarial assumptions of a fund. These impacts are well understood and trustees grapple with them day in and day out as they make investment decisions. These impacts are closely monitored and carefully measured. Trustees typically have an array of tools, benchmarks and consultants to help them in this essential task.

But all investments have other impacts. They may create or destroy jobs. They may alter the mix of skilled, high-paying jobs and unskilled, low-wage jobs available in the economy. They may favor some geographic regions over others. They may favor ownership over lending, equities over bonds. They may encourage some industries to expand and others to contract. These impacts are less well understood by most investors. They are not usually assessed before an investment is made and rarely measured after money has been committed.

There is growing recognition among trustees and other institutional investors that these secondary or collateral impacts matter and should be considered within the investment decision process. In an increasingly sophisticated world of investment options, investors more and more often find themselves in the enviable position of choosing between two or more equally attractive investment alternatives–be it between different equity managers, between different real estate funds or between domestic and international opportunities.

When faced with choices that offer equal likelihood of successful investment or rate-of-return outcomes, trustees have an opportunity to consider how their investment program can maximize these other outcomes and impacts. To do so, however, trustees need to be able to assess secondary and collateral impacts, which in turn requires new tools, analysis and a way of looking at investment opportunities.

The concept of *economically targeted investments,* also known as *ETIs,* emerged in the 1980s as the first step in trustees' efforts to do precisely this. In the early 1980s Randy Barber, and others, were calling for the creation of "financing mechanisms" that would permit labor-related pools of capital to invest in ways that were consistent with their ideals and aspirations. Such investing was initially perceived to be *social investing,* later referred to as *vested interests, job-creating* or *targeted investing.* More recently it has been called *economically targeted investing (ETI).* By whatever name, the goal has always been to "do well, by doing good."

Originally, this concept was used as a way of legitimizing an analysis that went beyond traditional financial measures. To counter claims that they were investing according to social or other "non-economic" criteria, trustees had to think long and hard about what they were trying to do. The notion of ETIs grew out of an understanding that it was both appropriate and effective to think about collateral benefits when designing an investment program. It was a way of giving intellectual weight to a more sophisticated approach, an approach which went beyond the narrow questions posed by traditional money managers. Today, the concept of ETIs is well accepted and a routine part of the process for many trustees. It is a concept that may be easier to apply in some asset classes than others, but it is a way of looking at the universe of all potential investments, which can uncover value in new ways.

As the investment programs of pension funds become more sophisticated and expand into new asset classes (like venture capital and international equities), it becomes even more important to understand the multitude of impacts created by every investment.

Trustees should evaluate investment options with reference to these impacts and should pursue those investment options that provide the best total package of benefits to plan participants.

ETIs as a Source of Value

The concept of ETIs has "worked" because the individual investments made under its banner have often "worked." These investments have achieved good risk-adjusted rates of return, captured secondary or collateral benefits for the funds and their participants, and contributed to the overall financial health of pension funds. If this were not the case, the concept would have dried up and blown away by now. In fact, ETIs have proven to be a source of value for those funds that have done the hard work to find the best alternatives.

When first developed, the concept looked like something new and "different," something outside of the established approaches applied to pension fund investing. Over time, it has become easier to see the concept of ETIs as being functionally similar to other investment "styles" or strategies of active management. Some equity managers follow a "value" style of investing while others look for "growth" stocks. Similarly, real estate managers often bring subtle differences to the process of selecting real estate projects, be it a preference for residential construction over commercial, or "Sun Belt" versus "Rust Belt" markets. ETIs, too, can be evaluated as an investment style or strategy, one that attempts to weigh the impact of investments on a host of concerns such as job creation or retention, community development, union versus nonunion construction, or preference for a state or region.

An investment manager who pursues ETIs as a style of investment has a job identical to traditional managers who may not be interested in collateral benefits. The ETI manager must evaluate the financial strength of the investment; the likelihood that the investment will achieve its financial targets; and the downside if the investment fails to perform as expected. Traditional considerations like liquidity, pricing and security apply to ETIs just as they do in traditional strategies. However, ETI managers must bring additional information to the decision-making process. They must answer questions beyond those posed by traditional analysis. Depending on the details of the manager's strategy, such questions might include:

- ◆ Where the investment is being made
- ◆ If new jobs will be created
- ◆ What kind of jobs these will be

- How the investment will affect the community within which it is located
- How it will affect communities that may lose facilities or jobs
- Who in the community should be consulted about the investment and its impacts
- What opportunities this investment will create in the future.

These questions require the ETI manager to go the extra mile to evaluate the investments under consideration and to measure impacts that previously might have been overlooked.

Note that no information from traditional financial sources needs to be sacrificed when bringing this new information into the decision-making process. Any decision can only be *enhanced* by the availability of more information.

Critics of the ETI are justifiably quick to point out that such investments are not automatically successful merely by virtue of being "targeted." A focus on ETIs does not always lead to "better" investments. Advocates of ETIs admit that ETI managers must strike the right balance between traditional financial indicators and other sources of information about collateral impacts. Moreover, collateral benefits rarely rescue a project that does not make financial sense in traditional terms. ETI practitioners understand that the traditional financial measures come first; every deal should only move forward in the decision-making process if it meets traditional measures of value. The assessment of collateral benefits can be made at any point in the analysis, but rate of return still "rules."

But one of the benefits of the ETI framework is to recognize that no investment should be judged on its expected rate of return alone; risk also matters. ETI proponents note that what trustees should seek are investments with acceptable "risk-adjusted" rates of return. That is, investments with more modest returns may be equally acceptable, if those expected returns are more predictable and stable than other, higher return options.

Further, the ETI framework allows investors to choose between investment options that offer equal or comparable rates of investment return. The key insight in the ETI approach is to say that if two investments have a reasonable expectation of similar returns, then investors have the right to consider which of the two offer further secondary benefits of value to plan participants.

The definition of those *secondary benefits* is a challenging question, one that ultimately trustees must decide for themselves, based on their industry, their business experience and the needs of their plan participants. No single answer works in every situation and no "cookie-cutter" approach can relieve trustees of the responsibility for thinking carefully and clearly about their goals and their participants' best interests. But having established the needs of the participants, trustees can then compare investments and select those that offer the best potential outcomes when measured across a range of considerations.

Examples of ETIs

Real estate has been the asset class best known for ETIs. One example can be found in the years immediately following World War II when the Electrical Workers in New York City invested in apartment buildings suitable to local union members working in the rapidly growing electrical industry, a project named "Elechester" in recognition of the industry's role in the community. Today, real estate funds with billions of dollars under management have demonstrated that ETI investing can combine solid investment results with collateral benefits.

Some real estate funds premise their investment strategies on the idea that high-quality construction of institutional grade real estate projects leads to superior investment returns. If such projects generate work for skilled tradespeople and union contractors, such collateral benefits should be given consideration in the investment decision process. Other funds believe that well-managed properties, using a stable and skilled maintenance workforce, maintain property values and promote tenant satisfaction over the life of a building. These approaches are not necessarily the only means of creating value in real estate. But they are equally valid when compared to other strategies that emphasize other concerns.

Those funds that invest with an ETI strategy are usually easy to find because investment managers tend not to be shy and retiring types. A fund with an ETI approach will be quick to explain its strategy and may base its marketing efforts around its success at achieving collateral objectives. With the number of funds increasing by the week, trustees should remember to ask all the traditional due diligence questions of their prospective managers, along with all the nontraditional questions about the managers' approach. Like past performance, an ETI focus is no guarantee of future investment success.

The Regulatory Response to ETIs

A trend of this importance was bound to catch the attention of regulators and legislators. The history of ETIs has been matched by dramatic changes in regulatory sentiment. At times indifferent, opposed or supportive, federal regulators have had a complicated and evolving relationship to the investment initiatives of pension fund trustees.

As noted above, ETIs have been around a long time (although the name *ETI* is relatively new). Following the passage of ERISA in 1974, trustees and their advisors read federal pension law to prohibit consideration of collateral benefits when making investment decisions. Few "targeted" investments were attempted and traditional strategies ruled the day. Few investment managers had enough experience to understand how to do the analysis required, ask the additional questions and make the right decisions. After all, it has always been easier to ask fewer questions than more. ERISA required all fiduciaries in the pension arena to reexamine their business practices and investment process, and in doing so it cooled the environment for nontraditional investments. Flawed investment strategies, especially on the part of a multiemployer Taft-Hartley fund in Florida that invested almost entirely in real estate, were taken as proof that ETIs did not work. Generally, the attention of federal regulators in this period was elsewhere and their attitude toward ETIs was one of benign neglect.

By the 1980s, trustees and money managers had grown accustomed to the stricter regulatory environment created by ERISA. Some began to think more carefully about collateral benefits and strategies that might earn good returns while capturing collateral benefits. Several real estate funds were established that explicitly sought out construction projects that used union contractors and created building trades jobs. These funds slowly built a track record of investing and a way of selecting projects that was prudent, diversified and successful. During the real estate collapse of the early 1990s, these funds regularly posted returns better than those real estate funds that paid no attention to collateral issues.

During this period, federal regulators noticed these early moves toward ETIs and they grew wary. Regulatory pronouncements in the 1980s warned trustees to be careful and to think twice before trying anything new. For example, James D. Hutchinson, the first administrator of Pension and Welfare Plans in the U.S. Department of Labor, expressed his disquiet about the trend in 1979 when he tried to define three categories of investment policy:

1. *Totally neutral investment policies:* These policies focus on the financial aspects of investment alternatives only. Under this policy, the investment decision makers analyze tradi-

tional investment considerations, which often include labor relations practices, legal compliance and other factors that impact on bottom-line earnings. If the investment decision maker has a valid basis for considering these "socially and economically responsible" indicia, then their consideration is valid on purely economic grounds. However, under a totally neutral investment policy, these noninvestment factors *cannot* override basic financial investment decisions.

2. *Socially sensitive investment policies:* These policies and practices include an initial analysis by the investment fiduciary of traditional financial investment considerations. However, once this traditional financial analysis is concluded, the fiduciary then selects among financially comparable investment opportunities by considering other, noneconomic, factors. These policies premise that *if everything else is equal*, the investment decision will be based on the noneconomic considerations.
3. *Socially dictated investment policies:* These are investment practices and policies that permit the sacrifice of safety, return, diversification or other financial criteria or are undertaken to further some objective other than the interests of plan participants.

The second definition provided by Hutchinson, that of *socially sensitive investment policies,* is clearly recognizable today as a reasonable description of ETIs. Even given the antipathy of the regulators to ETIs, this definition contemplated investment strategies that considered and valued collateral benefits. But regulators' "body language" made it obvious that ETIs should be avoided.

Such pronouncements gave plenty of ammunition to critics of the emerging experiments in "targeted" investments. This hostile regulatory environment created the backdrop against which the concept of ETIs was forged and ensured that anyone brave enough to proceed knew they had to succeed–or else.

By the 1990s, a new administration had taken office and with it arrived a team of regulators less hostile to "targeting" and assessment of collateral benefits. Appointed by a former Arkansas governor who encouraged ETIs in his state, PWBA Administrator Olena Berg in 1994 encouraged pension plans to:

- Invest in companies whose management invests in developing the value of human capital
- Become a source of long-term capital for companies that will stimulate jobs

- ◆ Recognize the appropriateness to make ETIs consistent with ERISA's prudence and exclusive benefit rules
- ◆ By such investment activities promote a more productive, healthier economy that will serve the interests of plan participants.

Then-Labor Secretary Robert Reich testified at a Joint Economic Committee hearing on ETIs, "[p]ension plan fiduciaries who invest funds in an ETI are acting well within their legal responsibilities so long as the ETI generates a competitive risk-adjusted rate of return, and so long as the ETI is an otherwise appropriate investment."

This thaw in regulatory opinion culminated in the Department of Labor's Interpretive Bulletin 94-1, *Economically Targeted Investing,* issued June 17, 1994. (See Appendix F.) The DOL reviewed previous advisory opinions and prohibited transaction exemptions involving investments that produce "collateral" benefits and set forth certain broad principles:

- ◆ ERISA does not exclude the consideration of collateral benefits in a fiduciary's evaluation of a particular investment opportunity.
- ◆ Arrangements designed to bring areas of investment opportunity that provide collateral benefits to the attention of plan fiduciaries will not in and of themselves violate Section 403 or 404 of ERISA, where the arrangements do not restrict the exercise of the fiduciary's investment discretion.
- ◆ Plan fiduciaries can be influenced by collateral factors that are not related to the plan's expected investment return only if, commensurate with risk and rate of return, such investments are equal or superior to alternative available investments.
- ◆ Fiduciaries who are willing to accept reduced returns or greater risks to secure collateral benefits are in violation of ERISA.

The specific terms of this interpretive bulletin did not differ materially from Hutchinson's definitions in 1979. But the message could not have been more different–regulators approved and encouraged innovative investments and trusted trustees enough to make prudent and fiduciarily sound decisions.

The Department of Labor even went so far as to commence a data collection project designed to track individual investments classified as ETIs in the hopes that such data would demonstrate that ETIs worked. However, in 1995 Congress killed the tracking project, not by legislating it out of existence, but rather by eliminating the funding required to collect the data. At that point, advocates and critics within the federal government had fought one another to a draw and no actions of any consequence have emanated from Washington since then.

The regulators' withdrawal from the debate is probably the best thing that could have happened. Trustees are left to themselves today to decide whether to consider ETIs, how to select them and by what means to measure the results.

Investment Criteria

Enough ETI or "worker-friendly" investment products have emerged to allow trustees today to make an informed choice among solid alternatives. To help trustees, the AFL-CIO published a report in October 1999 titled *Investment Product Review: Report of the Investment Product Review Working Group*. This report for the first time attempted to catalogue "worker-friendly" products and to assess the extent to which these products achieved their own self-stated goals of creating jobs and maximizing collateral benefits.

The working group was convened by the AFL-CIO Executive Council and included over 20 union and pension fund representatives. According to the report, "[t]he Working Group established four sets of criteria for Real Estate, Public Equity, Private Capital and International Investments and a committee to work on each." By doing so, the working group demonstrated that the possibilities for ETIs had grown far beyond the traditional confines of real estate. The working group surveyed investment managers and conducted an unprecedented series of interviews in which the committee members applied the criteria to the manager's strategy and holdings. Each manager was given a "grade" that applied to the manager's success at realizing collateral benefits. The working group went to great lengths to disclaim any attempt to evaluate the financial performance of these investment products and went so far as to include a disclaimer to that effect on every page of the report.

As useful as the grades may be when trustees are comparing investment alternatives, the real value of the review lies in the "Product Criteria" buried in an appendix to the report. There, the working group spelled out the standards it applied to investments in each asset class. The working group created road maps for those who seek to undertake their own evaluation of ETIs. The criteria can serve as a starting point, one that needs to be built upon if pension fund trustees want to tap the full potential offered by those ETIs available today and those that will emerge tomorrow. The Product Criteria are reproduced in Appendix G starting on page 285.

The report concluded that the ETI approach had been generally effective. The report's own words serve as an excellent summary of the value of seeking out investments with collateral benefits.

> We have learned through this process that pro-worker investments provide collateral benefits to many constituencies, including workers, their unions, their employers and their communities. A pro-worker real estate investment enlarges the membership base of benefits funds, builds a skilled workforce and reduces quality problems facing contractors. Similarly, a private capital investment that creates high-wage jobs benefits workers, communities and the entire economy by enlarging the tax base. When worker capital makes high-road investments, workers are not the only beneficiaries.

(Forward to the *Investment Product Review,* published by the AFL-CIO, October 1999.)

New Asset Classes

Although real estate has been the traditional terrain for ETIs, new frontiers have emerged. An increasing number of multiemployer funds are considering venture capital and private equity, a field long explored by large public employee funds. Those trustees that have delved into this asset class quickly learn that an even greater degree of due diligence, monitoring and oversight are required by trustees. They have also learned that there are opportunities here to define the "rules of the game" under which companies operate.

Venture capitalists, banks and life insurance companies have long attached conditions to the investments they make. These conditions relate to management authority and discretion, capital structure, and business strategy of those companies that receive an infusion of early equity. Pension fund trustees are beginning to consider what kind of venture capital investments are appropriate for their funds. They are also weighing the possibilities of attaching their set of conditions. One idea might be to invest in those small and emerging companies with responsible and sophisticated labor relations policies, under the assumption that such management practices increase the likelihood of a startup company's success, especially in service industries where the quality of the service is directly affected by the commitment and satisfaction of employees at all levels.

New measures of collateral benefit will have to be defined and new strategies for achieving such benefit will have to be tested. The experience in other asset classes, like real estate, suggests that this is both possible and practical. It also suggests that the collaboration between trustees and innovative investment managers will succeed in extending the concept of ETIs into new fields.

ETIs in Other Countries

Interest is growing in real estate investing by U.S. pension funds in properties located outside the United States. In its initial stages, those funds that seek international diversification likely will not insist on an ETI approach. But it is equally likely that those who investigate the possibilities will find both new issues to analyze and new possibilities for targeting and collateral benefits.

These investigations will inevitably involve U.S. pension trustees in dialogue with their counterparts in other countries who manage privately funded retirement plans. This dialogue will undoubtedly start with the realization that foreign investors have been coming to the United States for years and already have substantial holdings of U.S. stocks, bonds and real estate. Any international dialogue will quickly move to the topic of how foreign investors pick their purchases in the United States and the investment standards they should apply. U.S. investors are likely to find that they will need to think about how their investments affect workers in foreign countries at the same time that foreign investments have consequences for workers here.

Conclusion

ETIs represent a broader and more sophisticated view of value than is found in traditional investing. ETIs must identify and assess a range of impacts associated with any investment, and the ultimate decision on which investments to accept turns on trustees' understanding of their participants' needs. The questions raised by this type of investing are profound. They require both trustees and managers to think long and hard about the sources of value in capital markets and the techniques needed to capture that value.

ETIs have always been around in one form or another, passing under names that have evolved through time. They have existed despite regulatory hostility at times. ETIs have become less distinct in recent years just as they have become more accepted. Ironically, the growing diversity of real estate funds and venture capital strategies makes it harder to be sure what is an ETI and what isn't. Many investors today take for granted the need to consider investment impacts across a range of issues. These investors do not put money into a project unless and until they are satisfied that they know how such projects affect plan participants.

Ultimately, the concept of ETIs may be viewed by future observers as a transitional one–from a period where investors were discouraged from pursuing multifaceted investment strategies to a period where all investments are evaluated on the basis of optimizing investment return *and* collateral benefits. The concept has played a crucial role in getting trustees this far. Where trustees choose to go from here is an open, and fascinating, question.

Chapter 19

Corporate Governance/ Proxy Voting

Contributed by Richard C. Ferlauto
American Federation of State, County and Municipal Employees (AFSCME)

What Is Corporate Governance?

Corporate governance is the interaction among the board, the executive management and the shareholders for the purposes of strategic planning, determining the corporate structure and monitoring the management of the corporation. Corporate governance allows shareholders to influence issues significant to the company such as election to the board of directors, board structure, company capitalization, mergers/ acquisitions and certain executive compensation issues. In addition, an important aspect of ownership is the ability of shareholders to submit resolutions at annual meetings dealing with a broad range of issues so long as they are consistent with SEC (Securities and Exchange Commission) requirements.

The regulatory and legal framework for corporate governance is primarily derived from three places:

- ◆ State corporation law establishes company bylaws, and creates the legal framework for the governance and capital structures of a particular company.
- ◆ The stock exchange on which a security trades is a self-regulation mechanism, which establishes certain disclosure and governance practices that a company must comply with in order to qualify for listing.

Exhibit 19-1

POOR CORPORATE GOVERNANCE TIPS THE BALANCE OF POWER AT THE CORPORATION

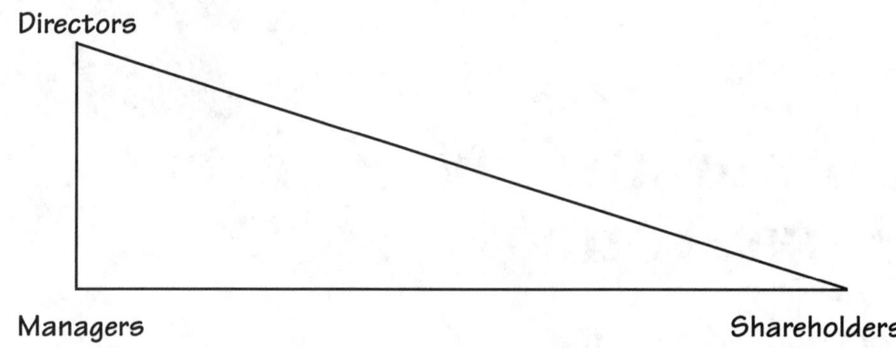

- The SEC regulates annual reports and proxy materials, with special attention to corporate disclosure and the proxy process. In addition, the SEC is the arbiter of shareholder activity by determining what shareholder proposals may appear on the proxy statement.

When corporate governance procedures are heavily skewed against shareholders, shareholders have limited input on important strategic and leadership questions concerning the future of the company. Bad corporate governance often leads to undeserved CEO pay, ineffective systems for financial monitoring, and corporate transactions that make no sense to shareholders. While the Sarbanes-Oxley legislation that was passed in response to the scandals at Enron and WorldCom has created a stronger regulatory environment through better disclosure, it does not give shareholders more influence in the corporate governance power triangle. (See Exhibits 19-1 and 19-2.)

Corporate governance is effective when there is an equitable division of power among shareholders, directors and managers. Such arrangements provide the required accountability and transparency need to produce long-term shareholder value.

Studies confirm that corporate governance creates shareholder value.

Proxy voting is meaningful only if better corporate governance does increase shareholder value. Does it? Not surprisingly the answer is *yes. Corporate Governance and Equity Prices,* a long-term study by Paul Gompers of Harvard Business School published by the well-respected National Bureau of Economic Research, describes a

Exhibit 19-2

EFFECTIVE CORPORATE GOVERNANCE CREATES VALUE

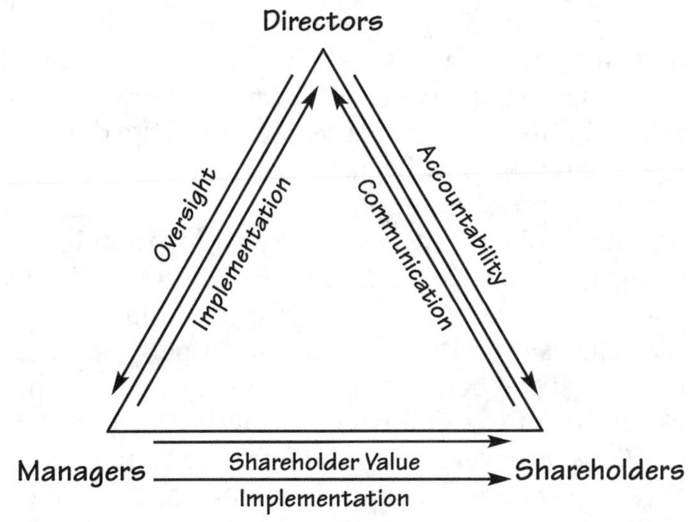

"striking" link between corporate governance and stock prices. The study evaluated 1,500 companies on 24 corporate governance points. They found that companies with strong shareholder rights turned out to generate as much as 8.5% more in annual returns in the 1990s than those with weak shareholder rights. Weaker shareholder rights were associated with lower profits, lower sales growth, higher capital expenditures and a higher amount of corporate acquisitions. Other empirical studies, including those by Tim Opler and Jonathan Sokobin of Ohio State University,[1] and Diane Del Guercio and Jennifer Hawkins of the University of Oregon,[2] found statistically significant improvement in operating profitability and share returns after they became the focus of shareholder activism.

Why Proxy Voting?

Proxy voting can influence the long-term performance of public companies by improving corporate governance practices. All multi-

1. *Does Coordinated Institutional Activism Work? An Analysis of the Activities of the Council of Institutional Investors,* 1997, Ohio State University working paper.
2. *The Motivation and Impact of Pension Fund Activism,* 1998, University of Oregon working paper.

employer plan and single employer plan trustees, as well as many public fund trustees, have an explicit fiduciary duty on behalf of their funds to vote proxies as a strategy to increase the value of their invested assets. A *proxy* allows shareholders to give voting instructions and grant voting authority to other responsible parties, most often corporate management, to vote their shares at a shareholders meeting. In this way, proxy voting is the fundamental action taken by shareholders to ensure an effective system of corporate governance because they can take part in important decisions without attending their company's annual meeting.

Those shareholders who use proxy voting to influence corporate behavior engage in what we call "active ownership." They actively use their ownership power as a way to improve their companies' long-term value. This is important because most pension funds have obligations to pay retiree benefits that are many years in the future. For example, the time horizon for most Taft-Hartley and public pension systems is 30 or more years. So funds need to be patient investors and should have in place asset management policies that comport with the responsibility to pay retirement benefits many years in the future. Active ownership is used to help ensure that public companies are managed to create an asset value over a fund's long-term time horizon. For example, shareholders can use the proxy vote to throw out entrenched managers that are mishandling the company, to seek greater director accountability through annual elections, to demand CEOs get paid on the basis of performance or to prevent ill-advised mergers.

The Impact of Aggregated Assets

Although the hundreds of thousands of individual stock investors may be lone voices against unresponsive corporate directors (many proxies of individuals go straight to the circular file), pension systems and other institutional investors have the size and ownership positions to be significant players in the corporate boardroom.

The market value of public traded companies exceeds $17 trillion. Of this total, all institutional investors have about $8 trillion invested in the stock market or 48% of all publicly traded securities. Retirement savings in pension funds account for approximately 25% of the assets. Public pensions and Taft-Hartley funds combined directly invest more than $2 trillion in the stock market. Multiemployer plans have about half of their assets equaling about $200 billion invested through Wall Street. (See Exhibits 19-3 and 19-4.)

Exhibit 19-3

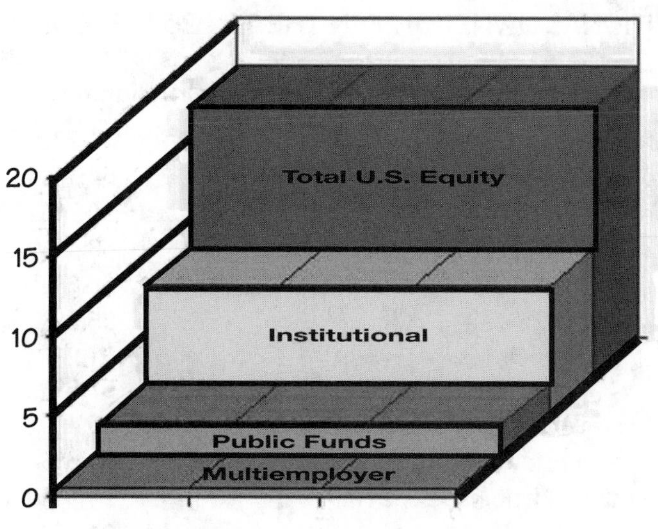

Exhibit 19-4

DISTRIBUTION OF RETIREMENT SAVINGS

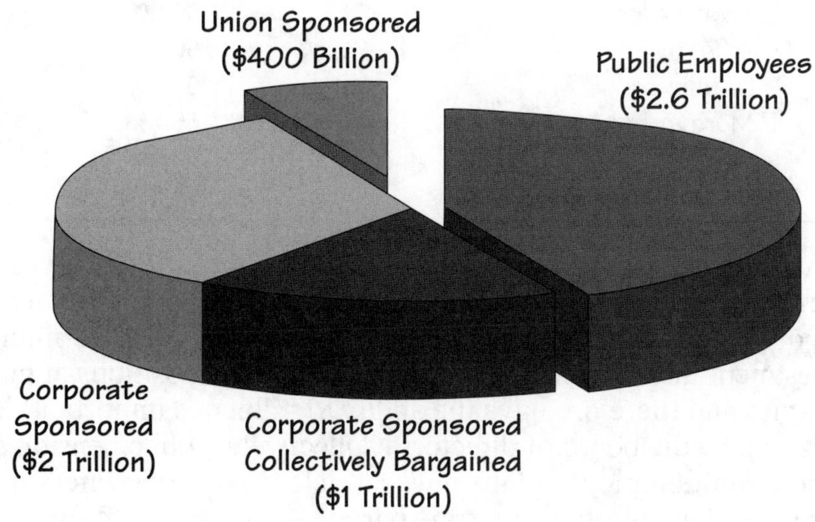

Exhibit 19-5

INSTITUTIONAL OWNERSHIP IN THE TOP 25 U.S. COMPANIES

Company	**Institutional Ownership**
General Electric	51.7%
Microsoft	54.1%
ExxonMobil	50.7%
Pfizer	63.4%
Citigroup	64.3%
Wal-Mart Stores	35.2%
American International Group	61.2%
Intel	57.3%
Cisco Systems	60.1%
Bank of America	86.5%
International Business Machines	54.5%
Johnson & Johnson	61.8%
Berkshire Hathaway	17.8%
Procter & Gamble	56.9%
Coca-Cola	58.3%
Altria Group	68.0%
Verizon Communications	52.8%
Merck	58.1%
Wells Fargo	66.4%
ChevronTexaco	59.6%
PepsiCo	66.3%
Dell Computer	61.3%
JP Morgan Chase	65.1%
Home Depot	60.9%
SBC Communications	51.8%

At this magnitude of investment, large institutional investors dominated by pension funds have become the majority owners in many of this country's largest companies. A relatively small number of investment institutions control substantial share positions at major companies and therefore have the ability to influence important decisions taken by the board of directors. Collectively, public pension systems and multiemployer plans have sufficient level of ownership to call for more accountability, transparency and responsibility from public companies. In fact, on average, 5% of a company is owned as the retirement asset of Taft-Hartley and public pension funds. (See Exhibit 19-5.)

The largest institutional investors, such as TIAA-CREF (Teachers Insurance and Annuity Association–College Retirement Equities Fund), CalPERS (California Public Employees Retirement System) and NYCERS (New York City Employee Retirement System), incorporate proxy voting as a fundamental part of their investment operations because they view active ownership as a proven technique for generating higher portfolio returns. In a similar manner, multi-employer plans and ERISA plans should think of proxy voting as a strategy for achieving long-term shareholder value and not purely as an ERISA compliance measure.

Characteristics of Active Owners

We have suggested that pension funds need to be active owners because they are patient investors with longtime horizons. Pension funds with obligations to pay retiree benefits are interested in generating and sustaining shareholder value for the fund for 30 years, not for the next quarter's earnings report. Indeed, it has been the short-term focus of active managers that has been blamed for the stock and accounting manipulations that led to the corporate scandals that began with Enron and continues today. With a long-term view, issues such as brand reputation, external liabilities and workforce productivity become significant factors in company performance and the ability to generate earnings over time.

Active ownership is a strategy of buying and holding a stock and seeking to improve it through corporate governance, rather than doing the Wall Street Walk. Indeed, trading in and out of stocks in the short term–the active management approach–may not be the best one for pension systems. Institutional investors have grown so large that they need to invest across the full range of public markets to be appropriately diversified. These large funds are prevented from selling out of securities because such a move would adversely affect all stockholders and other remaining positions that the fund might have. Selling a stock, and even picking winning and losing stocks in an actively managed portfolio, are not options for a large holder of public equity assets. In fact, many funds rely on *indexing,* a passive investment strategy that reflects a broad-based stock index such as the S&P 500 or the Russell 3000 to be appropriately diversified in the market. Indexing fees are much lower than the fees for actively managed portfolios. The turnover costs due to portfolio churning are large and not often compensated for by superior performance. Only one in four active managers has beaten its index in the past five years. So pension

Exhibit 19-6

Active Ownership	Active Management
◆ Patient Investor	◆ Buys or Sells
◆ Engages Company Management	◆ Management Rules
◆ Promotes Effective Corporate Governance	◆ Quarterly Earnings Paramount
◆ Evaluates Long-Term Shareholder Value	◆ Lowest Cost Approach to Boosting Stock Price
◆ Quality, Reputation, Investment Creates	◆ Stock Picking
◆ Indexing	
◆ Relational Investing	

systems choose to passively invest the bulk of their assets. Currently public pension funds put about 70% of their equity holdings in indexed portfolios. (See Exhibit 19-6.)

Pension funds not taking the Wall Street Walk increasingly are turning to corporate governance reform through proxy voting as a strategy increasing long-term shareholder value. They seek the engagement of corporate leadership, given their large ownership positions, rather than selling out.

Proxy Voting Under ERISA

The Employee Retirement Income Security Act of 1974 (ERISA) defines the fiduciary law that governs Taft-Hartley and corporate plan sponsors. The fiduciary duty to vote proxies was first described by the Avon letter, issued by the Department of Labor in 1988, which explicitly states that stock ownership rights including proxy voting are plan assets. Plan fiduciaries are obligated to vote proxies with the duty of loyalty and duty of care established by ERISA for the stewardship of all plan assets. The *duty of loyalty* requires that the voting fiduciary exercise proxy voting authority for the exclusive benefit of plan participants and beneficiaries. The *duty of prudence* requires that proxy voting be exercised with the care, skill, wisdom and diligence that a similarly situated prudent person with knowledge in such matters would use.

The Labor Department provided additional guidance on proxy

voting in a January 1990 letter to Robert Monks, the founding father of shareholder activism. The Monks letter states that an investment manager has the proxy voting authority and responsibility, unless the manager is expressly precluded from doing so in the plan documents. In this case, the plan document would have to reserve authority and responsibility to the plan sponsor or redelegate it to another fiduciary, such as a proxy voting service registered under the Investment Advisors Act of 1940. The letter also requires that the voting fiduciary take reasonable steps to reconcile the proxies they receive with shares held on the date of record.

The release goes on to state that in "certain situations it may be appropriate for a fiduciary to engage in activities intended to monitor or influence corporate management if the fiduciary expects that such activities are likely to enhance the value of the plan's investment." This is especially true for plans invested in index funds where assets cannot be easily disposed of and are invested with a long-term time horizon. The fiduciary voter, whether the plan sponsor or the investment manager, should be cognizant that monitoring extends beyond simple proxy voting to include other types of engagement of corporate managers.

On July 28, 1994, the Department of Labor released Interpretive Bulletin 94-2 (IB 94-2) relating to the voting of proxies by ERISA plan sponsors and investment. This release reaffirmed previous DOL actions such as the Avon and Monks letters and for the first time released codified requirements in the form of an interpretive bulletin published in the *Federal Register.* IB 94-2 goes well beyond previous interpretations by DOL of ERISA and proxy voting. DOL has made it clear that voting policy guidelines must be in place for recurring issues and that nonroutine issues must be addressed by consistent procedures and criteria. And, company-specific analysis must be performed, as rote or rubber stamp voting procedures are neither appropriate nor acceptable. Moreover, proxy voting responsibilities call for "active" monitoring of portfolio companies and communicating concerns about company performance and practices to boards of directors and top management.

DOL explicitly cited several areas for active monitoring and shareholder communications. These issues specifically named in IB 94-2 include:

- Independence and expertise of outside director candidates/ management directors
- Assuring the board is provided sufficient information to carry out its duties

- Policies with regard to acquisitions and mergers
- The extent of debt financing and capitalization
- The appropriateness of executive compensation
- Long-term business plans
- Workforce training investment
- Financial and nonfinancial measures of corporate performance.

Interpretive Bulletin 94-2 makes clear that ERISA funds can request their managers to follow specific guidelines and that shareholder activism to improve shareholder value is consistent with the duties under ERISA.

The evolution of DOL's regulatory framework, from its view of the fiduciary in general trust law through IB 94-2, has elevated proxy voting to a basic element of investment management.

The Voting Process

With the growing emphasis on proxy voting as a matter of fiduciary concern, institutional investors need to have a full understanding of both corporate governance policy issues and the best practices in proxy voting processes and procedures.

A plan sponsor has a number of choices when it comes to how to structure its proxy voting responsibility. According to ERISA the fiduciary responsibility for proxy voting resides with the investment manager unless the named fiduciary otherwise delegates this responsibility. ERISA allows proxy voting to be fully delegated to any investment advisor registered under the Investment Advisory Act of 1940. Proxy voting delegated to investment advisors shields fund trustees from liability caused by the imprudent use, or failed execution, of the proxy. By law, proxy votes must be cast for the exclusive economic benefit of plan participants and plan beneficiaries. In all cases plan sponsors retain the responsibility to monitor proxy voting and maintain voting records.

Within this legal framework, plan sponsors may decide to:

- Allow the investment manager to keep the proxy responsibility, using their own proxy policies; ERISA requires fiduciaries to vote consistently. Managers may not vote on a specific issue that would otherwise conflict with their voting guidelines, and they may not accept specific instructions for specific company votes.
- Direct the investment manager to use a specific voting policy or specific voting agent. Investment managers that outsource

to a voting agent service or implement policies at the direction of a plan sponsor still retain their fiduciary responsibilities. According to DOL, "An investment manager would not be relieved of its fiduciary responsibility merely because it follows directions of some other person as to the voting of proxies, or delegates such responsibility to another person." (IB 94-2.) An investment manager, however, may retain a proxy voting service to advise on votes cast and/or to implement a voting program.

- Redelegate the proxy responsibility to a proxy voting service that can create a customized policy or use a recommended policy such as the AFL-CIO voting guidelines. Plan sponsors that decide to use a service as a voting fiduciary should make sure that the delegation is proper by reviewing and adjusting their plan documents if necessary.
- Retain the proxy voting responsibilities internally, as do some of the larger pension funds, including a number of public funds.

Questions to Consider When Deciding Who Gets Voting Authority

1. Will the portfolio investment manager vote proxies in the best interest of plan participants?
2. What voting policies does the proxy service or investment manager use?
3. Does the manager have expertise in corporate governance or use a subadvisor that does?
4. Does the benefit of redelegating proxy voting from the manager to another voting fiduciary outweigh the benefit of managing the vote as part of the portfolio investment strategy? I.e., is the fund indexed or heavily traded?
5. Investment managers include the cost of voting in their fees, so what benefit is derived from paying for another voting fiduciary?
6. Will the fund's value be enhanced by aggregating its voting power with other like-minded plan sponsors through a proxy voting service?

All holders of record will be sent a proxy statement from the company. Federal proxy rules generally require that shareholders receive both a proxy statement and an annual report in a timely fashion to allow them to make informed voting decisions. In this document, parties soliciting shareholder votes provide shareholders with information on the issues to be voted on at an annual or special shareholders meeting. The soliciting party generally presents arguments as to why shareholders should grant them their vote. The information that must be disclosed to shareholders is set forth in Schedule 14A of the Securities Exchange Act of 1934 for a proxy solicited by the company and in Schedule 14B of the act for proxies solicited by others.

For the voting fiduciary, the process of voting can be segmented into four distinct components, which can be managed in one operation or broken out for the purposes of efficient execution among service providers.

Company and Issue Research

The essence of an informed proxy vote is a well-developed understanding of the company's performance and corporate governance practices. Important information includes how the company performs compared to its peer group and standard indices. The composition of the board, governance provisions, capital structure, antitakeover provisions and corporate governance all need to be considered. This information is contained in the company proxy materials and other SEC filings.

Proxy Voting Policies

ERISA plans should be voted according to written voting policies. As discussed above, plan sponsors may decide to use their manager's policy or use the guidelines that were developed by the AFL-CIO in conjunction with leading Taft-Hartley plans. No matter which voting policies are used, they should explain and direct voters on routine issues and offer a framework for nonroutine circumstances. Many investment managers choose to use an external service for research and voting, but retain their own proxy policies and voting process. DOL encourages, but does not require, funds to adopt proxy voting guidelines that are consistent with their investment policy.

> Maintenance of statements of investment policy is not specifically required under ERISA. The Department, however, believes that such statements serve a legitimate purpose. . . . A statement of investment policy that includes a statement of proxy voting policy may increase the likelihood

that proxy votes are consistent with other aspects of the investment policy. Moreover, in plans with multiple investment managers, a written proxy voting policy may prevent (where such prevention is desirable) the managers from taking conflicting positions on a given voting decision. One purpose of this interpretive bulletin is to clarify that maintenance of a statement of investment policy, including a statement of proxy voting policy, is consistent with the fiduciary duty of prudence under ERISA Section 404(a)(1)(B).

Interpretive Bulletin 94-2, U.S. Department of Labor, 1994 (29 CFR Part 2509).

Voting Execution

Proper vote execution depends upon a well-functioning relationship between the proxy voter and the custodian bank or master trustee. While "beneficial owners" are obligated to make voting decisions, the custodian banks of funds are the official recordholders for shares and must sign the proxy cards. A valid proxy card requires two separate items: a valid signature supplied by the custodian and the vote supplied by the institutional voter. It is important for funds to clarify with their bank custodians the delegation of proxy voting authority so the appropriate voting materials may be forwarded to the voting fiduciary. Often securities are held in the street name/nominee name. Holding a customer's stock "in street name" is when broker-dealers, banks or voting trustees register the shares held for customer accounts in their own names. Such a system makes it more difficult to obtain shareholder information. Note that often the legal owners are not the beneficial owners of the stock and therefore may not have the power to vote or direct the voting of the stock.

There may be some confusion over who has the responsibility for a specific vote when a security is traded. The New York Stock Exchange's policy is that a transfer is not effective until settlement, which occurs three days after the trade. On the similar issue of securities lending, the lending of a security does not relieve the fiduciary of the responsibility for voting that stock. Since lending securities may make it impossible for fiduciaries to vote, it should be taken into consideration before a lending program is created.

Reporting

DOL makes it clear that the delegation of proxy voting to the investment manager or a proxy service does not relieve the plan sponsor from all responsibilities or potential liabilities. Plan sponsors have a continuing duty to monitor proxy votes. This can be accomplished through review of voting reports and requiring that reports contain a rationale for all nonroutine items. Plan sponsors should review reports for voting inconsistencies, missed votes and discrepancies with policy guidelines.

What Plan Sponsors Should Require From Investment Managers or Proxy Voting Services

1. Written proxy voting policies, which may be updated and supplemented from time to time
2. A proxy committee composed of senior staff members to review policies and make final decisions on nonroutine issues
3. Application of a consistent voting program
4. Portfolio-specific voting reports with narrative rationales for every nonroutine vote
5. Reconciliation reports that match votes cast with ballots received
6. Monitoring for any potential conflicts of interest with systems to deal appropriately with such issues
7. Registration under the Investment Advisory Act of 1940 (for proxy services) with an annual review of the firm's disclosure information (Form ADV)
8. Participation in the annual AFL-CIO Key Vote Survey.

Best Practices for Plan Sponsors

- ◆ Establishment of a proxy committee, or the inclusion of proxy duties in investment committee responsibilities
- ◆ Annual review of proxy policy
- ◆ Written proxy voting policies and voting procedures including any delegation of voting authority included in your plan documents
- ◆ Regular review of voting reports including procedures for monitoring against cross voting, missing votes, votes against policy
- ◆ Recordkeeping for compliance with DOL.

Exhibit 19-7

CONTINUUM OF ACTIVE OWNERSHIP

Level 1: No Governance Standards Fund	Level 2: Management Governance Fund	Level 3: Strong Standards Fund	Level 4: Active Promoters of Beneficiary Interests
Management is subcontracted entirely to service providers	Trustees Inactive Basic Stewardship Standards in Place	Comprehensive Approach to Corporate Governance	Shareholder Activism Corporate Accountability Initiatives

Proxy Voting Guidelines

Plan sponsor proxy voting behaviors run the spectrum of ownership activities that range from acquiescence, to investment advisors that vote consistently with company management to active engagement of company boards through corporate monitoring, voting, shareholder communications and sponsoring shareholder resolutions. Each fund needs to determine where it belongs on the spectrum within its understanding of the best way to create long-term value for fund assets. (See Exhibit 19-7.)

Many Taft-Hartley fund sponsors are adopting proxy voting policies modeled from guidelines developed by the AFL-CIO Office of Investment, reflecting the best practices of active ownership. The orientation of these policies is long-term shareholder value creation by promoting accountability to shareholders and community stakeholders. These model proxy policies have been designed to provide a general framework and guidance on a broad range of corporate governance issues. They primarily emphasize corporate accountability to shareholders and stakeholders by shining bright lights on boardroom practices such as creating independent boards, setting executive pay levels, establishing annual elections and requiring shareholder votes major corporate actions.

These guidelines also consider workplace issues–as a component of maximizing shareholder value, fully consistent with ERISA–that affect corporate performance, including:

- ◆ Corporate policies that affect the security and wage levels of plan participants
- ◆ Corporate policies that affect local economic development and stability
- ◆ Corporate responsibility to employees and the local communities in which the firm operates
- ◆ Workplace environmental safety and health issues.

The Department of Labor's Interpretive Bulletin 94-2 makes clear that in addition to proxy voting, it is appropriate for pension fund fiduciaries to engage companies on matters such as executive pay, workforce practices and business strategic plans if they believe it will contribute to long-term shareholder value.

> "Issues may include such matters as consideration of the appropriateness of executive compensation, the corporation's policy regarding mergers and acquisitions, the extent of debt financing and capitalization, the nature of long-term business plans, the corporation's investment in training to develop its work force, other workplace practices and financial and non-financial measures of corporate performance." (IB 94-2)

Key Vote Survey

Before the beginning of every proxy season (late June), the AFL-CIO Office of Investment distributes a list of 35 to 40 shareholder resolutions appearing on annual meeting proxies. The resolutions are selected to reflect the broad range of corporate governance resolutions that will be voted on in the season ahead. At the end of proxy season, trustees are asked to distribute a key vote survey for response from their asset managers.

Trustees can use the survey as part of their procedures to comply with the ERISA requirement for monitoring the proxy vote. It can be equally important to asset managers and their ERISA compliance officers. Survey results can help answer questions about whether or not current proxy policies are purely rubber stamps for corporate directors, and whether or not they take seriously the DOL's direction to add value through the use of the proxy asset. Managers could use the results to compare their votes to others in the market and to other institutional ERISA-based proxy policies. Perhaps the survey's most important function is as a tool to help establish best practices for plan sponsors. Rather than simply viewing the survey as a manager scorecard, trustees could use it as an opportunity to review their proxy policies and procedures to be sure that they are in full compliance with their responsibilities.

The survey draws trustee attention to voting guidelines to examine the content of proxy voting policies, or the lack thereof, and focuses trustees on their obligation to discuss proxy policies with their asset managers and plan consultants in order to know and understand their voting guidelines. The survey establishes a system for ensuring that votes are consistent across managers and do not cancel themselves out. And, it is a way to focus on companies that break the rules of good corporate governance and therefore increase their performance risk. Trustees might find it quite appropriate to require that their fund consultants incorporate proxy guidelines in their plan documents, query managers about the use of appropriate voting policies and include the key vote survey results in manager searches and evaluations.

Some funds may consider more active engagement strategies, which may include submission of shareholder proposals, candidate nomination to corporate boards, active engagement of board members through shareholder communications, and shareholder securities litigation if there is suspected fraud.

No matter how much of an "active owner" strategy a Taft-Hartley or public pension plan decides to embrace, proxy voting is the building block of good corporate governance to enhance long-term shareholder value in the plan portfolio. Plan trustees have a responsibility to make sure that an effective proxy voting program is in place.

Chapter 20

The Investment Management Program

The investment funding process begins with the trustees, who are charged with the overall stewardship responsibility. Determined to ask the right questions and resourcefully armed with a knowledge of basic investment principles, and an appreciation for the long-term historical risk/return characteristics of the various asset classes, the trustees begin their challenge of creating an effective *investment management program* by an examination of the plan's internal factors. They are then in a position to adopt investment performance objectives appropriate to the plan's funding requirements. With the performance objectives in mind, and with an awareness of which classes and subclasses of securities can best facilitate the attainment of those objectives, they can next turn to the selection of the funding vehicles and choosing investment managers to supervise the portfolio. Since portfolio management is "investment engineering" it is important that you have an organized approach to solving your fund's unique investment riddle.

> If you fail to plan, you're planning to fail!
>
> *Robert A. Hewitt Jr.*

Policy Adoption

The full board of trustees can debate the investment issues, or an investment committee comprised of board members can be delegated to examine various alternative courses of action for subsequent recommendations to the full board. If a committee is used then it is important that the other board members are fully briefed on all of the issues and facts related to the decisions they are asked to make; after all, ultimate fiduciary responsibility falls on *each* trustee.

Regarding policy adoption, Allen Biller in addressing an International Foundation meeting raised the following questions:

- Who is going to do it?
- Is policy going to be set by the entire board or by a committee of the board?
- If by the latter, does the full board subsequently formally discuss and ratify it?
- What's the composition of the committee?
- Obviously, in multiemployer plans, it's going to represent both sides. How are members to be selected?
- Is the formulation of investment policy delegated to your advisor or consultant (if you have one)?
- If it is so delegated, what oversight and review does the committee or the full board maintain? This is especially important if the advisor is the investment manager himself.
- Decide who is going to do what right at the beginning.

It has been my observation that smaller groups are more effective in adopting policy than larger ones. This can be facilitated by designating a subgroup of the more knowledgeable (in the investment area) trustees to examine and debate the issues for further recommendation to the larger body.

Larger funds may have a full-time *investment coordinator* to assist the board; all funds, large and small, are encouraged to consider retaining an *investment consultant* as an additional board source.

Portfolio Structure

One major decision that must be made early on in the development of the program is, how passive (indexed) or how active will the plan's portfolio be? (See Exhibit 20-1.)

The range of choices includes:

1. Using only accounts that replicate the market's returns (passive approach)

Exhibit 20-1

STRUCTURING THE INVESTMENT MANAGEMENT PROGRAM

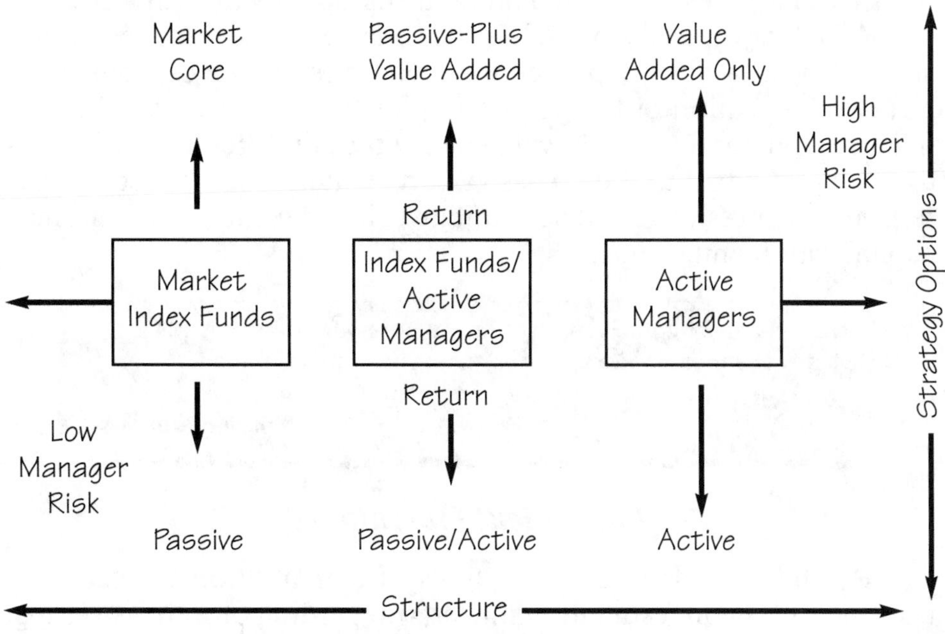

2. Using accounts that replicate the return of a tailored benchmark (passive-plus approach)
3. Using accounts that are managed within the discretion of an investment manager (active approach)
4. Using a combination of the above (passive/active approach).

Until the advent of index funds, *only* active management structuring was an option. Now you can combine active and passive vehicles in the same portfolio. The majority of plans, however, still choose to use only actively managed accounts permitting their managers significant discretion in their portfolio practices. Such value-added operations generally seek returns above the market's rate of return. Because most managers are seeking such returns, all managers cannot be successful in achieving the sought-after market-plus returns. Thus, active management operations have the element of manager risk inherent in their approach.

At the other extreme, the so-called passive approach fully embraces the use of market index funds. A pension portfolio comprised of market index funds has zero manager risk, but part and parcel with such an approach is the requirement to fully accept market risk. Since the market portfolio by definition must accept 100% of the interim negative returns on its way to producing the sought-after long-term return, the trustees must be committed emotionally to such a strategy.

A halfway house approach is the so-called passive/active or passive-plus value-added approach that combines the use of index funds as the core portion of the portfolio, plus the selective use of active managers attempting to add value above the core's return. Such managers operating around the passive core could include those characterized as aggressive growth, quantitative, income, international, small capitalization and so forth.

> Put the bulk of your holdings into a core portfolio that will track the market average. Then put the remainder into a package that will be intensively managed.
>
> *Wilson and Cummin*

Investment Operations

Exhibit 20-2 sets forth the lines of demarcation between the trustees and the investment manager(s) regarding objectives setting, policy adoption and risk management.

Exhibit 20-3 provides insight into the four areas of management operations: policy, strategy, tactics and trading; who is responsible for these activities; and the trustees' oversight responsibilities for each activity.

There are many ways to make money, but being disorganized is usually not one of the profitable options. Hopefully, the following chapters will help you as you organize your approach to finalizing the investment policy statement.

Exhibit 20-2

ROLES OF PLAYERS IN INVESTMENT PROCESS

	Trustees	Manager(s)
Goals and objectives	Assure success in funding process	Produce markets' return (passive) or add value above markets' return (active)
Policy and strategy	Structure the program	Implement the program
Risk management	Defensive; control risk	Opportunistic; exploit risk

Exhibit 20-3

FOUR AREAS OF INVESTMENT MANAGEMENT OPERATIONS

Decision	Time Horizon	Implemented by	Trustees' Role
Policy	Ten years or more	Trustees	Assure success in long-term investment funding process
Strategic	Full market cycle	Asset allocator (consultant or balance manager(s))	Confirm manager(s) adding value above markets' return
Tactical	Six months to one year	Investment manager(s)	Confirm timing moves add value
Trading	Today or tomorrow	Securities trader at investment manager(s)	Assure value received for dollar spent

Chapter 21

Developing Investment Policy Statement–Asking the Right Questions

> An investor who has all the answers doesn't even understand all the questions.
>
> *Sir John Templeton*

You don't need to worry about whether your fund will identify, adopt and implement investment policy that is appropriate to your long-term funding needs, as long as the trustees are *asking the right questions* and are objective when developing policy in response to the questions. Each and every trustee will not agree on all the answers; however, the relevant issues need to be identified, discussed, debated, differences resolved and a consensus reached.

The issues to be discussed fall into three categories:

- ◆ What are the compelling forces that will drive investment policy?
- ◆ What is the appropriate risk/return posture for the portfolio?
- ◆ What is the trustees' approach to managing the plan's investment management activities?

Questions that will lead to the identification of the compelling forces driving investment policy address both plan *internal factors* and the investment markets' *external characteristics.*

Some of the questions to be asked of the advisors are:

- ◆ What are the implications of the current actuarial assumptions?
- ◆ Are the current actuarial assumptions realistic?

- ◆ What is the profile of the benefit payments stream in relation to contributions and investment income?
- ◆ Are vested liabilities expected to grow? If so, at what rate?
- ◆ What is the expected trend of unfunded vested liabilities?
- ◆ Will the benefit level have to be increased to meet anticipated industry levels?

The actuary, of course, is the primary source of the information needed to answer these questions.

After identifying the expected emerging pattern of cash flow needs, the trustees can turn to how the plan's portfolio can be structured to meet these cash flow needs.

Key questions to be raised and answered are:

- ◆ What are the liquidity requirements of the fund?
- ◆ How important is it to increase current income to the fund?
- ◆ How important is it to attempt to seek growth in value of the fund?
- ◆ What implications does inflation have on investment policy and participants' benefits?
- ◆ How much volatility in principal value or variability in return are the trustees willing to tolerate?

After examining the internal plan factors and how the portfolio can be structured given the characteristics of these factors, the trustees can turn to an examination of the capital markets themselves, and how the various asset classes can be used in the portfolio as benefit funding vehicles. Risk and reward tradeoffs are considered; will the fiduciaries be satisfied with achieving the markets' rates of return, or do they want to attempt to achieve returns, with the accompanying volatility, above the markets' returns? This decision has an impact on the investment management structure adopted.

Creating the ultimate portfolio will require addressing further questions:

1. Which asset classes to include in the portfolio
2. What policy weights to assign to those classes over the long term
3. What short-term strategic weights to assign to these classes.

> *Genius is 1% inspiration and 99% perspiration.*
>
> *Thomas Edison*

Initial issues to be discussed related to retaining investment managers include:

1. What investment management services are we seeking?
2. What are the appropriate performance benchmarks?
3. What period of time is deemed reasonable to judge performance results?

Such a suggested "seek and search" process by the trustees, together with the participation of their advisors, consultants and managers, can be very arduous and time-consuming. Nonetheless, the exercise of this disciplined approach to "know thyself and thy fund" *prior* to developing the investment policy statement is crucial to success.

> Before everything else, getting ready is the secret of success.
> *Henry Ford*

In the ensuing chapters we will address the subjects of

1. Investment performance objectives
2. Asset allocation
3. Portfolio guidelines
4. Investment managers
5. The investment policy statement
6. Monitoring, reevaluation and modification.

Hopefully, these chapters will help you in your quest to *find the right answers* for your fund.

Chapter 22

Developing Investment Policy Statement–Investment Performance Objectives

What are investment performance objectives? They are the long-term risk/return targets you and your fellow trustees adopt after

- Examining the *internal* demographics and financial characteristics of your plan; the present and probable future, and
- Becoming familiar with the *external* financial characteristics of the securities markets; the past, present and probable future.

If the objectives are appropriate, and achieved, the investment management program will successfully contribute to the overall benefit funding goals of the plan.

The *overall* objectives, or goals, of a benefit plan will vary from fund to fund. Obviously, goals of a defined benefit plan differ from those of a health and welfare plan. Defined contribution plans have their own set of objectives. At the outset, trustees must understand and arrive at a consensus as to what the plan is intended to achieve in the final analysis. For example, a pension plan might have some or all of the following basic goals:

- To provide participants an adequate retirement income when added to income from other sources.
- To assist retirees in coping with inflation. (This, of course, implies periodic or automatic benefit increases.)

- ◆ To provide benefits competitive with those of other organizations in the same labor market.
- ◆ To meet the obligations of collective bargaining agreements.
- ◆ To provide above-average benefits in the industry or geographic area.

It is reasonable to expect that even among similar types of benefit programs, such as pension or welfare, the goals of individual plans will vary. Thus, trustees must first have a clear understanding of what their *plan's goals are* because this will have a decided effect on their portfolio's *investment objectives.*

Purpose of Plan

In attempting to carry out their fiduciary responsibility for fund investments, trustees should have a clear understanding of the major types of employee benefit plans and how the needs of each type of plan may affect investment objectives.

ERISA distinguishes between two major types of employee benefit plans: welfare and pension. An *employee benefit welfare plan,* as defined by Section 3(1), includes plans that provide not only the traditional hospital-medical-surgical benefits in the event of sickness, accident or disability, but also plans that provide death benefits, unemployment or vacation benefits, apprenticeship or other training programs, day-care centers, prepaid legal services and "any other benefit described in Section 302 of the Labor-Management Act of 1947." Clearly, this definition sweeps in most jointly trusteed benefit programs.

An *employee benefit pension plan,* as defined in Section 3(2) of ERISA, includes any plan, fund or program established or maintained by an employer or employee organization that provides retirement income to employees or that results in the deferral of income by employees "for periods extending to the termination of covered employment or beyond." Thus, all pension and profit-sharing plans, and many stock bonus, thrift and savings plans, fall under the scope of ERISA regulation.

Welfare Plans

The distinction between a welfare plan and a pension plan is perhaps so basic that it may be all too easily overlooked. Yet the difference is critical when it comes to developing a set of investment objectives. In the case of a *welfare* plan, most of the income received during the year is spent. When reserves are established, primary emphasis must be given to the objective of preserving capital so that it is available when needed to pay benefits. A secondary objective may be to generate investment income that can be used to help defray the administrative expenses of operating the trust.

Welfare reserves generally fall into three major categories: (1) *economic reserves,* which are reserves that are held to offset premium or administrative cost increases, either anticipated or unanticipated, during the term of the collective bargaining agreement; (2) *eligibility reserves* accumulated by trusts with extended liability or an "hour bank" system that permits workers to build up hours in excess of the minimum required for eligibility so that hours can be drawn on to retain eligibility when employment is down; and (3) *self-insured reserves,* which are set up by self-insured plans for "incurred but unreported claims." In addition, self-insured plans often establish *contingency reserves* to handle catastrophic or unanticipated adverse claims experience.

Prior to ERISA, the reserves held by health and welfare trusts were often invested by the fund administrator in savings accounts or short-term investments such as certificates of deposit (CDs) or Treasury bills. This discretion given to the fund administrator was usually very narrowly defined. However, with the passage of ERISA, administrators have become more reluctant to assume even this limited responsibility because of the potential liability exposure. Most welfare trusts have sought outside investment advice, not only to reduce liability exposure but to enhance the yield from the reserves in an effort to meet rising administrative expenses.

In setting their investment objectives, welfare plans have to recognize that the liquidity needs of a welfare plan are generally much more immediate than those of a typical pension plan. Indeed, new demands on available cash resources may develop over relatively short periods of time due to unemployment, marked increases in medical care costs or sharp swings in claims utilization. Many of these factors lie well beyond the control of the welfare fund trustees, and such factors must be carefully weighed when the trustees establish their investment objectives.

Pension Plans

By contrast, pension plan trustees are generally in a position to commit assets to long-term investments because of the extended period between receipt of employer contributions and payment of benefits. However, among pension plans, investment objectives will be affected by the type of pension plan that is in operation.

There are two basic types of pension plans with which trustees should be familiar: (1) defined benefit plans and (2) defined contribution plans, sometimes referred to as *money purchase* or *employee's own money* plans. Needed here is a look at the characteristics of each type of plan and how these characteristics impact on investment decision making.

Under a *defined benefit* plan, the plan designer has established a *fixed* monthly benefit, such as $10 for each year of credited service, or 2% of contributions required to be made. In arriving at the cost of the fixed benefit, the actuary has to make certain assumptions about investment return, employment, turnover, retirement rates and other factors that are likely to affect the flow of money into and out of the fund.

Most Taft-Hartley funds are defined benefit plans. Under a Taft-Hartley pension plan, labor and management negotiate the amount of contributions in the economic wage package, but the level of benefits is defined in the plan. The level of benefits provided under this type of plan bears a direct relationship to the employer contribution rate and the various actuarial assumptions, including the investment return assumption. If investment return falls short of the assumed return for a Taft-Hartley pension plan, there are no corporate profits or other company assets which can be tapped to make up the deficiency. To the extent that the investment results fall below the actuarial needs of the plan, new monies to make up the deficiency can come from only two major sources: (1) increased employer contributions when the collective bargaining agreement is up for renegotiation or (2) a reduction of benefits. In other words, the source of contributions is not open-ended.

This operating characteristic of a Taft-Hartley fund obviously imposes some additional constraints on the trustees as they try to keep the relationship between cash flow and outflow in balance. There simply are no hidden coffers from which Taft-Hartley trustees can draw to make up the difference between anticipated and actual investment return. By contrast, corporate plans at least have the option of passing some or all of any unanticipated costs of their retirement plans along to the consumer in the form of increased prices for goods or services to sell, and there are company assets to tap if investment return falls short of the mark. Trustees of Taft-Hartley pension plans must keep these factors constantly in mind as they develop their investment policy.

A second type of retirement plan is the *defined contribution* or *employee's own money* plan. This category includes substantially all profit-sharing, money purchase, individual retirement account, employee stock ownership, thrift or savings plans. Under a defined contribution plan, the amount contributed by the employer–which is really part of the employee's wage package–is placed in an individual account for each participant, and the benefits are based solely upon the amount accumulated in the participant's own account. The rate of contribution may be fixed–usually as a percentage of employee earnings or as a percentage of profits–or the contribution may be determined on a discretionary basis by a company's board of directors.

The employer's contribution together with the employee's contribution under a contributory plan (i.e., a plan that provides for both employer and employee contributions) plus the employee's share in the investment experience of the plan provides the eventual retirement income. The amount that can be accumulated by the time of retirement depends upon such factors as length of service, the amount of contributions and the investment experience of the plan. Pension plan benefits generally are paid out in the form of a monthly benefit for the life of the participant.

Although the contribution is defined, the exact amount is not fixed by the plan. Consequently, it is not possible to predict with any certainty the amount of retirement income a participant will receive under a defined contribution plan. However, as with other types of pension plans, actuarial calculations are made to estimate the amount of contributions and investment return necessary to fund a specified level of benefits which it is hoped can be paid to participants at retirement.

> A nickel ain't worth a dime anymore.
>
> *Yogi Berra*

For those defined contribution plans where the trustees set investment objectives, the trustees must be mindful of the fact that safety of the principal may be the most important goal for whatever amount has been contributed. A defined contribution plan is often called an *employee's own money* plan. Trustees of a defined contribution plan have a narrower range of investment options compared with trustees of other types of pension plans.

Marc Gertner, in a presentation to an International Foundation Investments Institute, outlined the differing characteristics of defined benefit and defined contribution plans:

Defined Benefit Plans	Defined Contribution Plans
Benefits “guaranteed.”	No guarantee as to benefits.
Benefits not adjusted for investment gains or losses.	Amount at retirement or termination of employment directly related to investment success.
Benefits payable for life.	Benefits payable only until account is exhausted. Pension plans require a joint and survivor annuity option.
Preretirement death benefits are required for vested participants who die “while actively employed.”	Total balance of fund paid at death.
Credit for past service permissible.	No credit for past service.
Disability benefits for life available.	Lump sum at disability if option available. Benefits only until account is exhausted.
Employer liable for unfunded vested liability.	No employer liability beyond making contributions. No employer obligations for contributions in profit-sharing plans.
Requires actuarial valuations to meet funding requirement.	No actuarial valuations needed.
No individual accounts; however, “cash balance” plans are defined benefit plans that *do* have individual accounts.	Individual account for each participant.
PBGC premiums due.	No PBGC premiums due.
Greater certainty of benefits.	Less certainty of benefits but opportunity for enhanced benefits if investment performance warrants.
Plan bears the investment risk.	Participant bears the investment risk.

Internal Factors

Among the most critical questions that the trustees must answer before deciding on specific investment objectives are the following: How much money will be coming into this fund over the next five to ten years? What will be the financial obligations during the same period of time? Only by "guesstimating" what the fund's cash flow needs are can the trustees set realistic investment objectives and select the investment program most likely to produce needed income at the proper time. The answer to these questions requires a cash flow projection. Usually, the plan actuary and/or consultant is responsible for developing that projection.

If the plan's cash flow is projected to be positive (net income exceeds disbursements) for the foreseeable future, the investment policy need not be overly concerned with restricting the use of relatively illiquid investments. On the other hand, if the cash flow is projected to be negative (disbursements exceed income) for some period of time, a different program may be indicated. In this case, the investment policy may call for reduced emphasis on assets that are illiquid or that do not generate cash currently.

In summary, plan internal factors that must be considered when developing performance objectives include:

- ◆ Workforce demographics
- ◆ Predictability of contributions
- ◆ Turnover rate
- ◆ Funding status
- ◆ Cash flow projections.

Although the trustees must rely on the professionals serving the fund to collect the data necessary to define the plan's probable future profile, the trustees are in the best position to discuss and debate any issues arising related to the impact the internal factors will have on setting performance objectives.

External Factors

Whereas internal factors dictate the needs of your plan, it is the *external factors* (economic environment and the securities markets) that ultimately will determine the limitations on funding the future benefit payments through investment return. Although the trustees have the superior insight on the internal factors, the investment professionals, by training and experience, have the superior insight regarding the external factors. Capital market studies performed by consultants and investment managers can assist the trustees in arriving at reasonable risk/return expectations for portfolios in the aggregate and their components. Such studies are updated periodically, permitting the trustees to compare expectations to reality. Thus, you and your fellow trustees are encouraged to seek the counsel of the consultants and managers before finalizing the performance objectives.

The key economic variables influencing your investment returns in the future will be:

- ◆ Inflation
- ◆ Interest rates
- ◆ Growth of the economy (GDP)
- ◆ Tax policy.

You are encouraged to observe these trends over time. Their impact on the securities markets will in turn impact the values of the securities in your portfolio and the portfolio's overall return. You and your fellow trustees will observe the link between the economic variables, market movements and what can be reasonably expected from a diversified portfolio. Such insight will enable you to quantify the performance objectives of your plan.

Investment Planning Horizon

When setting your performance objectives it is important to identify over how long a period of time the monies can remain invested.

To determine the "footprint" of your future cash flow requirements, the trustees should periodically request from the actuary a projection of the most probable financial profile of the plan. You will then find out the short, intermediate and long-term benefits funding requirements. As previously mentioned, most defined benefit plans can more profitably leverage their investment planning horizon than they do:

- ◆ Wrong policies

  Desire to "beat market" quarterly

  Overemphasis on liquid investments

  Distress over short-term fluctuations.

> Pension plans, which generally are accumulating funds for benefit payments in the future, are in a particularly good position to be long-term, patient investors.
>
> *David George Ball, Former Assistant Secretary of PWBA*

Exhibit 22-1

THE POWER OF TAX-FREE COMPOUNDING
How $1,000 Invested Each Year Grows Over 40 Years

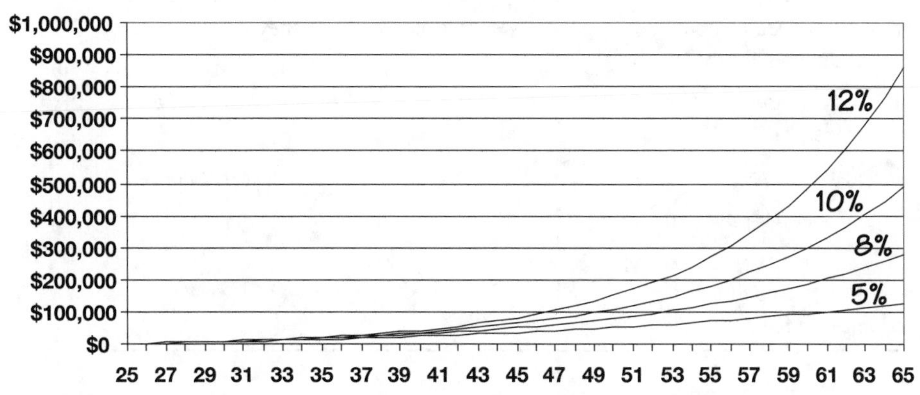

Investing Age

Assumes contributions at the beginning of the year, with a total of 40 contributions made.

- Correct policies
  Seek long-term increase in value.
  Sacrifice liquidity for higher return.
  Accept volatility for higher return.

Exhibit 22-1 demonstrates the power of tax-free compounding when monies are committed for the long term and not disturbed. Exhibits 22-2 and 22-3 reflect the different investments to be considered when the planning horizon is short (as is the case of health and welfare plans, and mature pension plans), or long (as is the case with most defined benefit plans).

It is axiomatic that every employee benefit plan has investment objectives that are *unique to its own set of characteristics*. These differing characteristics affect the planning horizon, the types of investments that are appropriate and the mix of those investments. However, one can generalize about the differing conclusions in objective setting when addressing the three types of funds, i.e., health

Exhibit 22-2

MATCHING ASSETS TO INVESTMENT PLANNING HORIZON

Time Horizon of Goals—Short Term (0-2 Years)

What to Look For	Tradeoffs	Investments to Consider
• Price that doesn't change or only changes slightly	• Lower overall returns	• Money market funds
• Maturity of no more than two years	• Vulnerable to inflation	• Short-term CDs
• Moderate yields		• Short-term bonds
• Regular income payments		
• Easy access to your money; no withdrawal penalties or redemption fees		

Exhibit 22-3

MATCHING ASSETS TO INVESTMENT PLANNING HORIZON

Time Horizon of Goals—Long Term (Over 5 Years)

What to Look For	Tradeoffs	Investments to Consider
• Records of highest long-term returns or highest yields	• More short-term price swings	• Long-term bonds
• Capital growth potential	• Less liquidity	• Real estate
• Returns that consistently outpace inflation	• Don't invest if you may need to sell out early	• Common stocks
• Maturity or investment horizon of at least five years		• Gold, silver or other hard assets

and welfare plans, defined benefit plans and defined contribution plans. Exhibit 22-4 examines these three plans and the differences in objectives when the factors of liquidity, liability matching, market risk and financial risk are examined.

Adoption of investment performance objectives is influenced by the conflicting goals to preserve principal value, produce current income, enhance principal value, preserve purchasing power, produce capital gains and enhance purchasing power. To the degree one emphasizes the performance objective of value enhancement over value

Exhibit 22-4

FACTORS IN OBJECTIVE SETTING
Health and Welfare—Defined Benefit—Defined Contribution Plans

Risk Factor	H&W	Defined Benefit	Defined Contribution
Need for liquidity	High priority due to potential for adverse claims experience	Minimum required, unless it is a mature plan	Uncertain benefit payout timing demands require liquidity-reserves
Need to match liabilities with maturing assets	Potentially shortened payment schedule requires liquidity	Deemed desirable to protect surplus—some matching is desirable	There are no surplus/deficit constraints
Need to control market risk	Highly desirable to provide redemption, if needed, at little or no loss of principal	Largely a decision of trustees, since they are "responsible" for any shortfall	Participants/beneficiaries bear the risk; they generally opt for limited fluctuations in their accounts
Need to control financial (credit) risk	Highly desirable to forego return from credit risk exposure to preserve principal value	"Prudence" generally requires high-quality portfolio	Participants/beneficiaries generally opt for very high-quality portfolios to assure principal protection

preservation, one must be willing to move out on the risk/return spectrum. The wider the range of alternatives granted the investment managers, the less control the trustees have over the stability in portfolio values.

Objectives to preserve and enhance principal value, produce current income and preserve purchasing power would most probably encourage the use of money market accounts, fixed income accounts, equity income accounts and real estate accounts. Performance objectives to enhance purchasing power and produce capital gains would most probably encourage the use of real estate accounts, balanced (stock and bonds) accounts, growth and income accounts, growth stock accounts, capital appreciation accounts, small company growth stocks accounts and even venture capital.

Your investment consultant or investment manager can play "what-if" games with you in determining your risk/return goals. An interactive computer program that combines historical returns, varying inflation assumptions and various asset mixes will give the trustees a feel (it is still as much an art as a science) for the risk/return trade-offs in portfolio construction.

Very few boards still express their investment performance objectives using a single absolute number. An 8% absolute target return would seem reasonable and attainable in a stable pricing or disinflationary environment; it would be less meaningful and attainable in higher inflation periods. Trustees also adopt relative return objectives: return relative to inflation, return relative to chosen referenced benchmarks, return relative to other funds, etc. The acceptance of relative return objectives recognizes the inherent market constraints that exist in the management of institutional portfolios.

Knowing what you are trying to accomplish through your investment program is the beginning of success. The empirical process that leads to such success includes:

- ◆ Examining the plan's internal factors
- ◆ Being acquainted with the opportunities and limitations of the securities markets
- ◆ Identifying the plan's *true* investment planning horizon
- ◆ Positioning the portfolio at the highest risk/return level that the analysis justifies and
- ◆ *Staying* the course!

Chapter 23

Asset Allocation

Introduction

The asset mix, that is, the proportion of a portfolio that is invested in various asset classes, is the principal determinant of the portfolio's long-run investment returns. It is also the principal factor determining the volatility of the portfolio's returns. Because investment risk and return are positively correlated, all investment decisions involve a fundamental tradeoff between returns (greed) and risk (fear). The greater the return we wish to achieve, the more risk we must bear. A successful long-term investment policy must not only target the appropriate rate of return, but also must confine risk (portfolio volatility) to a level that does not exceed the trustees' tolerance. In addition to the discomfort (heightened fear) brought about by an excessively risky investment policy, such policies tend to produce maximum damage to portfolio values and trustees' nerves at market bottoms and often thus result in selling at those times when market values and opportunities are the greatest and most of the downside risk in the market has already been suffered.

> *Greed and fear interfere with good investment thinking and with sound asset allocation.*
>
> *Claude N. Rosenberg Jr.*

Because we get paid for bearing risk in the markets, an excessively risk-averse investment policy can produce inferior investment returns and ultimately it too may impair the fund's ability to pay benefits. Stability of investment returns, that is, avoiding portfolio volatility, carries a premium in the form of opportunity cost. Higher long-run returns are sacrificed in favor of the reduced volatility. Because portfolio stability is purchased at the expense of higher returns, the trustees should avoid purchasing more stability than necessary.

Every investment decision should have as its objective either the enhancement of the portfolio's return, or the reduction of its risk, or both. Because asset mix is overwhelmingly the dominant factor in both the portfolio's expected return and its risk level, the asset allocation guidelines are the heart of any comprehensive investment management policy. In the long run, the investment success of the fund will be determined more by the trustees than by their investment managers because it is the trustees who determine what assets the fund will hold and, in many instances, how much is allocated to each asset class.

The purpose of an asset allocation analysis is to determine the efficient (expected investment returns are maximized relative to any specific level of risk) allocation of scarce investment resources and thereby provide a sound framework for diversifying the fund's wealth across asset types. The purpose of diversification is not primarily to increase returns, but rather to achieve a desired level of return with a minimum amount of risk. A byproduct of the determination of the optimal diversification for the fund as part of an asset allocation exercise is the assurance that the fund does not assume unnecessary risk in pursuit of returns.

Several studies have confirmed that the asset allocation choice is the primary determinant of long-run risk and return. One such study concluded that 93% of the long-term account performance resulted from asset deployment activities. Security selection decisions had an impact on only 7% of the long-term total account performance. It would appear from such studies that fund fiduciaries would be well advised to spend time, effort and money in the search for the most effective asset allocation for their fund.

Unfortunately, the record shows that trustees have spent the bulk of their investment management fees on management that emphasizes security selection activities, not asset allocation activities. Instead of focusing on the important asset allocation decisions, many trustee boards have been observed to be ill-advisedly engaged in practices leading to:

1. An excessive hiring of "winning" managers and firing of "losing" managers
2. Excessive turnover in the portfolio in an attempt to add value
3. Inordinate emphasis on stock-picking activities
4. Assuming unrealizable expectations for returns based upon recent market experience and in ignorance of the long-term risk/return relationships in the securities markets.

> You can't repeal human nature by an act of Congress.
>
> Bernard Baruch

Although mentioned before, it bears repeating: Trustees should place their primary focus on seeking answers to the following questions:

1. Which asset classes to include in the portfolio
2. What strategic policy weights to assign to those classes over the long term
3. What tactical short-term redeployment is permissible (if any)
4. Which manager and management strategies to use within and/or across asset classes.

We will address the first three questions in this chapter and the fourth question in a following chapter on investment managers.

Which Asset Classes Should Be Included in the Portfolio?

For detail on the characteristics of the various asset classes you are referred to Chapters 7 through 17.

Exhibit 23-1 reminds us how important it is to be mindful of the differing wealth-building characteristics of the various classes of assets when held for long periods of time. Expressed in dollars, starting in 1925 and ending in 2003, Exhibit 23-1 shows that:

1. $1 invested in small stocks grew to $10,954
2. $1 invested in large stocks grew to $2,845
3. $1 invested in long bonds grew to $61
4. $1 invested in T-bills grew to $18
5. What cost $1 in 1926 cost $10 in 2003.

Exhibit 23-2 shows the historical *real* rate of returns, and the ranges of those returns, for the various asset classes.

Exhibit 23-3 shows how the assets correlate to one another.

Exhibit 23-4 shows the risk/return tradeoff, reflecting the increasing return and risk, as the stock component of a portfolio is pro-

Exhibit 23-1

HISTORICAL RETURNS ON FINANCIAL ASSETS (1926-2003)

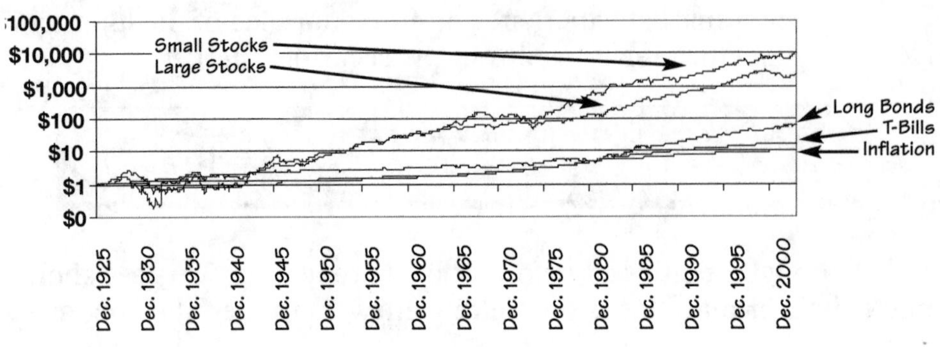

Source: Ibbotson Associates.

Exhibit 23-2

NORMAL RANGE OF REAL RETURNS FOR SELECTED ASSET CLASSES

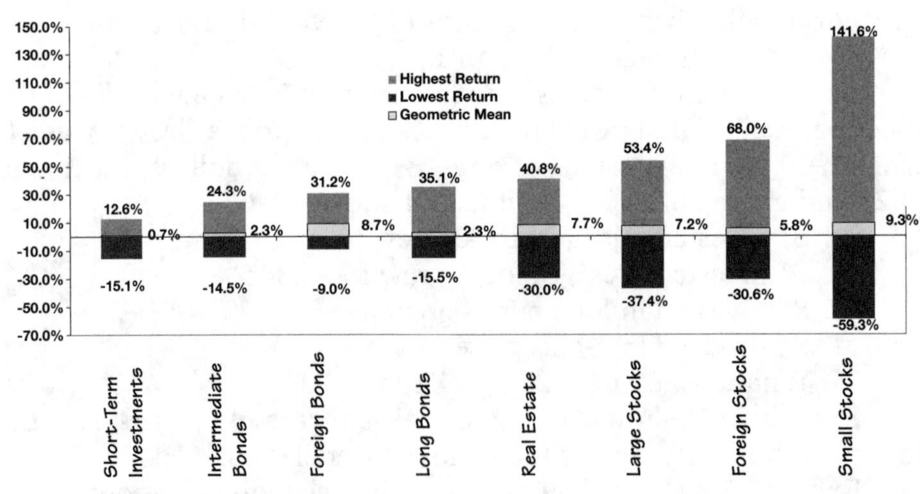

Source: Ibbotson Associates.

Exhibit 23-3

ASSET CLASS CORRELATION

	U.S. Stocks	Foreign Stocks	U.S. Bonds	Foreign Bonds	Real Estate	Short Term
U.S. stocks	1.0					
Foreign stocks	0.6	1.0				
U.S. bonds	0.2	0.1	1.0			
Foreign bonds	0.0	0.4	0.4	1.0		
Real estate	0.5	0.3	0.1	0.0	1.0	
Short term	0.1	0.0	0.1	0.0	−0.1	1.0

Source: Ibbotson Associates.

Exhibit 23-4

RISK/RETURN TRADEOFF: STOCKS AND BONDS PORTFOLIO OF U.S. STOCKS AND BONDS 1970-2003

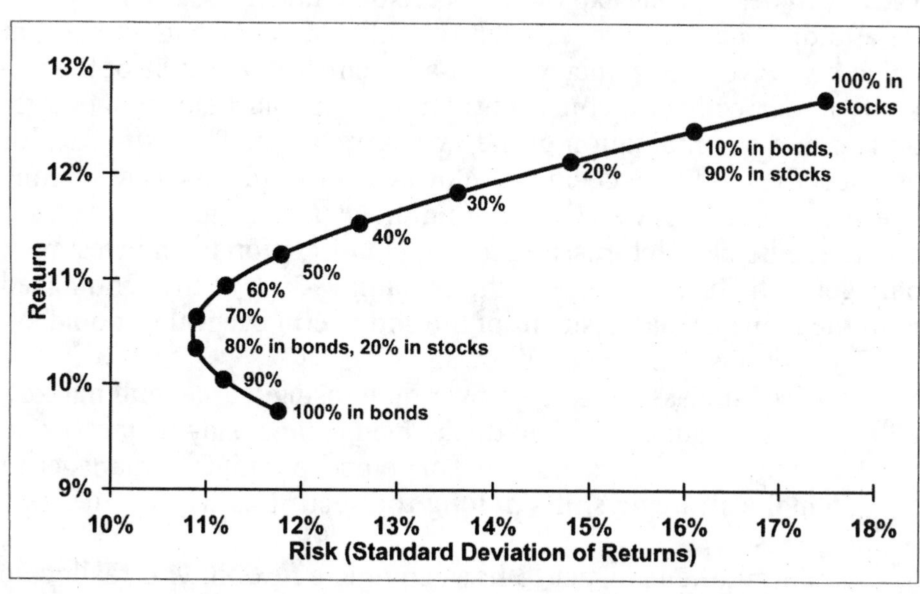

Source: Ibbotson Associates.

gressively increased and the bond component decreased. Since portfolio performance is determined by the combination of the rates of return, volatility and interrelationships between the various asset classes, it is particularly important that the trustees, together with their investment consultant, spend a great deal of time familiarizing themselves with the contribution the various assets make when added to the portfolio.

The assets you choose for the portfolio will be dictated by your tolerance for risk, which is determined by the investment performance objectives you have adopted. Exhibit 23-5 is an example of the differing portfolio profiles as they are matched to differing performance objectives.

What Policy Weights Should Be Assigned to the Classes Over the Long Term?

The trustees must address several fundamental policy decisions:

1. Once the asset mix is decided upon, it is to remain passively invested, or
2. Active management of the asset mix is permitted.

A fixed posture is constrained to accept the long-term risk/return tradeoffs in the markets. A flexible posture assumes that a management system can periodically exploit the occasional undervaluations that exist–and do it consistently enough to add value over and above that which a passive fixed policy would have achieved. Because of the difficulty in correctly and consistently timing the markets, many larger funds prefer a combination of the two approaches. That is to say, for instance, the fund may decide to allocate 80% of the assets to be fully invested at all times, weighted among the classes in accordance with long-term historical returns, and then grant discretion to an investment manager to tactically redeploy the remaining 20% of the fund based upon the manager's assessment of the short-term cyclical outlook.

The options then are as follows:

1. Keep the asset mix fixed over time (using market and market-plus accounts) or have the active manager stay fully invested within the asset class. This, of course, permits the manager to make strategic shifts *among* the securities within the asset class.
2. Permit the manager to have complete flexibility to reallocate at her or his discretion.
3. Adopt a combination fixed/flexible policy. The magnitude of flexibility you permit depends to a great degree upon (a) past

Exhibit 23-5

PORTFOLIO DESCRIPTIONS

Portfolio Objectives	Risk Tolerance	Investor Preferences and Practices
Aggressive growth	Well above average	Emphasis on future price appreciation and income growth. Long-run time horizon. Willingness to accept short-run fluctuations in portfolio value. Portfolio includes smaller capitalization stocks. Bonds include high-grade corporates and governments.
Long-term growth	Above average	Emphasis on future price appreciation and income growth versus current income. Long-run time horizon. Willingness to tolerate short-run fluctuations in portfolio value. Portfolio includes some smaller capitalization stocks. Bonds include high-grade corporates and governments.
Balanced	Moderate	Balanced emphasis on current income and on future price appreciation with income growth. Portfolio includes medium and large capitalization stocks. Bonds include high-grade corporates and governments.
Current income	Conservative	Emphasis on maintaining high and stable current income. Future price appreciation and income growth are less important. Portfolio emphasizes large capitalization stocks and government bonds.
Stable principal	Risk averse	Emphasis on stable portfolio value. Future price appreciation and income growth are unimportant. Short-run time horizon. Income fluctuations are undesirable. Portfolio emphasizes blue-chip stocks and government bonds.

Source: Robert W. Baird & Co. Incorporated, ©August 1994, *Baird Economic Outlook and Investment Strategy Perspective.*

experience in asset shift activities and (b) the confidence in your present manager to successfully redeploy the assets in the future.

For smaller funds that use one, or several, *balanced* managers: The manager most probably is given a range of flexibility within which he or she can make tactical asset mix shifts.

Exhibit 23-6

POTENTIAL RETURNS FROM ACTIVE MANAGEMENT

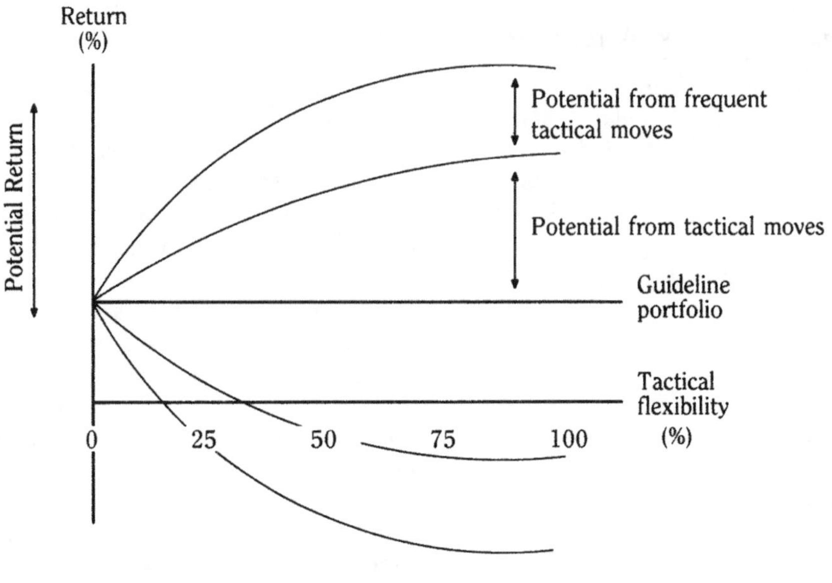

Exhibit 23-6 illustrates the potential impact on return from active (tactical) portfolio moves, depending upon the degree of flexibility permitted. There is *upside* potential and *downside* potential.

If the trustees adopt a policy to have the asset mix remain passive/fixed over time, they will still have to occasionally *rebalance* the portfolio back to its original allocation or its "drift" may eventually produce a vastly different risk/return profile than was intended. Rebalancing generally results in selling the recently "winning" securities and buying the "about to be winning" securities, a discipline that has proven to have had advantages.

John Bogle *(Bogle on Mutual Funds)* offers the following support for *passive investment, with occasional rebalancing:*

> We are thus led to put forward to most of our readers what may appear to be an oversimplified 50-50 formula. Under this plan the guiding rule is to maintain as nearly as practicable an equal division between bond and stock holdings. When changes in the market level have raised the common-stock component to, say, 55 percent, the balance would be restored

> by a sale of one-eleventh of the stock portfolio and the transfer of the proceeds to bonds. Conversely, a fall in the common-stock proportion to 45 percent would call for the use of one-eleventh of the bond fund to buy additional equities.
>
> . . . we are convinced that our 50-50 version of this approach makes good sense for the defensive investor. It is extremely simple; it aims unquestionably in the right direction; it gives the follower the feeling that he is at least making some moves in response to market developments; *most important of all, it will restrain him from being drawn more and more heavily into common stocks as the market rises to more and more dangerous heights.*
>
> Furthermore, a truly conservative investor will be satisfied with the gains shown on half his portfolio in a rising market, while in a severe decline he may derive much solace from reflecting how much better off he is than many of his more venturesome friends.

> We all have strength enough to endure the misfortunes of others.
>
> *Rochefoucauld*

What policy weights you adopt will to a large degree be determined by the trustees' "tolerance for pain." What is the worst-case scenario you can live with? Exhibit 23-7, based upon historical returns, shows the maximum *negative* return you can expect in any one year, depending upon your asset mix.

Market Timing Versus Asset Allocation

Many plans encourage market timing operations, not realizing there are significant differences between such short-term oriented activities and longer term oriented asset allocation activities. (See Exhibit 23-8.) Market timing operations can be very profitable if successful. Unfortunately, since you are competing against the wisdom of all other investors, consistently successful market timing operations have also proven to be elusive. Characteristics of *market timing operations* include the following:

1. Frequent manipulation of the positions in the portfolio
2. Transaction-driven results
3. Wide variability in returns achieved.

Characteristics of *asset allocation operations* include the following:

1. Low turnover in portfolio resulting from long-term commitment to holding assets
2. Market-driven results
3. Highest probability of achieving the returns you are given to expect from the asset class.

> Invest—don't trade or speculate. The stock market is not a casino, but if you move in and out of stocks every time they move a point or two . . . or if you continually sell short . . . or deal only in options . . . or trade in futures . . . the market will be your casino. And, like most gamblers, you may lose eventually—or frequently.
>
> *Sir John Templeton*

It is very difficult to win the "market timing game." According to Prudential Investments research, "miss the top twenty-six performing months for stocks and you may as well have invested in Treasury Bills." (See Exhibit 23-9.)

Exhibit 23-7

RESULTS FOR PORTFOLIOS HOLDING VARYING AMOUNTS OF STOCKS AND BONDS (1949-2003)

Portfolio	Composition	Number of Down Years	Average Loss in Down Years	Worst 1-Year Loss	Average Annual Return
Aggressive	100% stocks	13	−10.7	−26.5	12.2
Growth	75% stocks/ 25% bonds	12	−7.1	−19.0	10.9
Balanced	50% stocks/ 50% bonds	10	−3.9	−11.1	9.5
Income	25% stocks/ 75% bonds	5	−2.0	−3.5	7.9
Conservative	100% bonds	7	−1.5	−5.1	6.2

Source: Ibbotson Associates.

Exhibit 23-8

POTENTIAL RETURNS FROM ACTIVE MANAGEMENT

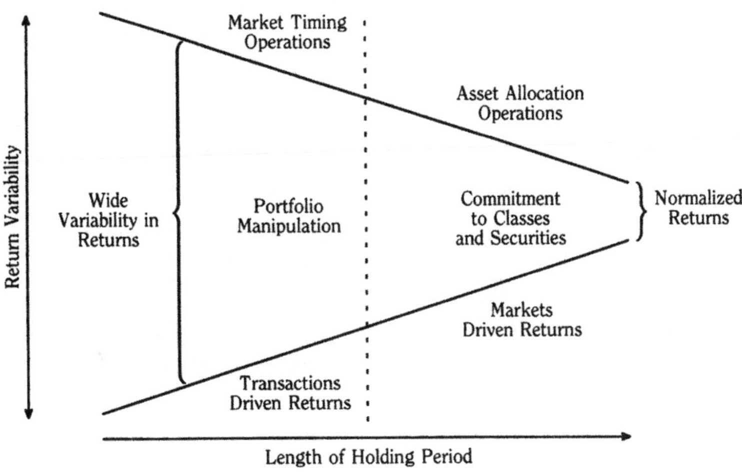

Exhibit 23-9

MISS THE TOP 18 PERFORMING MONTHS FOR STOCKS, AND YOU MAY AS WELL HAVE INVESTED IN T-BILLS

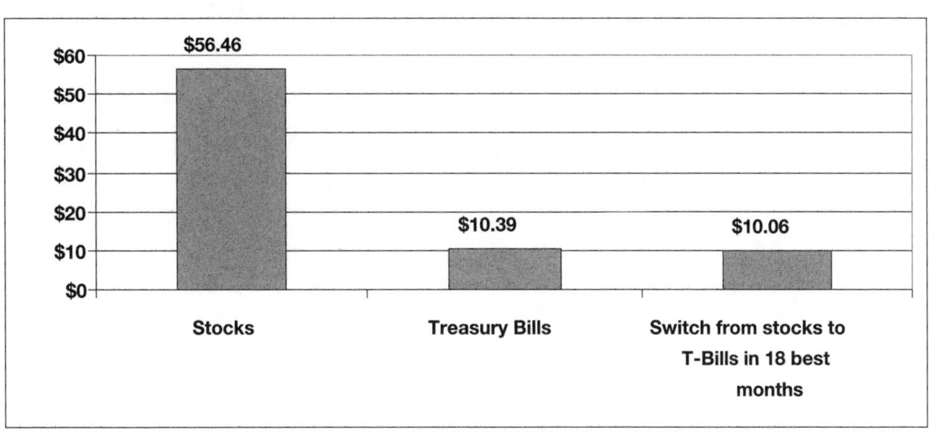

Source: Ibbotson Associates.

A $1 investment in the S&P 500 in January 1964 would have been worth $56.46 by the end of 2003. A similar $1 investment in 90-day U.S. Treasury bills would have only been worth $10.39. Suppose that instead of a "buy and hold" policy in the S&P 500 an investor shifted the balance from stocks into T-bills and then back again for 18 months over the 40-year period. This would be approximately 4% of the time. If the investor was unfortunate and the 18 shifts coincided with the 18 best monthly stock returns, the $56.46 would have shrunk to $10.06. To put it differently, *miss only the 18 best months of stock market performance in the last 40 years and an investor would have been better off holding T-bills over the entire period.*

This analysis leads to the following conclusions:

1. It is too late to become defensive once the bad news breaks.
2. While asset allocation can add value, it is not the place to make major shifts, i.e., movements of 0-100% in an asset class.
3. There are significant costs to being wrong in the "market timing game."
4. A balanced approach that matches expected returns with a risk level that can be tolerated is probably the best approach to follow.

Market timing involves high exposure to "manager risk." Asset allocation minimizes manager risk, preferring to substitute the assurance of the historical upward bias of the market to produce positive returns over time. Asset allocation operations are more akin to investing; market timing is a trading effort in the attempt to constructively exploit short-term cyclical events.

> Portfolio reallocations, specifically switching among stocks, bonds and cash equivalents while attempting to "time" the market, had a significant *deleterious* effect on portfolio performance for ERISA plans, endowment funds and public pension plans.
>
> *DOL Study (1968-83) of ERISA Plans*

The Allocated Portfolio

For the *small* fund, asset allocation may or may not be set by the trustees. If they retain a *balanced* manager they may choose to let the manager set the mix within certain percentage limitations. If specialty managers or mutual funds are used, then the trustees must adopt allocation guidelines.

Exhibit 23-10

INTERMEDIATE-SIZED PENSION FUND

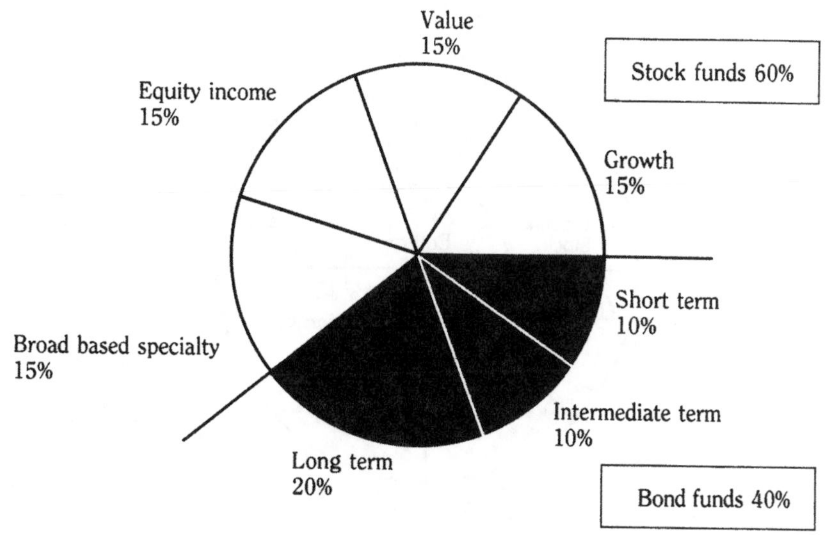

The *intermediate*-sized fund (see Exhibit 23-10) may choose to restrict its assets to stocks and bonds, further allocating within the asset categories to subcategories of those two classes. Several managers may be retained to cover one or more categories. Depending upon their confidence in the manager's ability to tactically redeploy the assets, the trustees may permit the manager to engage in shorter term asset-shifting activities.

Large pension funds are typically broadly diversified over many classes of assets using both passive and active portfolios. (See Exhibit 23-11.)

When establishing your asset allocation policy, seek to identify the most *appropriate* risk/return profile for the portfolio. Charles Ellis, in *Investment Policy,* challenges you and your fellow trustees to *stretch* out for the *golden ring:*

> Recognizing that higher returns are the incentive and reward for investors taking and sustaining above average market risks and that the highest returns, therefore, come from equities, clients should set their portfolio's asset mix at the highest ratio of equity exposure that their economic and emotional limitations can afford and sustain. To do their work well, clients must understand the turbulent nature of

Exhibit 23-11

LARGE FUND STRUCTURE

markets in the short term and the basic consistency of markets in the long term. This understanding will enable the effective client to increase his or her tolerance for interim market fluctuations and to concentrate on the long-term purpose of the portfolio. Soundly conceived, persistently followed long-term investment policy is the pathway to success in investing. The actions required are not complicated. The real challenge is to commit to the discipline of long-term investing and avoid the compelling distractions of the excitement that surrounds, but is superfluous to, the real work of investment.

Most Taft-Hartley boards of trustees do not devote sufficient time to the asset allocation decision, even though the implication of their asset mix on returns, benefits and contributions is enormous.

Appendix K, "The Asset Allocation Decision," contributed by Bryce Barnes, Quantel Associates, Inc., Clinton, New Jersey, demonstrates the value of increasing common stock in a portfolio.

Chapter 24

Investment Managers

An investment professional has to have certain inherent skills, intellectual and analytical resourcefulness leading to the exercise of sound judgment, a certain sense of skepticism, a balance between confidence and humility, and the ability to make decisions and the courage to back those decisions with a rational defense.

After asset allocation, the next most significant decision the trustees will make is selecting the investment manager(s) to implement the trustee's investment policy decisions. Two dominant factors contribute to successful investment programs:

1. The adoption of appropriate performance objectives, policy and guidelines and
2. Identifying and selecting investment manager(s) who will successfully implement the policy and guidelines.

There still may be a few trustee boards who adopt *and* implement the policy by buying and selling individual securities. Although trustees may be experts in their chosen fields, they are most probably laymen regarding investment matters. Thus, in my opinion, part-time, lay trustees should not be expected to supervise a portfolio of securities. There are literally thousands of variables that affect stock prices; the following are just a few questions portfolio managers must address:

1. Is the company well run?
2. Are profits growing?
3. Is the company's industry on the rise?
4. Is the company an industry leader?
5. Is the stock reasonably priced?
6. Is the balance sheet solid?
7. Is there some special "sizzle" about the stock?
8. Does the company invest in research and development?
9. Is the stock appropriate for the portfolio?

Wouldn't you agree that these are questions beyond the resourcefulness of even the "above-average" trustee?

> Next to doing a good job yourself, the greatest joy is in having someone else do a first-class job under your direction.
>
> *William Feather*

Because the "buy and sell" decisions in investment management operations are so technically demanding, trustees are advised to retain investment managers to provide discretionary supervision of the portfolio within the policy constraints adopted by the board.

The term *investment manager* refers to a fiduciary:

(a) who has the power to manage, acquire or dispose of any asset of a plan,

(b) who is a registered investment advisor under the Investment Advisers Act of 1940, or a bank as defined in that act, or is an insurance company qualified to perform investment services in any state, and

(c) who has acknowledged in writing that he is a fiduciary with respect to the plan.

An early interpretation of ERISA and its fiduciary standards suggested the need for outside professional investment management. As a result, many trustees opt for the designation of an investment manager to obtain the "safe harbor" of ERISA Section 405(d)(1). Section 405 provides that if an investment manager is appointed, then the trustees are not liable for any act or omission of the investment manager nor are they obligated to invest or manage plan assets assigned to the investment manager.

However, trustees who appoint investment managers must be prudent in the following ways: selection of the investment manager, establishment of investment objectives and monitoring the performance of the investment manager. With the alternative of lower fee index funds being available to trustees, it is now incumbent upon them, when seeking active management, to retain managers who give promise of being able to provide returns that are superior to the markets' returns in those asset classes where index funds provide an alternative.

Manager Qualifications

What distinguishes the *superior* investment management organization? First, it should be recognized that success in investment decision making is indifferent to the structure of the organization, its size or location. Whether the firm is organized as a bank, insurance company, mutual fund organization or independent counsel firm, the keys to its success are the *people* and the *process*. Of course, to the degree that any one of these four organizational types becomes more successful in attracting, compensating and motivating the best and brightest professionals, then that type of organization will eventually produce superior performance.

If structure is unimportant, what about size? Some studies support the conclusion that smaller firms (as measured by money under management) produce higher returns than do larger firms. Yet we all know of firms managing billions of dollars that have done very well. The higher relative returns attributed to the smaller firms may be more related to the risk/return profile of the securities the firms have chosen to emphasize, rather than to the firms themselves.

The smart manager, though, will limit the assets he or she attempts to supervise if the marketplace for the manager's selection universe imposes volume limitations on success. In any event, any "size" criteria used in selection of the manager should be carefully considered before automatically eliminating the larger management firms.

What about location? The location of the management firm is probably the least significant factor in the selection process. A manager in your own neighborhood may, over the longer term, provide you with the most resourceful counsel. At one time, a close proximity to Wall Street was considered important. Now, with improved global communications, a manager can be wired to receive whatever information is deemed important at any location. Some managers are successful in part because they have distanced themselves from the financial centers and cultivated a more objective environment for processing information.

If structure, size and location are relatively unimportant, what then are the characteristics of a superior manager? The firm should have developed an approach to investing that has proven successful in the past. It should consistently apply that approach and understandingly articulate it. The firm should have highly intelligent, insightful, well-trained, experienced professionals and motivate them with performance incentives. It should cultivate an environment conducive to creativity and innovation. It should target the investment management activities to attain the *client's* objectives and goals. And, finally, it should have resourceful quantitative support systems and should maintain a high standard of internal quality control in the delivery of the firm's investment management services.

It is not sufficient, though, for trustees to have identified the "superior" manager and allocated the trust fund monies to his or her discretion. Professionalism begets professionalism. Managers work harder (and more successfully) for those fund fiduciaries who comprehend and are supportive of the manager's efforts to add value. Becoming an insightful client should be the personal goal of each trustee. Instead of attempting to "manage the manager," the trustees need to lead the manager in the identification of the most critical issues related to the needs of the fund. Then the manager, with the professional support of the trustees, is free to strategically exploit his or her investment universe to the extent permissible within the guidelines established for the account.

Trustees in Their Role as Client

The science (art?) of investing is a complex discipline. It involves collecting and analyzing a myriad of variables. Culled from these variables are data the manager deems to be the most relevant in the quest to add value. Thus, to render the best service, the manager must be emotionally free to exercise his or her skills. Informed trustees acting professionally can "bring out the best" in the manager. In *Managing Your Investment Manager* (Dow Jones-Irwin, 1986), Arthur Williams III offers the following practical advice to fiduciaries who aspire to be good clients:

1. State your goals.
2. State your goals precisely.
3. Don't change your goals too frequently.
4. Don't compare yourself to others with different goals.
5. Provide your manager with cash flow projections.
6. Don't make surprise contributions or withdrawals.

7. Confide in your manager about internal preferences and (fund management) politics.
8. Don't fall for every fad.
9. Don't believe the performance figures of every person who walks in the door.
10. Don't expect miracles.

The Managers' Portfolio Management Process

Since the purpose of this book is to address issues related to *developing investment policy,* our discussion regarding investment managers will confine itself to the managers' potential to successfully implement policy through the application of their *investment process.* A manager's process begins with the *selection universe* and ends with the *valuation process* (buy and sell decisions).

The *internal process* undertaken by the manager results in what is *externally* identified as the manager's *style* of management. To better understand a manager's style of management, trustees can seek answers to the following questions:

- What is the manager's definition of how he adds value through portfolio management?
- Has it been independently verified that his management has been *consistent over time* with his defined approach?
- How is his management different in style when compared to other managers serving the fund?
- What internal controls are in place to assure consistency of style in the future?
- Are the same individuals managing the portfolios that produced past results?

Stock Managers

There are many styles of stock management. A manager's selection universe can include:

1. Growth stocks
2. Value stocks or
3. A blended portfolio.

While at the same time it can include:

1. Large capitalization stocks
2. Medium capitalization stocks
3. Small capitalization stocks
4. A blended portfolio.

The manager's valuation process can include sector rotation, market timing and contrarianism.

The importance of *all* the trustees understanding the manager's style cannot be overstated. Because the market has such a big influence on portfolio valuations, market forces can temporarily overwhelm a manager's value-added contribution from sector, industry and company choices. By understanding that such deviations in one period are necessary to position the portfolio for superior returns in subsequent periods, the trustees share in a joint commitment with the manager to the style.

It is possible that more funds fail to achieve their long-term investment performance goals through *miscommunication* among the trustees and their investment managers than through inept investment management. Programs are often ill-advisedly aborted at the wrong time in the investment cycle.

Since a recent study concluded that "the two most important reasons for manager termination were loss of confidence in the manager's process and inconsistent investment philosophy or style," it is all the more important that the trustees both understand *how* their managers supervise portfolios and correctly evaluate the results.

The single most significant contribution an active specialist manager can make is in selecting undervalued securities. The price of a security fluctuates around a mystical central value. If a manager pays too much of a premium above the intrinsic value, it will take either a bull market or unexpected good fortune for the firm, or both, to redeem the manager's decision. For the stock manager, this means having a strong company-research capability. For the bond manager, it may be strong credit research; for the real estate manager, it means strong demographics research. Thus, a key question for you when interviewing prospective managers is: Within the manager's style of management, how well does he compare with his peers in identifying undervalued securities?

Bond Managers

The management of bonds requires careful attention to the various risks in bond ownership. These risks include:

1. Credit risk
2. Interest rate risk
3. Inflation risk
4. Call risk
5. Reinvestment risk.

The active strategies in bond management include changing the duration of the portfolio in anticipation of the changes in interest rates, sector swapping activities and security swapping activities. Bond managers can also add value by including new markets (international) and new products (synthetics), and the application of a host of quantitative strategies.

The active styles are looking for a higher return but, of course, must also embrace higher risks. The more passive styles reduce risk but also sacrifice the potential for higher returns.

The following is an example of the stated philosophy and process of a successful "active" bond manager:

- ◆ The manager is willing to make portfolio shifts; such shifts are driven by his analysis of the longer term trends, i.e., changes in the social/political/economic environment.
- ◆ The manager is seeking consistency in investment performance results by avoiding extreme swings in the maturity/duration of the portfolio.
- ◆ The manager is seeking to add value from portfolio activities, which include the use of futures, options, his analysis of the future volatility in the bond market and his analysis of the relative values in the sector/coupon/quality sectors of the bond market.

Such a bond manager might, for instance, allocate money predominantly to Treasuries, with smaller allocations to other quality sectors in the bond market. He may also distribute his portfolio among governments, agencies, internationals, financials, industrials and public utilities to a greater or lesser degree, depending upon his analysis of the most attractive sector distribution to be made in the portfolio.

As in common stock investing, there are a number of managers who provide passive strategies, which include:

1. Liability matching
2. Immunization
3. Dedicated portfolios.

Real Estate Managers

Successful real estate investing requires attention to location, product and management. Therefore, a fund must retain a real estate manager with a resourceful research staff. Since real estate is a relatively inefficient market, a real estate management organization should, by processing information in an effective manner, ultimately acquire those properties whose configurations of attributes will assure relatively high demand. Building on a firm base of research capability, the manager must have developed a strategic approach compatible with the plan and have demonstrated the ability to acquire properties astutely through analytical talent and negotiating skills. An underrated resource of a manager is his or her property (asset) management capability, whether developed in-house or successfully retained and monitored. It also is important to determine that the principals of the firm have formed a team that enjoys industry peer group respect. It takes time and effort for brokers to develop marketing packages for complex properties. Those management teams who (a) have attracted a sufficient client base to provide continuing cash flow availability, (b) have available the diverse disciplines to evaluate a deal effectively and (c) can quickly respond to the offer to capitalize on a market opportunity will be afforded priority in being shown the more desirable properties.

Trustees could develop their own portfolio of properties; however, because Taft-Hartley funds lack sufficient real estate investment expertise, are limited both in cash flow required and access to real estate "deal flow," they are advised to access real estate investments by participating in commingled funds. Because real estate portfolio management is so technically demanding, most fiduciary insurance policies will not cover real estate investments, unless the investments are under the auspices of a qualified professional asset manager (QPAM).

A *commingled fund* is an investment entity comprised of more than one investor. Several investors agree to pool their money for investment purposes. In the real estate industry, the term *commingled fund* specifically refers to investment entities that have been established to serve as investment vehicles primarily for qualified plans.

Real estate commingled funds, as we know them today, came into existence in 1969. Such funds provide investors with experienced real estate investment management services and a high degree of diversification.

Commingled funds may use any of several legal entities as an operational vehicle. The entity selected should not have an impact on the performance results of a fund. A main point here is to make certain the type of entity utilized is authorized for use by your plan documents.

Some of the common entities utilized are:

- ◆ Insurance company separate accounts
- ◆ Group trusts

- ◆ Limited partnerships
- ◆ Real estate investment trusts (public or private).

Because of the legal requirements, the type of entity utilized is most commonly a function of the nature of the fund manager. Only insurance companies may use a separate account structure and only banks and trust companies may use a common trust structure. Other types of fund managers are usually limited to the group trust, limited partnership or real estate investment trust structures.

As in other investment areas, there are different types of commingled funds with differing investment objectives. There are two main types of funds: *open end* and *closed end.*

Open-End Commingled Funds

Such funds are analogous to open-end securities mutual funds. They are, at least theoretically, periodically "open" for new contributions or redemptions. Such funds normally reinvest all earnings. Profits are reflected in terms of increases in the value of the fund's unit (share) value. In order to realize a profit, the shares must be redeemed by the plan.

Share values in the open-end commingled real estate funds are a combination of the appraised fair market value of the assets plus retained earnings. Most funds report on a quarterly basis and allow redemptions or new contributions based on the reported share values. The investor should ensure that the reported value of the shares is at least a reasonable value upon which to base a purchase or sale.

The "advantage" of the open-end structure is that it provides a certain level of liquidity for an asset that is relatively illiquid. One of the reasons many employee benefit plans give for not investing in real estate is its perceived illiquidity. The open-end funds were structured to resolve that issue.

However, the liquidity of most funds has been more theoretical than real. None of the sponsors of such funds can *guarantee* the redemption of shares. The capital for redemption comes from the fund itself. If there is capital available to redeem shares, they will be redeemed. If not, shareholders must wait until there is sufficient capital available to do so. After all, real estate is an *illiquid* asset and should only be added to a portfolio if a truly long-term holding period can be assumed for that portion of the assets.

Since funds reinvest earnings, they take on the nature of an index fund if they continue to buy through all cycles of the market.

There is also the potential for dilution due to new contributions coming into the fund, which will be reinvested at current market rates. Open-end funds, by nature, are large. Thus, they can provide an investor with a much greater degree of diversification than smaller closed-end funds.

Closed-End Commingled Funds

Closed-end commingled funds are structured to allow a one-time infusion of capital at their formation and then are "closed" to new investors. These funds are "blind pools" in the sense that there are no assets in the fund prior to capital contributions by the investors.

Usually, such funds have a specific term, such as ten years, and earnings and proceeds from sale are distributed rather than reinvested. Investors buy the assets "at cost," rather than on appraised values, since the assets are acquired after the formation of the fund, and no new shares are sold thereafter.

Closed-end funds may target their investment strategy much more precisely than open-end funds because they do not reinvest earnings or accept new contributions. They may select a specific opportunity at a particular point in a market cycle, make the investment and then do not dilute that position by investing in other phases of the cycle. For this reason, such a structure is more adaptable to an opportunistic approach than is an open-end structure.

The closed-end structure was not designed with liquidity as an objective, even though all such funds have some form of redemption mechanism. Rather, it is based on the premise that *real estate is a long-term investment.*

An investor should examine a closed-end fund's investment strategy carefully because it will tend to be more specialized than that of an open-end fund. The investor should also consider whether the amount of diversification offered is reasonable in light of the plan's overall real estate investment position.

Exhibit 24-1 compares the differing characteristics of open-end and closed-end funds.

Manager Diversification

If a fund uses a multimanager system, each of whom manages a portion of the aggregate portfolio, how many managers are sufficient for diversification of "manager risk"? A 20-30% holding limit for each manager suggests that "four or five managers adequately diver-

Exhibit 24-1

OPEN-END FUNDS OR CLOSED-END FUNDS

	Open-End Fund	Closed-End Fund
"Window" to invest	Opened quarterly	Open only during subscription period (6-12 months)
Portfolio disclosure	Prospective clients can "kick the tires," if desired	"Blind pool"—only strategy is identifiable
Pension plan buys	Units valued by appraisal process	Portfolio assets at cost
Diversification	Broad—geographic property type and "time"	More specialized and targeted —stage of development —type of properties —geographic concentration
Liquidity	Withdrawals at discretion of participant, within portfolio limitations	Liquidation at discretion of manager, over long period (up to 12 years)
Management	Expertise and approach is critical to results	Expertise and approach is critical to results

sifies a fund's exposure to manager-induced risk." Exhibit 24-2 illustrates the impact on manager-induced risk by adding additional managers. Adding a fourth manager to a fund presently utilizing three managers would reduce risk by about 8%. It is clear from the exhibit that the incremental risk reduction from diversification beyond five managers is not substantial.

Since 90% of the managers' returns are market-induced, and adding more managers results in additional fees and trading costs, an excessively managed program adds an insurmountable, costly load factor on the program. An excessive number of managers also stretches the trustees' allottable time to perform their monitoring activities. Information overload can prevent focused oversight of the managers' activities.

How much an investment manager is involved in policy development varies from plan to plan. Smaller plans, with one manager (balanced?), may lean heavily upon the manager for input. Conversely, a large plan with many managers, utilizing an investment consultant, may develop its overall policy statement exclusive of any

Exhibit 24-2

DIVERSIFICATION BENEFIT OF AN ADDITIONAL INVESTMENT MANAGER

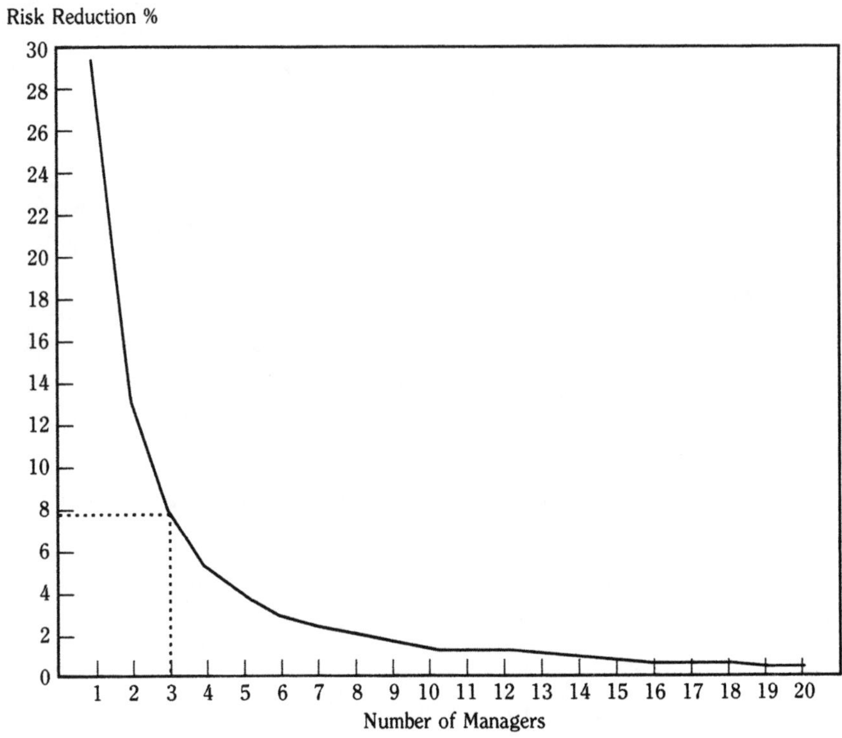

dialogue with a manager, reserving any policy discussions with managers to their own subpolicy statements.

Nonetheless, policy adoption and manager selection go hand in hand. For your policy decisions to be successful, they must be *successfully implemented* by a manager. The most successful managers cannot make up for ill-advised policy decisions. Conversely, the best-intentioned policy will fall short of its performance objectives if either miscommunicated by the trustees or misimplemented by the manager.

Chapter 25

Investment Guidelines

We have learned that *asset mix* has the most significant impact on portfolio return and that the *investment manager* is the key to successful implementation of the trustees' policy decisions. Following closely in importance to these is the subject of guidelines. The net effect of the guidelines detailed in the policy statement is an expression of the *risk posture* that the trustees are comfortable with. The guidelines are statements of trustee preferences regarding portfolio composition and portfolio management practices.

When considering the specific guidelines for the portfolio, or for a given investment manager, the trustees must not only involve themselves but should also seek input and advice from the fund's actuary, the administrator, the consultant and from the investment managers involved. Prior to adopting the guidelines for a specific investment manager, there should be mutual agreement among parties that the guidelines are acceptable. Then, at a later date, the manager cannot claim that investment results were impaired by one or more of the guidelines.

In developing guidelines, a number of questions arise. The most significant are: What are the fund's *liquidity* needs? How much *marketability* should securities in the portfolio have? How much *diversification* should be sought in the portfolio? What *quality* of securities should be permitted? How much *turnover* is acceptable? A host of other questions can be raised, but let us first deal with these crucial ones.

Instead of trying to define the liquidity needs in a dynamic investment situation, the trustees simply may wish to require the investment manager to consult periodically with the trustees and their advisors, especially the fund actuary, in order to determine a proper level of liquidity. Therefore, it may be inappropriate to state at the onset the specific percentage of fund assets that should have liquidity as their primary objective.

The trustees should consider carefully the amount of marketability needed and provide only the required level. By and large, pension fund fiduciaries have overemphasized the need for marketability.

Both the language of ERISA and the Conference Report incidental to the law emphasize the importance of *diversification*. Needless to say, in a volatile market environment, those plans that have been diversified adequately probably have the best chance of producing acceptable results. Just how much diversification a plan should embrace can only be answered by each board. Certainly enough diversification to protect the plan from the potential of "large losses"; not so much as to generate excessive fees, or transactions costs, or to dilute "value-added" contributions from astutely selected managers.

Guidelines addressing diversification preferences include statements regarding:

- Classes of investments
- Geographic dispersion
- Industries permitted
- Dates of maturity
- Management systems.

The trustees need to concern themselves with the "quality" (financial soundness) of the fund's investments. Even though the Department of Labor in its prudence regulations has encouraged a total portfolio approach, many trustees are more comfortable if each and every investment added to the portfolio passes a minimum quality test.

Turnover refers generally to the amount of buying and selling of portfolio securities over a period of time. Most studies indicate that the ability to trade stocks and bonds successfully with some consistency over various stock market cycles is rare. Excessive turnover, unfortunately, often produces results less than what could have been achieved with a passively supervised portfolio of similar quality assets.

The so-called frictional costs (fees, commissions and market impact) are often of such magnitude in a high relative turnover account that the manager finds it very difficult to produce a superior rate of return over less actively traded portfolios. Therefore, it may be helpful to have some mutual understanding as to acceptable turnover levels.

> What always impresses me is how much better the relaxed, long-term owners of stocks do with their portfolios than the traders do with their switching of inventory. The relaxed investor is usually better informed and more understanding of essential values; he is more patient and less emotional; he pays smaller annual capital gains taxes; he does not incur unnecessary brokerage commissions; and he avoids behaving like Cassius by "thinking too much."
>
> *Lucien D. Hooper, Forbes columnist*

Other general items that may be considered by the trustees when establishing investment guidelines include the acceptable conversion period allowable before the effective date of monitoring the performance of new managers, details on classes of investments authorized, the designation of brokerage business for specific services and the rates considered acceptable, and stipulation as to how the voting of the proxies will be accomplished.

For actively managed bond accounts, guidelines may include percentage limitations on exposure to any one industry, company or issue. Other restrictions can include the use of futures, foreign securities, convertibles, minimum quality threshold, private placements, commingled funds, mutual funds, insurance company separate accounts, commercial paper and certificates of deposit.

For the actively managed common stock accounts, the guidelines may include the following: minimum diversification requirements; percent limitation on the securities held in any one industry or company; and limitations on the use of stock options, puts or calls.

Some additional restrictions may cover the use of foreign securities, letter stock, mutual funds, insurance company separate accounts, short sales, commingled funds, convertibles, preferred stock and limited market capitalization.

Since most funds participate either through commingled accounts or through limited general partnerships, guidelines are dictated by the vehicle through which the plan invests in mortgages or real estate. Some of the areas that may be considered in such a decision are: (1) the type of properties, (2) the strategic investment process, (3) the geographic distribution and (4) the choice of leveraged or unleveraged vehicles.

If the trustees feel uncomfortable about certain types of securities–such as foreign stocks, oil leases, puts and calls, or whatever–they should, at the very least, require the manager to seek their approval before such purchases are made. The risk associated with certain types of investments certainly cannot be totally overlooked by the trustees, and there may be good reasons for the trustees to place specific limits on certain high-risk investment alternatives.

As a general rule, however, trustees are well advised to grant broad discretion to the manager to apply his or her management expertise to the portfolio to the fullest extent possible. Exclusionary guidelines may unnecessarily prohibit the manager from contributing his full resourcefulness to the portfolio. After all, *before granting discretionary supervisory responsibilities* to the investment manager it is assumed that the trustees have performed, or have had a qualified firm perform, sufficient due diligence to determine that the manager has *internal controls* in place to assure the delivery of an investment "product" that will meet standards acceptable in the industry.

> Money is like an arm or a leg—use it or lose it.
>
> *Henry Ford*

Each trustee board must adopt its own set of guidelines. Appendix D, Checklist of Elements for Inclusion in Investment Policy Statement, may be helpful to you and your fellow trustees.

Chapter 26

Investment Policy Statement

"If an employee benefit plan does not have an investment policy statement, it does not have an investment policy." Now, that is a harsh statement, but it represents a strong sentiment of truth. The absence of a cohesive written statement results in a loose aggregation of ideas. A loose aggregation of ideas results in a fuzzy understanding of what your objectives are, and until you go through the arduous task of finalizing a statement, the investment manager may be seeking objectives incompatible with the needs of the plan, or the investment vehicles selected for your plan may be inappropriate, given its needs. If a policy is not reduced to writing, it is not mutually understood, and the absence of understanding between the trustees and the professionals is the most significant cause of poor investment results.

The investment policy statement becomes the overall "game plan" from which all substrategies and implementation of those strategies evolve. Investment decisions will then be in concert with the needs of the plan, and your stewardship role will have been fulfilled as you have effectively articulated the "'management of risk" directives. Cohesive investment policy fosters good understanding between all participants in the process. Lines of demarcation are carefully drawn, permitting appropriate accountability and adjustments in the review, reevaluation and modification process. Diverse areas–the requirements of ERISA, fiduciary responsibility, acceptable performance, diversification and discretion delegated to managers and attitudes toward ETIs–need to be addressed. Without the development of policy and its subsequent reduction to a written statement, the plan may flounder in a dynamic economic environment, like a ship without a rudder.

Perhaps the reason so many plans suffer from a lack of finalizing a written statement is that the process is a very arduous task. Nonetheless, all fiduciaries and co-fiduciaries must be willing to make the effort. In addition to the members of the policy committee or board, others who would be logically involved in the process leading to the finalizing of an investment policy statement are legal counsel, the actuary, administrator, investment manager and independent consultants, as deemed appropriate.

Such an empirical process is an ongoing effort. The policy and evolving strategies of the plan must respond to the dynamic political, social and economic environment within which they are found. The policy statement for the plan in the aggregate then becomes the steppingstone for the individual policy statements for the separate investment managers.

Reducing a plan's investment policy to a written statement provides legal protection, improves communication and provides instructions to investment managers.

For legal protection. If the fund is ever subjected to a compliance audit by the Department of Labor, chances are the investigating officer will begin his examination of the investment program by simply asking, "May I see a copy of your investment policy statement?" Needless to say, it will be comforting to be able to go to a file and pull out a copy of such a statement for review. Since ERISA requires that "care, skill, prudence, and diligence" be applied in the investment decision-making process, it is presumptuous to think that this requirement could be met without succinctly written directives. A written statement also draws together the funding policy and the investment management program in such a way as to give credibility to the commonsense approach used by the trustees in fulfilling their stewardship responsibility.

For improving communication. One of the natural byproducts of the drafting process is that it opens the door to improved communication between the trustees and their professional advisors. The drafting process itself requires a high degree of interaction and communication among the principals involved. As a result, there is likely to be a better flow of information among all parties and a more reliable base of information upon which to develop, evaluate and modify a sound investment policy.

Wrestling with the probability of achieving investment expectations, as expressed in the performance objectives, adds an element of reasonableness in the minds of the trustees and provokes increased understanding between them and the investment managers. A mutual understanding of the appropriate risk posture of the fund and of the related portfolio guidelines adopted goes a long way toward arriving at mutually acceptable marching orders. The inevitable debate among those writing the policy statement about certain policies that will arise will be constructive toward refining the consensus conclusions.

For instructions to investment managers. The preamble of the written statement provides the retained investment manager(s) with important background information related to the plan, identifies the unique requirements of the plan and otherwise informs them of the basic goals and objectives of the trustees. Liquidity and cash flow requirements are stipulated. The manager can more easily respond to the performance objectives when he or she has, in fact, agreed with the reasonableness and probability of achieving those objectives.

It is important to point out that a statement of investment policy differs importantly from a statement of investment objectives alone. An investment *policy* prescribes acceptable courses of action; a policy can be acted upon, implemented. An investment *objective* (such as a performance standard) is a desired result. A manager cannot implement an objective; he can only pursue a course of action, consistent with investment policy, that he believes offers a reasonable likelihood of realizing the objective. Therefore, in drafting instructions for an investment manager, primary emphasis should be on stating the investment, or risk, policy clearly.

Smaller funds that use a "balanced" manager may find it sufficient communication to provide the manager with a copy of the fund's overall investment policy statement. Funds that have a multi-manager structure, particularly those that use specialist managers, may find it helpful to provide each manager with a policy statement that is specifically directed to his or her account. Without such a tailored statement the manager may fail to recognize how the assets he or she manages are merely a part of an aggregate portfolio; the attainment of its objectives is dependent upon a consistent application of his or her style of management in the portfolio he or she manages.

The statement prepared for the fund in the aggregate generally includes at least the following elements:

1. Background information on the fund

2. Identification of fiduciaries
3. Organizational structure
4. Cash flow requirements
5. Lines of authority and delegation
6. Diversification of the portfolio
7. Active/passive strategies
8. Definition of assets
9. Performance objectives
10. Guidelines
11. Brokerage
12. Voting of proxies
13. Trusteeship/custodianship.

The statement related to each investment manager would include background information; future fund and cash flow projection; investment objectives; portfolio guidelines; reporting requirements; voting of proxies; and review, evaluation and modification methods.

To assist you, your fellow trustees and your advisors, the following sample policy statements are included for reference purposes:

- Appendix A–Sample Investment Policy Statement–Defined Benefit Plan
- Appendix B–Sample Investment Policy Statement–Defined Contribution Plan
- Appendix C–Sample Investment Policy Statement–Health & Welfare Plan.

These samples were provided by Terrence S. Moloznik, National Electrical Benefit Fund (NEBF), and are intended to provide you with a "general overview" of the structure and contents of policy statements. Any statement adopted by your plan would *specifically* address *your* objectives, policy and guidelines preferences.

In Appendix D, a checklist of potential elements to include in policy statements is provided. Obviously, all these items are not included; only those that address the needs of your plan.

Every plan's statement is unique to its own requirements. It need not be lengthy, but it does need to exist; to be effective, it must be current. It is a tough job to finalize a written statement with all the players involved in the process and the diversity of interest and opinions they bring to the table. Nonetheless, the effort may very well produce higher rates of return for your fund, without even incurring greater portfolio risk!

Chapter 27

Monitoring, Reevaluation and Modification

> Succinctly put, the acid test of prudency in investment decisions is the adequacy of the methodology used, not the investment results achieved.

No expression of investment policy should be written in stone. Because of the dynamic natures of the plan's population and the social-economic-political environment, there should be periodic reevaluations of all facets of the program. Frequent policy reexamination can be done both formally and informally and may well lead to modification of the existing written investment policy statement. Formal review should be conducted, if not annually, at least biannually. Extraordinary events may require that the policy statement be revisited between formal review dates.

> It's important to remove yourself from the details and look at the Big Picture. We must constantly assess our investment policy and determine how it interrelates with the goals and objectives of paying pensions to plan participants.
>
> *David Blitzstein*

Some of the questions that the trustees should address as part of their monitoring process are:

1. Does the actuarial database now reflect different characteristics?
2. Has there been a change in the cash flow requirements?
3. Do the expected returns of various classes of investments suggest a change in asset allocation?
4. Have the investment managers, in fact, been executing their program in concert with the original guidelines?

As these and a myriad of other questions are addressed, the trustees may perceive a need for modifications to the statement and/or program.

Trustees often focus their oversight activities entirely on the performance of their investment managers, when, in fact, they should begin with *their* stewardship activities: What has been their contribution to asset enhancement from the trustees' asset allocation decisions? Have they included the "right" styles of management? Are the guidelines too restrictive? Have the trustees negligently retained a manager who should be terminated? Did the trustees stay committed to their original policy, or did they "panic" when the market hit a "bear" cycle? Only after a disciplined self-examination should the trustees reevaluate the investment manager.

> If you don't profit from your investment mistakes, someone else will.
>
> *Yale Hirsch*

In the discussion with their investment manager regarding how the manager's performance is to be quantitatively measured and over what period of time, the trustees should consider a reporting system that has the following characteristics:

- Recognizes change in *market* value, as well as income received
- Takes into account any appreciation or depreciation that occurs during the period examined, whether *realized* through the sale of securities or left *unrealized by* holding securities
- Recognizes and adjusts for cash flow or asset transfers that are essentially beyond the control of the investment manager
- Covers a sufficient time period to permit meaningful results.

If trustees are to monitor the activity of their investment manager properly, they must know what has happened to the fund's money, both on an immediate and on a cumulative basis. This requires a clearly defined system of financial reporting. The frequency and form of the investment manager's reports to the trustees will vary somewhat from fund to fund, but the reporting requirements should be spelled out in the fund's investment policy.

The first step is to discuss with the investment manager the kinds of information that the trustees feel they need as a basis for tracking their manager's performance. Although the cost of generating the information is a factor that trustees must consider, they should initially ask themselves: What figures or percentages will give the best insight as to what kind of job the manager is doing? There's no simple answer to this question, but the following types of information would seem to be basic:

- A *dollar* breakdown by category of asset showing both cost and fair value
- A *percentage* breakdown of assets by category, calculated on the basis of both book value and fair value
- A *summary of transactions* since the previous report, showing the beginning balance at cost and fair value, the costs of new purchases, trading costs and the ending balance at both cost and fair value
- Annual income rate (in dollars) and yield (in percentages) for each sector of the portfolio and overall.

The system of financial reporting finally agreed upon should, at the very least, produce data on a timely basis that will help trustees answer a few basic questions:

- Are the fund's assets sufficiently diversified to avoid large losses?
- How much turnover of assets is there, and what has the turnover produced in the way of return?
- What rate of return is the fund experiencing on its investments?
- Are any assets lying idle when they should be invested?
- Are the liquidity requirements being met?

Trustees may wish to indicate in their investment policy that they expect their investment manager to furnish reports on a quarterly and/or annual basis that provide the data needed to answer these questions. It is a fundamental aspect of fiduciary responsibility to require the manager to meet with the trustees at least once a year for a comprehensive review of performance, and at such other times as the trustees feel necessary.

The point is that somewhere in the investment policy statement trustees should try to be as specific as possible regarding the type of information they want from their manager, in what form and how often. By being specific, trustees clearly demonstrate their intent to monitor the performance of their manager carefully and, in so doing, meet their fiduciary duties under ERISA.

Investment Management Controls

The trustees must also recognize that periodic review of the investment manager's activities and performance represents an essential element of the asset management process. It is one thing to formulate an investment policy and communicate it to the investment manager; it is quite another matter to check on its implementation. But formulation of the policy and implementation of the policy should be regarded as part of the same process because the former is really a futile exercise without the latter. Thus, trustees should establish specific procedures or controls designed to ensure periodic review of their manager's actions and performance. These procedures or controls should be set forth in the investment policy statement so that both the trustees and their investment manager are fully aware of their obligations. Such controls may include, but are not necessarily limited to, the following:

- Reviewing written reports prepared by the investment manager in accordance with the specifications set by the trustees regarding form and frequency
- Requiring regularly scheduled meetings with the investment manager to review the manager's adherence to the guidelines and objectives set forth in the investment policy statement as well as his or her performance
- Retaining an independent performance evaluation firm to measure:
  (a) The extent to which the investment performance met the fund's investment objectives, as set forth in the investment policy, and
  (b) How the fund's performance compared with that of other funds having similar characteristics and similar investment objectives
- Actively soliciting the counsel of the fund's various professional advisors concerning potential problem areas in the implementation of the investment policy. (For example, the fund attorney may be asked to comment on the extent of diversification in the portfolio, the actuary on whether the investment mix seems to be in line with the fund's cash needs, or the auditor on whether the investments are creating any contingent liabilities.)

The above listing is suggestive only. It is not complete, nor is every control necessary for every fund. The important point is that trustees must consider what controls they are going to impose on their manager in order to ensure his accountability.

As mentioned earlier, if the trustees elect to delegate their investment responsibility to an outside manager, and if they do so in part to reduce their own liability, then they must be in a position to demonstrate that they properly supervised the manager's activities. By setting forth specific review procedures in their investment policy statement, the trustees have taken a giant step toward fulfilling their fiduciary responsibilities.

Policy Review and Revision

Like the trust agreement or the plan document, periodic review and even occasional revision of the investment policy statement may be necessary in order to keep the policy responsive to the fund's needs. Indeed, there are many factors beyond the control of the trustees that might require policy changes. For example, a policy formulated during a period of full employment might have to be radically altered to cope with the problems generated by chronic unemployment. Or, passage of a major piece of federal legislation (like ERISA) may require some serious rethinking about the fund's investment management program. Or, continuous double-digit inflation might alter a fund's investment strategy. This list of unpredictable events could be easily expanded, but these few examples should be sufficient to illustrate how important it is for trustees to review their investment policy periodically.

> It takes plenty of talent, training, experience, decisiveness, perseverance and flexibility—admirable but scarce attributes all—to produce consistently superior investment results. But these attributes usually are required for success in any venture—certainly any competitive endeavor.
>
> *Harold B. Ehrlich*

Comparing and evaluating a pension fund's investment performance goes beyond simply assessing the rate of return as either "good or bad." The trustees should attempt to identify those factors that contributed to the returns generated, i.e., industry and sector factors, security selection and market timing decisions. Performance measurement activities should be a "schoolmaster" to the trustees, enabling them to make more insightful policy, strategy and manager selection decisions over time.

To effectively reevaluate their investment policy, and its implementation, the trustees need to go beyond the "number-crunching" activities. The annual or biannual review should be a comprehensive audit and assessment of their entire *procedural approach* to solving their "investment riddle." Without such a discipline, the plan's portfolio may drift away from being efficiently postured to meet the plan's long-term investment objectives.

Chapter 28

Custody

Contributed by Gerard M. Arnone
Comerica Bank

Say the word *custody* to most people and their eyes glaze over with visions of a huge vault door closing slowly on a room lined with metal shelves piled with stock certificates and a few loose dollar bills. An elderly security guard is sitting beside the door and might be coughing from the dust raised. It is not a very exciting picture.

But that's the way it was. Wall Street (the securities industry) was nothing but paper, paper and more paper that moved from brokerage house to brokerage house to banks by messengers carrying both securities and checks. The lines of these messengers at the various vault "cage" areas were as long as lottery lines when it hasn't been hit for weeks. And all of those certificates and checks were being watched over by that elderly security guard who probably had no idea that the unbelievable conglomeration of paper represented billions and billions of dollars in value.

It was all that paper and the signing into law of the Employee Retirement Income Security Act (ERISA) on September 2, 1974 that brings us to where we are today. Exhibit 28-1 shows the pre- and post-ERISA progression.

The fact is that the custody business has become an extremely dynamic piece of the exploding worldwide securities industry. An argument can be made that of all the talented team members that the

Exhibit 28-1

PRE-ERISA	POST-ERISA
— Single investment managers (usually bank trust departments or insurance companies) — Simple asset classes — Assets held by trust departments or insurance companies as part of the investment management process	— Multiple investment managers — Multiple plans — More volatile financial markets — Greater asset diversification — Governmental disclosure requirements — Assets still held by bank trust departments but under more demanding accounting and reporting structures

trustees have put together for the benefit of better plan performance (both investment and administrative/operational), the custodian is one of the most important, because it is the custodian that must successfully implement and execute the strategies of the others.

Exhibit 28-2 illustrates how far we've come from the static image of warehousing stock and bond certificates. The custodian is the trustees' representative at the hub of a large number of complex activities needed to implement the investment strategy devised by trustees' consultants and investment managers. Because of the diversity of investment programs, custodians do not just physically safekeep securities, but rather they keep track of their clients' securities at various central depositories and subcustodians. (A central depository is a custodian's custodian. Financial institutions like banks, broker-dealers, investment companies, etc., have formed and/or joined depositories to transfer securities among themselves with just a bookkeeping entry. This is often referred to as security immobilization.)

Other daily interfaces are with clients, investment managers and transfer agents, pricing vendors' input daily to assist custodians in valuing their clients' assets, which is no small task. Large custodians have tens of thousands of domestic issues to price, and when managers move to broad global investment for diversification purposes, the number of securities that need to be priced is increased many times. Combining all the above with greatly enhanced reporting capabilities, including online, real-time data center hookups, it's easy to see why the custodian is no longer just a warehouse for assets, but rather a very modern information processor.

Exhibit 28-2

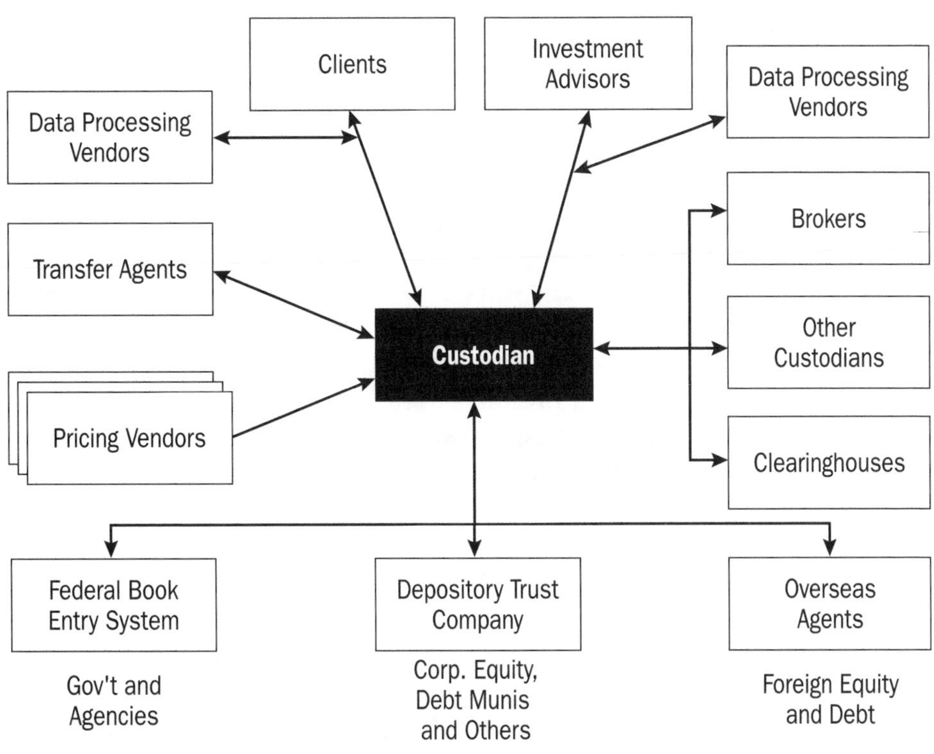

What Are the Duties of Your Custodian?

There are seven primary duties and a number of ancillary functions that your custodian can perform. The primary functions are discussed below:

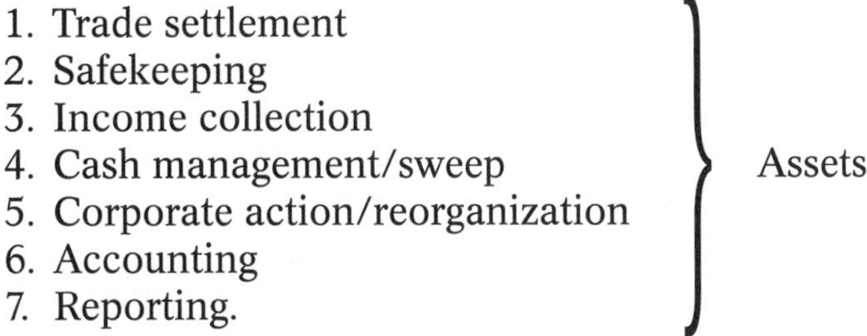

1. Trade settlement
2. Safekeeping
3. Income collection
4. Cash management/sweep
5. Corporate action/reorganization
6. Accounting
7. Reporting.

} Assets

Trade Settlement

Everything begins with a security transaction made on behalf of the trustees. Trustees hire investment professionals to manage the assets and custodian banks to implement the whole process. As such, the custodian is responsible for acting on the trade instructions from the investment managers and for providing them with important information like daily cash balances and corporate actions like stock splits and dividends. Custodian banks have become very good at working with investment management firms to service their mutual client.

Safekeeping

Remember the elderly guard? He's been moved to another job. Through technology and the establishment of various central depositories, custodians now can settle trades, move portfolios or move entire funds with the relative ease of pressing a button. This is one of those cases where the good old days aren't so good. Depositories have been a wonderful and very necessary addition to the custody business–In no way could the current daily trading volume of 400+ million shares be handled without central depositories. However, there are still some securities that are retained in the vault since they are not depository-eligible, e.g., individual mortgage contracts held by a fund.

Exhibit 28-2 on page 213 reflects the use of the two major depositories:

- ◆ The Federal Book Entry System (FBE)–used for all Treasury securities including Ginnie Mae (Government National Mortgage Association) and Fannie May (Federal National Mortgage Association) securities
- ◆ The Depository Trust Company (DTC)–the world's largest, used for domestic stocks and corporate bonds.

Income Collection

In this function, income due the fund is collected from the security's paying agent. Differences from late trades, taxes and security reconciliation items are resolved by sending "claims" to the paying agent. Income can be credited on either "payable" date or upon actual receipt. Obviously, the preferred method is payment on payable date in "Fed Funds," which is equivalent to cash that is available for investment. (See the Cash Management section below.)

Cash Management/Sweep

Cash management, which involves both balance management and income collection, is a very important subject. While it may appear to be a fairly simple function that is easily performed, it can be quite complex. Because of the total assets involved and the daily cash flows in the modern-day employee benefit fund, there are significant additional earnings to be gained with an intensive cash management program.

The *cash balance* is simply the amount of uninvested cash in the portfolio at the end of the business day. However, good cash management must also consider the income collection process. Income will be credited on an actual receipt basis (which usually is many days after the payable date), on the payable date or some combination of the two. The methods that custodians use reflect their operational capabilities and their approach to crediting income.

A first-rate custodian must be able to provide an effective cash balance management service for an employee benefit plan. The cash sweep vehicle used most frequently is a commingled or pooled portfolio of cash equivalent investments called a *short-term investment fund (STIF)*. Virtually every custodian bank has such a commingled vehicle. These STIF vehicles range from minimal to high risk. Depending upon the guidelines the trustees have in place, investment managers can choose the sweep vehicle of choice. Most Taft-Hartley funds will trend toward utilizing a STIF program with minimal risk. Those custodians that do not have STIF funds make use of master notes and other instruments of demand and commercial paper. Other banks use pools of government or agency securities, and sometimes government bills or notes directly. While the capital safety of government-backed securities is unquestionable, the rate of return is not as good as a well-managed STIF. The advantages of the short-term investment fund are those of a typical commingled fund, i.e., diversification, cash flow advantages, negotiated brokerage advantages, etc.

Corporate Action/Reorganization

A first-tier custodial bank will have a strong "re-org" unit that enables custodians to notify investment managers of recently announced corporate actions. It is paramount that the custodian communicates accurate information on a timely basis to ensure that investment managers have the information they need when a change with a security is pending.

As an example, to monitor whether a bond is being "called" prior to maturity, a re-org unit will scour the following as a daily source for pending or announced corporate action:

Domestic

- DTC and Financial Information Incorporation (PC-based system)
- Standard & Poor's
- NYSE letters
- *Wall Street Journal*
- Company correspondence
- Telestat (for stock splits and dividends)

Foreign

- Extel
- IDSI
- The WM Company (over 80 sources)
- Valorinform
- Subcustodians
- Reuters
- Telekurs
- Bloomberg.

Accounting

While accounting and reporting are considered the same by many, in actuality they are quite different. This section describes the accounting process within the bank, otherwise known as "posting to records."

There are three basic accounting systems (procedures) that custodians utilize to maintain their own records:

1. Delivery date (cash) accounting
2. Settlement date (contractual) accounting
3. Trade date (accrual) accounting.

The history of the trust industry includes the evolution from delivery to settlement and now to trade date accounting. Most people can easily understand accounting on a *cash* basis *(delivery date accounting),* and in fact it is still used today. "Give me my security and I'll give you your money" is the guiding principle. The custodian's records reflect only the actual movement of cash and securities so the so-called accounting is really just a snapshot of the trust's physical holdings on a given day. Looking at it from another angle, it's a picture of the security movement industry in general. It's not very accurate as an accounting (report), but it does fill the custodian's need to keep the trust "whole" at any given point in time, because you either have securities or cash.

But obviously, delivery date accounting is extremely deficient in the true accounting sense, and to a certain extent hampers the investment programs of money managers. The accountings aren't accurate since they do not reflect the true position of a trust at a given point in time. Investment managers may have made commitments to either buy or sell securities, but that is not yet identified on the custodian's books. In addition, the managers themselves keep a supplementary set of records (typically as of trade date) so that they are aware of the commitments they have made. Also, the investment managers are affected by the "fail" situation in the security movement industry. Under a delivery date system, the manager might sell a security today for settlement in three business days while also wishing to make a purchase with the proceeds from the sale. However, since there is always a danger that the buy transaction will settle before the sell transaction (creating an overdraft), the manager must wait until the sale proceeds are received before making the purchase; if the security to be purchased has increased in price in the interim, the trust has not realized that gain in value (lost opportunity).

A third major deficiency of delivery date accounting is that it makes the income collection process much more difficult to track. Since the transfer agent frequently doesn't know who owns a given security on the date when dividends are credited, the buying and selling custodians must clear this up in a costly manual process called claiming.

Settlement date, or *contractual accounting,* is a major improvement over delivery date accounting. A settlement date process means the custodian will record the purchase or sale of a security on the trust records on the contractual settlement date (usually the third business day after trade) regardless of the physical location of that security. As long as the custodian knows about the trade and considers it a good trade, the trust records will be credited. This is an enormous improvement because of the discipline that it applies to both the accounting and investment procedure. On the accounting side, the custodian is showing a much more disciplined and logical position of a trust's assets on a given day. As far as the investment process is concerned, settlement date accounting allows the investment manager to make a sale and a purchase on the same day, knowing in full confidence that in three business days the sale will produce proceeds that in turn will be used to settle the purchase, eliminating the possibility of overdraft and therefore eliminating the need to keep excessive cash balances available. Also, the discipline of settlement date accounting simplifies somewhat the procedure for tracking of income; and there is less possibility that a dividend will not be collected.

Trade date, or *full accrual accounting*, is the next logical step. Trade date accounting, which reflects ownership of a security on the date actually traded, has been used by mutual funds for many years; and investment managers keep their own records as of trade date. It was inevitable that trade date would become the goal in the securities industry, and it has become the most commonly accepted accounting methodology today.

Reporting

After the custodian has accounted for all the purchases and sales, reorganization issues, income collection and cash management earnings, it must be reported to the trustees and their professionals.

While actual and delivery date reporting is still utilized, most major custodian banks have adopted at least some form of trade date reporting package. Some have done it on an annual basis, some on a quarterly basis and others are rendering monthly security reports on a trade date basis. Where an online real-time link with the custodian's data center is available, trustees can create daily trade date positions.

Trustees should not fail to appreciate the complexity and difficulty of producing a trade date report. It requires the custodian to maintain duplicate and sometimes triplicate records. The "factory" of the custodian, the security clearance area, must be maintained on a cash basis. Obviously, no custodian is going to pay cash to a broker until the broker shows up with the security. On the other hand, the assumed discipline of a security clearance area is a contractual settlement date basis, because that is the way the securities industry strives to operate. As a custodian is made aware of a trade, various "pending" records have to be maintained, anticipating the settlement on a given day. Finally, the three sets of records are melded to create the actual trade date report for the plan trustees and investment managers.

There are two primary ways in which this information can be distributed: hard copy and online. A third method is the use of CD-ROM technology.

Reports are typically issued monthly, quarterly and annually. In special situations, interim reports are also available. Following is a list of what a custodian can supply:

Daily:

Daily Statement

Opening and closing balances
Complete purchase and sale information

Redemptions and maturities
Interest and dividends
Cash receipts and disbursements
Corporate actions (stock splits, tender offers, etc.)
Other transactions

Monthly, Quarterly and Annual:

Transaction Statement

Opening balances
Cash inflows and outflows by transaction types in summary and detail
All interest and dividend transactions
Noncash transactions
Closing balances
Detailed elements of the trades

Statement of Changes in Net Assets

Inflows in summary
Outflows in summary
Administrative expense in summary
Total net inflow/outflow
Net gain/loss on sales
Change in unrealized appreciation/depreciation
Net assets at beginning and end of period

Analysis of Earnings

Income collected and accrued for current and previous periods
Earnings by category (e.g., interest, dividends)

Statement of Assets and Liabilities (Schedule A)

Overview of total book and market values for all categories of assets and liabilities
Net assets
Percentages each category represents of net asset amount

Diversification of Assets (Schedule B)

Total book and market values by industry classification within security type
Percentage each industry classification represents of total book and total market and value of its security type
Accrued income

Statement of Assets (Schedule C)

Securities within industry classification
Total book and market values for each security based on fully committed positions
Unit book and current price

Percentage each security represents of total book, total market and market value of its security type
Accrued income

Statement of Liabilities

Call options written
Percentage each option represents of total options outstanding
Aggregates liabilities into major "payable" categories

Security Transaction Report

Acquisition/disposition by security
Book value, unit costs, unit proceeds, aggregate proceeds
Gain/loss on sales
Investment activity
Capital changes
Payments/maturities
Free receipts and deliveries

Brokerage Commission Report

List of brokers
Total commission by broker
Percentage of total commission by broker
Total commissionable trades by broker
Percentage total commissionable trades by broker
Annual broker commission information

5500 Reporting Package (Annual Only)

Ancillary Services

Five other custodial services are available as options to the primary custodian package:

1. Securities lending
2. Online services
3. Benefit payments
4. Performance measurement
5. Investment management.

Securities Lending

Although securities lending is not considered a true primary deliverable by a custodian bank, it has become the number-one option utilized.

Securities lending is a way for institutional investors to gain incremental income from their portfolios by lending securities to counter-parties. The counter-parties need to borrow securities for the following reasons:

1. Trade settlement. The counter-party needs to deliver a security not in his inventory. This may be a result of short selling or a fail to receive a portion of a security due on a block trade.
2. Trading strategies. The counter-party needs to deliver shares as a result of arbitrage, hedge and short-selling strategies.
3. Financing needs. Counter-party borrows securities to be used as collateral for repurchase agreement (repo) transactions. This would be less costly than traditional financing.

In the majority of cases, counter-parties borrow securities through a broker. The broker contacts a custodian bank that acts as a lending agent for either institutions with large portfolios or an institutional investor that lends directly. From the lender's point of view, the broker is the borrower, and the actual counter-party remains unknown. Brokers may also borrow for their own account. Exhibit 28-3 shows the process.

Exhibit 28-3

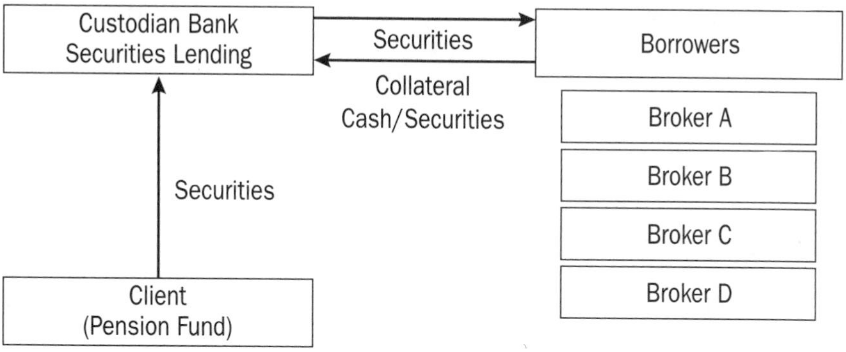

Securities may be lent either for a specific period of time (a *term* loan) or for an undefined period of time (an *open* loan). In any case, the lender may demand the return of the securities at any time. It is important to understand that within a securities-lending transaction the borrower has unrestricted use of the security, including the right to vote proxies. The lender retains all economic rights, i.e., all cash and noncash distributions.

Whenever securities are lent, the borrower is generally required to provide to the lender collateral that has a value of 102% of the borrowed securities (105% for international securities). This collateral is marked to market daily to maintain the required level. Generally, acceptable collateral includes cash, U.S. government securities and irrevocable letters of credit.

When cash is received as collateral it is placed in a high-quality, short-term investment fund (STIF) or money market mutual fund. Under certain circumstances, customized investment funds can be created with the goal of exceeding the standard money market rate. The lender's profit is the interest earned on the collateral reduced by two items, a rebate given back to the borrower (a common industry practice) and a fee earned by the custodian for implementing and monitoring the transaction. The profitability of the loan is directly related to the demand for the security and the rate of return on the investment.

Online Services

The ability to access information directly from a custodian's data center is becoming increasingly important to trustees and their fund office. With today's personal computers and the custodian's technological support, the possibilities are virtually limitless. Fund offices can view daily asset listings, pending trades, income projections and other data and often prepare customized board reports that can reduce consulting expenses.

Benefit Payments

A custodian can prepare and distribute monthly retiree checks and lump-sum payments, including all the tax filings.

Performance Measurement

The custodian's technological capabilities make performance measurement calculations simple. By servicing literally thousands of accounts, the compilation of complete and unique indices is a natural by-product. However, high emphasis should not be placed on this when considering a custodian since most funds use a consultant that provides this information as a part of its assignment.

Investment Management

In addition to cash management services noted earlier most, if not all, custodian banks offer comprehensive investment management services, from total passive products to very specialized investment vehicles.

Looking for a Master Custodian

While we have made the case for a dramatic change in the role of the custodian in the increasingly complex securities industry, it is still banks and limited purpose trust companies that provide the service. Indeed, the banks may have been the only institutions that possessed both the technical/data processing knowledge and the financial resources to participate in the metamorphosis of the custodian. Their technical knowledge was enhanced by the experience of implementing modern retail banking systems; the financial resources were committed to protect and hopefully grow their market share in the securities industry. And, let's face it, "custody," "trust" and "fiduciary responsibility" go hand in hand; the banks are good at it and want to protect their franchise.

There are over a thousand banks in the country that have some form of custodial service. They range from a simple warehousing capability for your stock certificates only to a truly global capability to settle a transaction on your behalf virtually anywhere in the world, and then safekeep, collect income and report almost instantaneously. While multinational corporations are the primary user of this premier service, all professionally managed funds are quickly moving in that direction.

It is incumbent on trustees to very carefully consider the qualifications of custodians before committing plan assets to their care, so a significant part of this chapter is devoted to the selection of a custodian.

Conducting a Search

Use of Consultants

The consultant industry has grown almost as fast as the custody industry. For many years, the role of a consultant was primarily that of a benefits advisor. The major actuarial firms employed a staff of consultants to assist the plan trustee in determining what benefits should be implemented and how best to do it. But with the advent of performance investing in the 1960s, the need arose to help determine how to achieve that performance. Some major firms were formed at that time, and their early work consisted primarily of performance measurement and evaluation.

Consultants became a clearinghouse for the performance data generated by the major investment managers in our industry. As multiple investment managers became commonplace, the problems associated with the administration and operation of multiple portfolios grew significantly. Therefore, it was a very logical step for the consultants to expand their expertise into the area of custodian banks.

The decision to use a consultant is typically made on the basis of the other responsibilities of the trustees, their sophistication in employee benefit services and whether or not the trustees want some type of a "buffer" between them and the selection process.

Consultants can perform a valuable service and can be a powerful tool. Because of their position as an impartial third party, and because of their implied power in directing business, managers and custodians make a considerable effort to influence them. Consultants who are forthright and capable are recognized as such, and many enjoy an open communications channel with the major custodians in our industry. Custodians are comfortable being candid in these situations and therefore the information gathered by these consultants is the best available. The expertise and the sophistication of the consultant should be used to ferret out information from those custodians who are not so open and candid.

Doing It Yourself

Some trustees have chosen to go it alone in selecting a custodian. This is not only a viable alternative but can actually be rewarding if the trustees have time to devote to the project. Doing it properly and thoroughly will not only increase their confidence in the final decision, but can also save a few dollars in a budget that may be tight.

Identifying the industry leaders in the custodian field is not a difficult task, but one that requires time and research. Custodians are more than accommodative in providing information on their services and products. Many custodians will place ads in the trade journals seeking business. Trustees need to be careful not to be unduly influenced by ad campaigns. Ads are good at determining who is aggressively seeking the business, but they are the shallowest documents for determining the capability of properly servicing the business. Trustees need to seek out the custodian who will be the right size provider for their fund.

If time is not of the essence, trustees have the option to just wait until they are contacted by custodians in their normal marketing efforts. The value of these initial presentations can be significant in terms of "education" when the custodian sends out a knowledgeable marketing/sales representative. Unfortunately, sometimes the meaningful education process has to wait until the trustees ask to see some of the administrative personnel back at the bank.

After sitting through some initial presentations and feeling ready to expand the scope of the study, trustees can contact the remaining prospective custodians they would consider. These meetings should be spaced over a number of days since daily pressures can cause trustees to be distracted in some presentations and miss important points. The general experience of these presentations is that new insights will be gained with each meeting. People express thoughts differently, and what may not have been appreciated in the previous meeting will suddenly become clear. More importantly, each new presentation will, of course, stress that particular firm's strong points. To the extent that these strong points are appealing, trustees should not hesitate to go back to custodians who have already made a presentation in order to clarify a certain item. In fact, there is much to be gained in finding an excuse to get back to the earlier applicants even if you feel you have a good understanding of what they have to offer. Calling up someone unexpectedly and putting him on the spot for quick information, especially information that he did not volunteer during the initial interview, is a very good way of testing the experience and responsiveness of the firm. After all, the custodian is seeking a long-term service relationship and responsiveness is the name of that game.

But your emphasis should be at the contact level. One of the advantages of a responsive organization is that particular questions can be answered at the contact level, i.e., with a single phone inquiry. The relationship manager who is the contact point for the plan trustee should be a decision maker, i.e., he or she should be able to commit the custodian for certain actions. If he or she cannot commit the custodian, then the trustees or staff are destined to be given the runaround every time a nonstandard question is asked. This can happen at both small and large banks and is not symptomatic of size. Indecision or nonaction is merely symptomatic of a custodian organization that is inexperienced and incapable of functioning on its own. The department head should be there for guidance only and not be necessary for day-to-day operations.

Questionnaires

The use of a request for proposal (RFP) in the custodian search has become commonplace, and it does have value. If the trustees have a significant number of banks to be considered, the RFP can be extremely useful in the initial weeding-out process. The RFP should be used as an information-gathering device, indicative of the bank's overall capabilities in the securities processing area and its capabilities of expressing itself in a coherent manner.

RFPs generally reflect the style of those who construct them. Whether it's a consulting firm or the trustees, a typical format is as follows:

- General statistics
- Organization
- Operations
  - –Securities processing
  - –Data processing
  - –Securities lending
  - –Global custody
  - –Performance measurement/evaluation
- Administration
- Training
- Reports
- Investments (including STIF)
- Benefit payments
- Fee schedule
- References.

Under the general statistics category, the trustees should be looking for not only total current statistics (trust department, employee benefit department, custody business specifically), but also for trends (first major custodial appointment and what the growth pattern has been). A range of the size of custodial accounts handled is also useful since it's an indication of their ability to be responsive to customers of various sizes. In looking at the general organization of a custodian, look closely at its independence and its link with the overall bank. Does the bank look at custodial services as a separate business? This is important because without the status of being a separate, profit-contributing business, it's doubtful whether sufficient capital will be allocated when that business needs resources.

Looking further into the organization, ask some specific questions on how the administrative account load is established. What will your account do to the existing organization, and if your account is sizable, how will the bank cope with it? The bank that is extremely aggressive in seeking new business very often takes liberties with the quality of service that it delivers to existing customers. Look at that particular bank's plans for handling new business, as well as maintaining and upgrading the quality of staff. Don't accept a general answer here, but pin the bank down to specific courses of action.

Evaluating reporting capabilities can be tricky. Because custodians call the same reports by different names and because custodians typically have, in total, the same amount of information spread out or allocated differently among different reports, it's extremely difficult to compare reporting packages without a personal interview. What you can and do want to get committed to writing is the timing of various reports. No matter what a custodian calls its reports, as long as they are rendered within a reasonable amount of time, trustees will have the information they need.

Significant questions should be devoted to ancillary investments offered by custodians, the most important of which is the short-term investment fund. This is a major area of leverage, and the performance aspect should not be overlooked even though the primary purpose of these funds is short-term liquidity. This area of the RFP is also the appropriate spot for asking questions about a custodian's index fund capabilities, fixed income capabilities, etc.

Pension payments is an area of great concern to the administratively oriented trustee. In this section questions should be asked not only on the volume of payments handled now, but more specifically on the input required by the fund office to set that procedure in motion, turnaround time for special requests, information, etc.

The section on fee schedules should include much more than the actual fee schedule. Trustees should supply adequate statistics and ask for a specific fee quote for their particular situation. Insist that the worksheets be included. This is important when dealing with custodians that have unbundled fee schedules and who therefore must make estimates in terms of activity, etc.

References are, of course, a very important part of the process. Ask for a spectrum of references going from large to small customers, from old to new customers and specifically for the size account you represent.

Organization of the data center is important, especially if you are considering a custodian that does not control its own data center (i.e., must share it with the commercial side of the bank). In fact, a shared data center is true more often than not because of the huge expense of running a modern installation. A custodian that maintains its own facilities has a very decided advantage over the competition. The operating configuration of the data center is less important but no less interesting. It's *not* a safe assumption that most major custodians are equipped to handle the volume of business that they are seeking. Trustees need to be assured that a custodian has the right systems in place and that these systems can handle the requirements of their fund. Staffing statistics in the data center are as important as they are in the administrative area, especially in terms of programming capabilities.

Key elements of the securities settlement process are important. A potential weak link in any custodian's operation is the manner in which information is gathered from the outside investment managers and brought into the custodian's shop for processing. The leading banks in this field are those that have put considerable time and effort into automating the process and the interaction with investment managers with central depositories and sometimes trustees.

There's a temptation to try to make the RFP as easy as possible for the custodian to answer and for the trustees to compare responses. Obviously, this would be accomplished by asking closed-ended questions (*yes* or *no*). This can be one of the biggest mistakes that a trustee can make when using an RFP. While there is a place for *yes* or *no* questions, the trustees should go out of the way to ask open-ended questions, questions that require thoughtful, complete answers. When asking such questions, a trustee has a unique opportunity to separate the salesmen from the technicians. If an RFP has asked the proper open-ended questions, a trustee has a better chance of getting back a response that reflects the thoughts and abilities of the administrative people who will be handling the account.

Examples of how questions should be asked are listed below:

WRONG

1. When are interest and dividends credited?
2. Do you give credit for fail float?
3. Do you have a quality control system?
4. Do you offer automated cash management?

RIGHT

1. Explain your system for crediting interest and dividends.
2. What is your system for fail float?
3. Describe your quality control system.
4. Describe your system for automated cash management, including all advantages and disadvantages.

See the sample questions for request for proposal on pages 232-233.

Interviews

The initial interview for a custodian should be in the trustees' office. First of all, the initial interview should cover a good number of custodians and it's simply more efficient to have the custodians do the traveling. Secondly, the initial interviews should be spread over a period of time so as not to interrupt daily work flow and, equally as important, to keep your mind fresh and open for each presentation. Third, final interviews are best held in the custodian's offices, as explained below.

After initial interviews and evaluating responses to the RFP, finalists can be narrowed down to between three and five. On-site visits are made for primarily two reasons:

1. You want to bring experts with you, possibly including a data center expert, to inspect physical facilities. Meet not only your main administrative contact, but also his or her backups. The environment in which these people work will give you an idea of what status they really have within the entire bank, questionnaire responses aside.
2. Visit the bank to meet some senior management of the custodian department. Typically, these people do not, and should not, have the time to travel around the country making final presentations. Their job is management, and a well-run trust department needs specialists in this area, not general managers. Trustees should meet with some of these senior people in order to get a better sense of their knowledge and commitment to the custody product.

Trustees should "load" the meeting. This should be done in terms of both the number and quality of personnel that come to the meeting. Obviously, the higher the ranking of a plan trustee that comes to the bank, the higher the ranking officer the bank will supply from the custodian department management. This makes for a better meeting to begin with and also provides another test for the bank personnel with whom you will be working on a day-to-day basis; i.e., you want to see how they operate in a highly charged atmosphere of senior people.

A tour of the facilities is mandatory and should include both the securities settlement operating area and the data center. Lastly, be sure to leave plenty of time for these interviews. Frequently, operating and administrative areas are geographically separated.

Post-Interview

Each interview is a learning process. Even if you had two interviews with a prospective custodian and have evaluated an RFP response closely, it is almost inevitable that additional questions will come up. This is partially true because each custodian will, of course, emphasize its strong points and these particular items may not have been covered at all with the other finalists. Therefore, don't hesitate to go back with any questions. This can be done over the phone and rarely is an additional meeting necessary. The custodians involved will not mind at all. In fact, the most capable ones will very much appreciate the diligence with which you are exploring the situation.

Fees

Fees are generally quoted in one of three ways or some combination thereof:

1. Transactional
2. Flat fee
3. Percentage of market value.

Transactional. The fee is calculated by applying a unit cost against different variables, i.e., number of portfolios, number of holdings, etc.

Flat Fee. This is a flat fee for all the services a custodian has agreed to provide, based on estimates provided by the trustees.

Percentage of Market Value. In market value fees, a basis point charge is applied against the market value of an individual portfolio or the total market value of the fund. (A basis point is one-hundredth of 1%.)

All three of these methods are used throughout the industry. Which one trustees might use is a matter of preference, since most custodians will quote fees on different bases when asked. No matter which method is used, a top-tier custodian will provide the same quality service that the trustees expect.

Current Trends

The metamorphosis of the custodial industry is very much a good news-bad news situation. In fact, each trend has a good news-bad news element.

Consolidation

Since custodians are banks, they cannot escape the pain of the current wave of consolidations in the banking industry. Even where the bank is remaining independent, some custodial/trust departments are selling their book of business rather than commit the many millions of dollars necessary to compete in the large trustee market. The bad news is that trustees will have a shrinking number of options from which to choose. The good news is that the remaining vendors are stronger and more likely to survive future threats to their businesses.

Extreme Price Competition

Some large custodians have adopted an aggressive market share philosophy. Since they believe that a very high market share is one of the keys to success, they have submitted low bids for some very large pieces of business, setting off a price war for "mega" accounts and causing other pricing to remain static if not decline slightly. The bad news is that some vendors of quality services are leaving the marketplace rather than compete on price. The good news is that trustees should have no problem in finding good services at fair prices.

Global Custody

As the world's economies become more interdependent, so does professional investing. Very few investment programs are domestic only. So when plan trustees decide that global investing has become appropriate for their plan, literally a whole new world is opened with regard to the custodianship of those assets, and having a custodian with global capabilities is becoming necessary and commonplace. The basic options are to allow each global manager to work with a custodian of his choosing (the common practice in the United Kingdom), appoint custodians in each country, appoint a single international custodian (for assets outside the United States) or appoint a single global custodian (the widely preferred choice). But asking your domestic custodian to accept global responsibilities is not without risk. The diligence that trustees exercise in evaluating domestic capabilities must be doubled and tripled when considering global investing.

The custodian must make arrangements for local (on site in the foreign country) trade clearance and settlement, currency exchange, local safekeeping, income collection, tax-reclaiming services, corporate actions, communications flows between the local market and themselves, and multicurrency accounting/reporting.

Since even the largest global banks/custodians do not have securities processing facilities in every country where investments are made, a custodian's network capabilities are paramount. Even where a global custodian is using its own branch facilities, networking is important because that branch, while having the parent's name on the door, is really a foreign entity.

Therefore, the most important elements to consider when selecting a global custodian are commitment to the business, experience of staff, data center/communications capabilities and the multicurrency accounting system utilized. Without these tools, a custodian's ability to provide a superior service to its clients in a reasonable time frame is severely hampered.

The good news is that the custodian community is meeting the challenge. The bad news is that the global custodian's fixed cost base is growing in order to satisfy demands for capabilities in all the world's markets. This will eventually set some prices too high for investors not utilizing the "emerging" markets.

Wholesale Outsourcing

Because no custodian does it all itself anymore (see Exhibit 28-2 on page 213), it has become competitively acceptable to outsource part or all of the securities operation. There are high-quality systems and/or domestic operations vendors available, and many of the larger global custodians lease or outsource part or all of their global network to competitors. The net result is good news for both the small investor and small custodian–Even a regional custodian can supply global services to local investors, thereby protecting its market.

Suggested Questions for Request for Proposal (RFP)

1. What is the procedure to monitor, advise and follow up on DKs ("Don't know the trade"–Street language denoting lack of knowledge of a particular transaction) and other fails? What is your policy for reimbursing clients for lost interest due to fails?
2. Is there anything special or distinctive about your safekeeping abilities that the board of trustees should know? If yes, please describe.
3. Do you credit all regularly scheduled dividend and interest payments on payable date, regardless of whether these monies have been received? If no, please explain your process. If yes, include discussion of errors and omissions and procedures used.

4. Describe the infrastructure you have built for providing investment accounting services. Be sure to include a description of your computer hardware configuration, a separate description of your software applications and a discussion of the staff dedicated to the accounting function.
5. Please provide a sample copy of all standard and optional accounting reports and custody statements for global accounts. Please indicate on the cover sheet of each report which are for standard services covered by the basic fee, and which reports are optional and available only for additional fees. The actual fees for the optional reports should be provided in the fee proposal.
6. Describe your procedures for sweeping uninvested cash balances from investment accounting into your short-term investment funds (STIFs). How many types of collateral STIFs (commingled, separate or customized) do you offer in the program? Provide investment guidelines for each. Provide a description of each as enumerated below.
   - Investment policy
   - Objectives and guidelines
   - Quarterly investment performance gross of fees
   - Indicate the fee (bpt) for each type of STIF or collateral reinvestment fund. Please specify how fees are handled. Are they deducted from the unit value or charged back to the fund?
7. Describe your securities-lending program. Do you offer "indemnification"? Describe your policies for accepting collateral and describe your required collateral margin.
8. Describe your proxy administration policies. What alternatives do you offer?
9. Describe your system of controls to assure the accuracy of the processing and reporting of the master custody division.
10. Describe your firm's commitment to service quality and customer service. Does your organization have a total quality management program? If yes, please describe. Do you survey your clients? If yes, provide the results for the last three years.

Chapter 29

Brokerage Services

Contributed by Mark Caropreso

So Where Have All the "Stockbrokers" Gone?

The stereotypical stockbroker, shouting buy and sell orders into phones in either hand, is much further from the reality on Wall Street than the 1980s movie bearing the same name as the famed financial avenue. While Messrs. Douglas and Sheen entertained us with the story of fast-paced lives filled with greed, intrigue and ill-gotten gains, we remember how it ends. In reality, successful brokers work hard on behalf of their clients to provide the best possible services in a very competitive environment that produces more efficiencies as well as product and service offerings to attract clients and earn business. So while the dual phone-wielding persona may be inaccurate, today's financial services representatives labor intensely in a fast-paced industry to serve their clients better, faster and competitively. If they don't, there is always someone else waiting to do so.

Today's stockbroker or "financial consultant" has been retooled. Further educated and specialized, they represent their respective firms' multitude of investment-related services to trustees. It is not just all about the trade or transaction. It is about the relationship and the value they can bring to the table.

The Trade

Perhaps the best place to start is at the end. At the end of every investment decision is the transaction. After the investment policy statement is drafted, after the asset allocation parameters are established, and after the investment managers are hired, eventually someone buys something. Stock or bond, mortgage-backed security or futures contract, a broker is involved in helping match buyers with sellers. The service most easily recognized by clients of brokerage firms is the execution of trades. Brokers buy and sell securities on behalf of their clients.

On behalf of their clients, brokerage firms execute the desired trade and coordinate payment for securities purchased or delivery of securities sold to be complete by the settlement date. Settlement day is the deadline for the buyer to be in receipt of purchased securities and the seller to be in receipt of the payment. For most trades this period is the third business day following the trade date. The industry refers to this as T+3. Some securities, like government bonds or option contracts, settle one business day after the trade date (T+1). When both buyer and seller agree, trades that would normally take time to settle can be settled the same day in order to expedite payment and/or receipt, though this is much less frequent. Brokers coordinate this process and are paid a fee for their service.

Cost Associated With Trading Equities

Typically, brokers are paid a commission to execute trades on behalf of their clients. If a client were to buy 100 shares of stock at $25 per share and the broker charged a commission of $0.10 per share, the total charge for the trade would be $2,510. The commission charge is broken out and shown as a separate line item on the client's confirmation receipt.

Trades executed in "net" terms do not always show the exact amount paid to the broker for the execution of the trade. Assume a client were to buy 100 shares of a stock at $25.10 net per share for a total of $2,510. We can see just how much the total transaction cost the buyer, but we are not sure how much was paid to the broker unless it is listed on the confirmation showing a "mark-up" or in the case of a sale of stock a "mark-down." The confirmation of a net trade often would show the total net price per share (including brokerage expense) and also disclose that the price includes a mark-up or markdown of a certain amount. The example above may read, "You bought

100 XYZ at $25.10 net. The price includes mark-up of $0.10 per share. Price to NASDAQ = $25 per share."

Not all net trades are reported this way, but it is important for trustees to realize that nobody works for free. While some trades reported "net" might not show exactly what brokers were paid, it would be incorrect to assume that no commission or fee was paid. Maybe "The best things in life are free;" but generally brokerage expenses are not!

Trading Bonds

The bond market is many times larger than the equities markets. Brokers and brokerage firms also handle bond transactions. It is not typical for bond buys or sales to be reported showing a commission. These trades are usually reported net of transaction charge. Bond investors purchase bonds quoted by price, in terms of their yield. The "face amount" is the maturity value of the bond. A $100,000 bond will fluctuate in value from day to day or even from minute to minute, but will mature at $100,000. "Par" is 100% of the face value. So par value of $100,000 face amount of bonds is $100,000. The "yield to maturity" is the amount of interest per annum an investor will receive for holding the bonds until maturity. Yield to maturity is typically how bonds are quoted. If a bond investor wants to buy $100,000 face amount of a specific 5% bond maturing in ten years and calls on two brokers for an offer price on the bond, the brokers would respond with the price (as a percentage of par) and yield (to maturity) of the bond.

For example, if broker A responds with an offer on $100,000 face amount of the bond, at a price of $103 net, yielding 4.622% to maturity; and broker B responds with an offer for the exact same bond, at a price of $103.5 net, yielding 4.56% to maturity, the investor would choose to buy the bond from broker A whose lower price produces a higher yield. In neither offering do we know what the broker is receiving in payment for procuring the bond on behalf of the investor, but we know it is something. The investor wants the bond and will select the best offering to produce the best resulting yield regardless of what the broker received. Broker A may have included a higher mark-up than broker B, but because he/she could find the bond cheaper, their offering remains the best execution for the investor. Perhaps both brokers had to pay the exact same amount to provide the bond to the investor. If that were the case, the lower price must be a function of a lower mark-up and therefore would be the best execution for the investor. Either way, the investor is generally more interested in the overall price of the bond that produces the best yield as opposed to just the cost component.

Not only is the bond market many times larger than the equity market, but also the individual bonds differ from one another in many ways. An investor buying common stock in XYZ Corporation has typically one option. In the case of large companies there may be hundreds of millions, even in excess of one billion, common shares outstanding for investors to trade. Each common share represents the same proportional ownership of the underlying company and has the same rights and value associated with it.

In the case of bonds, a company may have dozens, even hundreds, of different series of bonds. Each bond has different attributes. Different maturity dates, different interest rates or "coupon" amounts, different credit quality, different asset backings or different call features are just a few of the myriad ways bonds issued by the same entity could differ from one other. Because there are so many different bonds available and because each specific series of bond may be considerably smaller in size than outstanding common shares of the same company, bond investors need to be very careful and exercise significant due diligence in selecting and trading bonds.

A broker can be of tremendous help to investors attempting to purchase specific bonds to meet their needs. A broker who can find the appropriate bonds and offer them to an investor at the best price is adding value to that investor's portfolio. As mentioned earlier, the brokerage business is extremely competitive. This competition for the investor's business helps produce the best pricing. Just remember that nothing is free and that the competitor with the best offering is compensated for its efforts.

Many Specialized Professionals, Many Different Services

If the best place to begin this chapter was at the end, or the actual trade, perhaps the best place to conclude is back at the beginning. Beginning this chapter we pondered, "Where have all the stockbrokers gone?" Institutional brokers and traders that typically serve the needs of investment managers and institutional investors are much closer to the stereotype. They use many phones and computer screens to focus their efforts on executing trades on behalf of the investor. They work for pennies and fractions of pennies matching buyers with sellers to earn their fee. While transaction execution is still the backbone of the modern brokerage firm, the growth in business for brokerage firms is the result of their offering many different services beyond transaction execution. When was the last time you met an institutional broker or trader? Have you ever interviewed one for inclusion on your fund's team of plan professionals? The investment manager typically selects these brokers. Trustees rarely have contact with this part of the investment process.

Transaction fees can be viewed as assets of the plan and should be reviewed in an effort to reduce overall costs. Transaction fees may also be used to benefit the plan in other ways. Commission recapture programs, soft dollar arrangements to pay other services and all-inclusive fee arrangements are methods for trustees to receive some benefit for the plan dollars spent by investment managers trading their accounts.

Today's retooled "account executive" or financial consultant has left the execution of trades to the institutional trader and gone out to represent the multitude of other services offered by his/her firm to trustees. Most large brokerage firms offer many additional services important to the modern benefit plan.

Asset Management, Investment Management Consulting, Trust Services

In this day of continued financial service consolidation it is becoming harder and harder to find firms that offer only one service. Economies of scale producing more strategic combinations have resulted in the menu of services growing exponentially. I remember early in my career commenting, tongue-in-cheek, to my operations manager, "Al, someday we will all be owned by the banks." I just never thought it would happen so quickly. As a result of legislative changes, banks, brokers and insurance companies were permitted to combine and offer related services; the modern multifaceted financial services company emerged.

Top-notch asset management divisions are a part of most brokerage/financial services firms in today's world. Many highly regarded portfolio managers are available through these organizations. The largest investment management consulting organizations by number of clients and by value of consulting assets are divisions of large brokerage firms or major financial services companies. With the involvement of big global banks, clients can also access custodial and trust services in the same place.

It is important for trustees to recognize the various methods of purchasing the services related to the investment of plan assets. Recognizing the alternatives that exist in combining necessary services and the various providers of those services will assist trustees in selecting those most qualified at the best overall cost.

Being mindful of the potential for conflicts of interest is also important. Representatives working in firms that offer a myriad of services typically specialize in one area or another and generally refrain from competing for services where conflicts could arise. In cases where a representative provides investment management consulting services to a fund, it may be inappropriate to recommend an asset management division of the same firm if the representative would also benefit from employing the investment manager. Similarly it may be inappropriate for your investment manager to recommend a consultant that he/she feels will work to maintain the investment manager's employment, regardless of whether or not the manager and consultant share the same parent company. In all instances, full disclosure by professionals as to the manner in which they receive compensation should always be declared.

When selecting plan professionals, the integrity and objectivity of the individuals being considered is of utmost importance. The firm they represent and the services they provide are ancillary to the fiduciary relationship between the trustees and the individuals in whom they place their trust. There are many competent, honorable and professional individuals competing for benefits plan business. There are no monopolies on good products, good service providers or good individuals.

Trustees are charged with the duty of building a team of professionals that can best address their individual plan needs. There remains no clear-cut right or wrong way to accomplish this in every situation. When considering professionals for your team, keep an open mind and keep your eyes wide open. There may be no clear-cut answers in every case, but a trustee that does his/her homework will find the best-qualified professionals.

Chapter 30

Concluding Thoughts

In our attempt to solve the investment riddle of our respective employee benefit plans we often strike out in random fashion in a number of directions. This disorganized approach to problem solving often leaves us puzzled as to why our plan is always grappling with unsuccess. The seeds to the solution in solving our investment riddle should include the following:

- ◆ An organized approach
- ◆ Increasing our knowledge of investment fundamentals
- ◆ Adopting the appropriate planning horizon
- ◆ Placing the emphasis on "risk management," i.e., asset allocation and
- ◆ Adopting and implementing a written policy statement.

By demonstrating expertise, independence and care, you should be led to policies, procedures and operatives enabling you to:

1. *Multiply* your *efforts* many times by effectively tapping the resources of the plan professionals serving the fund.
2. *Maximize* your *return* by applying constructive investment principles that have stood the test of time.
3. *Minimize* your *risk* by adopting guidelines that will narrow the range of probable portfolio results.
4. *Attain* your *goals* by focusing on your objectives, insight-

fully measuring portfolio performance and modifying your program, as necessary.

What are the incentives for conducting yourself in such a "procedurally prudent" manner?

1. *Personal satisfaction* for having fulfilled the stewardship responsibilities that others have entrusted you with and
2. Any audit of your plan by a compliance officer from the Department of Labor will be just another event, not a crisis!

All of us, past and present, who have contributed to this guidebook wish you and your fellow trustees EVERY SUCCESS in all of your plan endeavors.

> It is not ourselves, but our *responsibilities* we should take seriously.
>
> *Author unknown*

Appendix A

Sample Investment Policy Statement–Defined Benefit Plan

Provided by Terrence S. Moloznik
National Electrical Benefit Fund (NEBF)

Investment Policy Statement of Defined Benefit Pension Plan

This benefit plan was established in 20_____. It covers the full time employees of the organization. The Plan is governed by an eight member Board of Trustees. The current members are ________________. Contributions to the Plan are made on a monthly basis and the contribution rates are collectively bargained, usually over a three year term. Assets are held in a segregated trust fund out of which benefit payments are made. Growth in the fund results from a combination of contributions and the return achieved from investing the accumulated reserves in the total fund.

I. PURPOSES OF THIS STATEMENT

The purposes of this Statement of Investment Policy are to:

1. Articulate the Trustees' views of the Plan's investment objectives and tolerance for risk.
2. Formulate policies to assist the Trustees with, first, developing a suitable asset allocation; second, selecting appropriate investment managers or commingled funds within the framework of that asset allocation; and third, prudently monitoring and evaluating the performance of such managers or commingled funds.

II. INVESTMENT OBJECTIVES

The Plan shall seek to achieve the following long-term investment objectives:

1. A long-term rate of return in excess of the annualized inflation rate, defined as the average annualized compound rate of the CPI calculated on a five year moving average.
2. A long-term rate of return that meets or exceeds the assumed actuarial rate as stated in the Plan's actuarial report.
3. A long-term competitive rate of return on investments, net of expenses, that is equal to or exceeds various benchmark rates on a moving three year average.
4. Maintenance of sufficient income and liquidity to pay monthly retirement.

III. POLICY

Consistent with the above, the Trustees will determine from time-to-time a suitable asset allocation that seeks to control risk through portfolio diversification and takes into account, among possible other factors, the above-stated objectives, in conjunction with current funding levels and economic and industry trends.

The Trustees will select various investment managers and/or commingled funds and allocate the assets of the Plan to seek to achieve the stated investment objectives and to control risk. The assets subject to each such investment manager or commingled fund shall constitute an "investment account."

The Trustees will establish reasonable guidelines for each asset class and investment account, specifying (as applicable) acceptable and/or prohibited investments, limits on asset and asset class exposures, risk constraints and investment return objectives. To the extent Plan assets are placed in commingled funds, the practices of such funds as identified in the fund prospectus shall be materially consistent with this Statement.

The Consultant and Plan staff will monitor the activity and performance of each investment account and the Plan as a whole and report to the Trustees on a periodic basis.

IV. ASSET ALLOCATION

The strategic target asset allocation will be as follows:

Asset Class	% of Portfolio
Equities	45%—+/— 5%
Fixed Income	40%—+/— 5%
Cash	5%—+/— 5%
Real Estate	10%—+/ —5%

To further control risk the Plan will also diversify by equity style. The Plan will maintain a passive core equity portfolio based on the S&P 500 Index. Complementing this core will be several active equity managers that utilize specific styles of equity management, such as value and growth. Additionally, equities classified as large-cap, mid-cap and small-cap will be included as part of the diversification strategy. The Plan will also seek prudently to invest in a diversified portfolio of equity real estate and will view real estate as a long-term investment and inflation hedge.

V. GUIDELINES

A. Equity Securities

1. Investment Objective

Equity investments are intended to provide a real rate of return over a market cycle (generally three to five years), and therefore to contribute to the Plan's "purchasing power" and long-term capital growth. In addition, each active equity investment manager is expected to produce a net return that is equal to or exceeds an appropriate benchmark index (i.e., S&P 500, Russell 2000, etc.) based on the individual investment account style and to outperform the median performance of other equity managers of the same or substantially similar style, on a gross return basis over a three year period.

For purposes of performance measurement, rate of return shall mean total rate of return, that is, investment income plus realized and unrealized capital gains and losses. It shall be calculated on a time-weighted basis by linking dollar-weighted monthly rates of return.

2. Diversification

   To assure a prudent degree of diversification and avoid excessive risk, equity investment accounts shall not exceed the following limits:

   a. No more than 5% of the investment account total assets in the securities of any one issuer; and
   b. No more of the account's total assets in any one industry than specified in a separate written agreement with the manager pursuant to a system of classification to be agreed upon with each equity security manager.

3. Permitted Activity

   Unless specifically recommended otherwise by the Trustees in writing, selection of equity funds or managers shall not be subject to restrictions or requirements (beyond those imposed by law or prudence) pertaining to:

   a. Turnover, except that turnover will be monitored by the Consultant and shall be subject to guidelines applicable to each investment account;
   b. Realizing gains and losses;
   c. Use of convertible securities; and
   d. Use of (i) securities of foreign-based companies that are traded on a major U.S. exchange in U.S. dollars and (ii) ADRs. "ADRs" are American Depository Receipts. These are listed and freely tradeable on major American exchanges and represent ownership in major, non-American corporations.

4. Prohibited Activity

   No equity investment manager and no commingled fund in which the Plan invests shall in the aggregate substantially engage or invest in the following:

   a. Foreign investments defined as securities that are not denominated in U.S. dollars and/or that are traded solely on an exchange outside the U.S.;
   b. Short sales, unless part of a market neutral strategy, specifically approved by the Trustees;
   c. Options or futures contracts, unless specifically approved by the Trustees;

d. Commodities, unless specifically approved by the Trustees;
e. Restricted stock or letter stock;
f. Non-marketable securities except for securities subject to Rule 144A; and
g. Margin transactions, except in conjunction with a strategy specifically approved by the Trustees.

B. Fixed Income

1. Investment Objective

Fixed income investments are intended to provide a positive rate of return over a full market cycle, (generally three to five years) and to provide a regular supply of cash flow. The fixed income managers are expected (a) to produce a net return that is equal to or exceeds the return of an appropriate benchmark index (e.g., Lehman Brothers Government/Corporate Index, Lehman Brothers Aggregate, etc.) based on the individual style of the fixed income account over a three year basis and (b) to outperform the median performance of other fixed income managers that are of the same or substantially similar style management on a gross return basis over a three year period.

2. Diversification

To assure a prudent degree of diversification and avoid excessive risk, fixed income accounts shall not exceed the following limits:

a. No more than 5% of the investment account and Plan's total assets shall be committed to the securities of any one issuer at the time of purchase, with the exception of securities issued or guaranteed by the full faith and credit of the United States or AAA-rated securities issued by government-sponsored enterprises (as to which there is no limit);
b. No more of the investment account's total assets shall be committed to any one industry than as agreed in a separate set of guidelines with each fixed income manager or as stated in each commingled fund's prospectus.

3. Permitted Activity
   Unless specifically approved otherwise by the Trustees, in writing, selection of fixed income funds and managers shall not be subject to restrictions or requirements (beyond those imposed by law or prudence) pertaining to:
   a. Turnover, except that turnover will be monitored by the Consultant and shall be subject to guidelines to be applicable to each investment account;
   b. Realized gains and losses; and
   c. Maturity, coupon, quality and issue selection.
4. Prohibited Activity
   Unless specifically approved otherwise by the Trustees, in writing, no fixed income manager shall engage or invest in the following and no commingled fund in which the Plan invests shall in the aggregate substantially engage or invest in the following:
   a. Repurchase agreements against securities which are not permitted to be held in the portfolio;
   b. Short sales;
   c. Options or futures contracts;
   d. Commodities;
   e. Non-marketable securities, except securities subject to Rule 144A;
   f. Margin transactions or any borrowing of money, except for emergencies, such as a need for a commingled fund to meet redemption requests;
   g. Foreign investments, defined as securities that are not denominated in U.S. dollars and/or that are traded solely on an exchange outside the U.S.;
   h. More than 15% of the fixed income portfolio in securities with a less than investment grade rating;
   i. Non-FDIC insured bank deposits; and
   j. Portfolios that have an average maturity and duration exceeding 10 years.

C. Short-Term Investments

1. Investment Objective

   Short-term investments are intended to be conservative and meet any necessary disbursements of the Plan and to accumulate funds for future investment. The short-term investments will be expected to provide net returns at least equal to the Salomon Brothers U.S. Treasury Bill Index on a one year moving average.

2. Permitted Activity

   Short-term investments are a permitted class of assets provided they fall within one or more of the following categories:

   a. U.S. Government securities (backed by the faith and credit of the U.S. Government) and U.S. Agency obligations;
   b. Certificates of deposit, maturing within 12 months, of any domestic bank meeting the capital standards mandated by the FDIC Improvements Act of 1991, provided that such certificates of deposit from one institution shall not represent more than 5% of the assets of the short-term investment account;
   c. Commercial paper, maturing within 9 months, of any domestic issuer, provided that such commercial paper shall be rated not less than A-1 by Standard & Poor or Prime 1 by Moodys;
   d. Repurchase agreements secured by U.S. Government or U.S. Agency obligations;
   e. High grade bankers acceptance; and
   f. Commingled accounts offered by banks or mutual funds that are designed for cash management strategies.

3. Prohibited Activity

   Unless specifically approved otherwise by the Trustees in writing, no short-term investment account shall engage or invest in any of the following and no commingled fund in which the Plan invests as a short-term vehicle shall in the aggregate substantially invest or engage in the following:

   a. Options or futures contracts;
   b. Non-marketable securities; and
   c. Margin transactions or any other borrowing of money except for emergencies, such as a need for a commingled fund to meet redemption requests.

D. Miscellaneous Investment Related Issues

1. Securities Lending

   The Plan will be authorized to engage in a prudent securities lending program to generate additional income. Collateral must be in the form of cash, letters of credit or securities of like kind and have a market value of at least 102% of the securities being lent.

2. Voting of Proxies

   The Trustees have delegated the right to vote common stock shares to the investment managers. All proxies must be voted in the long-term, economic interest of the Plan participants. Each investment manager is required to send a copy of its written proxy policy and guidelines to the Trustees and to submit quarterly reports on its proxy voting activities.

3. Periodic Review of this Statement

   The Trustees shall review this Statement annually. Changes to any portion of this Statement will be made to the extent such changes would be in the interest of the Plan participants.

BY: ____________________________
Chairman

BY: ____________________________
Secretary

Appendix B

Sample Investment Policy Statement– Defined Contribution Plan

Provided by Terrence S. Moloznik
National Electrical Benefit Fund (NEBF)

Investment Policy Statement of Defined Contribution Plan

This defined contribution plan was established in 20___ to provide a retirement program for employees of the organization. The Plan is governed by a four member Board of Trustees. The current members are _________________. Contributions to the Plan are made by the employee and matched by the organization. The Trustees offer a combination of investment choices to provide participants with a means to diversify their investments to meet their individual needs and risk tolerances.

I. PURPOSES OF THIS STATEMENT

The purposes of this Statement of Investment Policy are to:

1. Articulate the Trustees' objectives for structuring a retirement investment program suitable to the long-term needs and risk tolerances of each Plan participant.
2. Formulate policies for selecting appropriate investment managers, commingled and/or mutual funds or other suitable investments within the framework of that structure.
3. Establish objectives for prudently monitoring and evaluating the performance of such investment program.

II. INVESTMENT OBJECTIVES

The Plan's overall investment program and individual investment options provided to the participants shall seek to achieve the following long term investment objectives:

1. A long term rate of return in excess of the annualized inflation rate, defined as the average annualized compound rate of the CPI calculated on a five year moving average.
2. A long term competitive rate of return on investments, net of expenses, that is equal to or exceeds various benchmark rates on a moving three year average.
3. An investment program flexible enough to meet the varying needs of participants and provide each individual with the ability to construct a diversified portfolio to meet their long term investment goals.

III. POLICY

Consistent with the above, the Trustees will determine from time-to-time suitable investment options for the investment program that seek to control risk through portfolio diversification. The Trustees will select, offer to participants and monitor a range of investment options through the investment program with the intent of meeting the "safe harbor" of Section 404(c) of ERISA and applicable regulations. The selection of such options shall take into account the risk/return and other financial characteristics of the other investment options, so that individual participants who seek investments materially different from those offered through one of the options may select amongst a range of reasonable alternatives. These investment options can include separately managed accounts, commingled accounts offered by trust companies, mutual funds and insurance products.

The Trustees will periodically monitor the investment options to ensure that they remain suitable for the investment program and provide reasonable long term performance relative to their risks.

IV. GUIDELINES

Investment guidelines for commingled trusts, mutual funds and insurance contracts will be identified in the governing documents of such investment. To the extent that assets are placed in these funds, the practices of such funds as identified in the fund prospectus or contract shall apply. Discretionary investment accounts, when used, will be guided as follows:

A. Equity Securities

1. Investment Objective

   Equity investments are intended to provide a real rate of return over a market cycle (generally three to five years), and therefore to contribute to the participants "purchasing power" and long term capital growth. In addition, each active equity investment manager is expected to produce a net return that is equal to or exceeds an appropriate benchmark index (i.e., S&P 500, Russell 2000, etc.) based on the individual investment account style and to outperform the median performance of other equity managers or funds that use the same or substantially similar style of equity management on a gross return basis over a three year basis.

   For purposes of performance measurement, rate of return shall mean total rate of return, that is, investment income plus realized and unrealized capital gains and losses. It shall be calculated on a time-weighted basis by linking dollar-weighted monthly rates of return.

2. Diversification

   To assure a prudent degree of diversification and avoid excessive risk, equity investment accounts shall not exceed the following limits:

   a. No more than 5% of the investment account total assets in the securities of any one issuer or affiliated group.
   b. No more than 4.9% of the outstanding stock (or of any single class thereof) of any one issuer.

3. Permitted Activity
   Unless specifically recommended otherwise by the Trustees in writing, selection of equity funds or managers shall not be subject to restrictions or requirements (beyond those imposed by law or prudence) pertaining to:
   a. Turnover, except that turnover will be monitored by the consultant and shall be subject to guidelines to be applicable to each investment account;
   b. Realizing gains and losses;
   c. Use of convertible securities;
   d. Use of (i) securities of foreign-based companies that are traded on a major U.S. exchange in U.S. dollars and (ii) ADRs, up to a combined maximum of 15% of all equity securities. "ADRs" are American Depository Receipts. These are listed and freely tradeable on major American exchanges and represent ownership in major, non-American corporations.
4. Prohibited Activity
   Unless otherwise approved in writing by the Trustees no equity investment manager shall engage or invest in the following, and no commingled fund in which the Plan invests shall in the aggregate substantially engage or invest in any of the following:
   a. Foreign investments securities and ADRs beyond 15% of the total equity allocation;
   b. Short sales, unless part of a market neutral strategy, specifically approved by the Trustees;
   c. Options or futures contracts, except for purposes of hedging within a commingled fund;
   d. Commodities;
   e. Restricted stock or letter stock;
   f. Non-marketable securities; and
   g. Margin transactions or any other borrowing of money, except for emergencies, such as a need for a commingled fund to meet redemption requests or in conjunction with a market neutral strategy.

B. Fixed Income
   1. Investment Objective
      Fixed income investments are intended to provide a positive rate of return over a full market cycle, (generally three to five years) and to provide a regular supply of cash flow. Fixed income investment accounts are expected to (a) produce a net return that is equal to or exceeds the return of an appropriate benchmark index (e.g., Lehman Brothers Government/Corporate Index, Lehman Brothers GNMA, etc.) based on the individual style of the fixed income account over a three year basis and (b) outperform the median performance of other fixed income managers or commingled funds that use the same or substantially similar style of fixed income management on a gross return basis over a three year basis.
   2. Diversification
      To assure a prudent degree of diversification and avoid excessive risk, fixed income investment accounts shall not exceed the following limits:
      a. No more than 5% of the fixed income investment account and Plan's total assets shall be committed to the securities of any one issuer or affiliated group at the time of purchase, with the exception of securities issued or guaranteed by the full faith and credit of the United States or AAA-rated securities issued by government-sponsored enterprises (as to which there is no limit);
      b. No more of the fixed income investment account's total assets shall be committed to any one industry than as agreed in a separate set of guidelines with each fixed income manager or as stated in each commingled fund's prospectus.
   3. Permitted Activity
      Unless specifically approved otherwise by the Trustees in writing, selection of fixed income funds and managers shall not be subject to restrictions or requirements (beyond those imposed by law or prudence) pertaining to:
      a. Turnover, except that turnover will be monitored by the consultant and shall be subject to guidelines to be applicable to each investment account;
      b. Realized gains and losses;
      c. Use of convertible securities;

d. Use of securities of foreign-based companies that are traded on a major U.S. exchange in U.S. dollars, up to a maximum of 15% of all fixed income securities in the portfolio.

4. Prohibited Activity

Unless specifically approved otherwise by the Trustees in writing, no fixed income manager shall engage or invest in the following and no commingled fund in which the Plan invests shall in the aggregate substantially invest or engage in any of the following:

a. Repurchase agreements against securities which are not permitted to be held in the portfolio;
b. Short sales;
c. Options or futures contracts, except for hedging within a commingled fund;
d. Commodities;
e. Non-marketable securities;
f. Margin transactions or any other borrowing of money, except for emergencies, such as a need for a commingled fund to meet redemption requests;
g. Foreign fixed income securities beyond 15% of the total fixed income allocation;
h. Securities with less than an investment grade rating, unless specifically authorized;
i. Non-FDIC insured bank deposits; and
j. Portfolios which have an average maturity and duration exceeding 10 years.

C. Short-Term Investments

1. Investment Objective

Short-term investments are intended to be conservative, to assist in meeting any necessary disbursements from the Plan and to accumulate funds for future investment. The Plan will offer a short-term investment vehicle as an alternative asset class to those participants who desire a very conservative investment option. The short-term investments will be expected to provide net returns at least equal to the Solomon Brothers U.S. Treasury Bill Index on a one year moving average.

2. Permitted Activity

   Short-term investments are a permitted class of assets provided they meet the following guidelines:

   a. U.S. Government securities backed by the full faith and credit of the U.S. Government and U.S. Agency;
   b. Certificates of deposit, maturing within 12 months, of any domestic bank meeting the capital standards mandated by the FDIC Improvements Act of 1991, provided that such certificates of deposit from one institution shall not represent more than 5% of the assets of the short-term investment account;
   c. Commercial paper, maturing within 9 months, of any domestic issuer, provided that such commercial paper shall be rated not less than A-1 by Standard & Poor or Prime 1 by Moodys;
   d. Repurchase agreements secured by U.S. Government or U.S. Agency obligations;
   e. High grade bankers' acceptance; and
   f. Commingled accounts offered by banks or mutual funds that are approved for investment by tax exempt organizations.

3. Prohibited Activity

   Unless specifically approved otherwise by the Trustees in writing, no short-term investment account shall engage or invest in the following and no commingled fund in which the Plan invests as a short-term vehicle shall in the aggregate substantially invest or engage in the following:

   a. Options or futures contracts;
   b. Non-marketable securities; and
   c. Margin transactions or any other borrowing of money except for emergencies, such as a need for a commingled fund to meet redemption requests.

D. Miscellaneous Investment Related Issues

1. Securities Lending
   The Plan may engage in prudent lending of securities to generate additional income. Collateral must be in the form of cash, letters of credit or securities of like kind and have a market value of at least 102% of the securities being lent.
2. Periodic Review of this Statement
   The Trustees shall review this Statement annually. Changes to any portion of this Statement will be made to the extent such changes would be in the interest of the Plan participants.

BY: ______________________________
Chairman

BY: ______________________________
Secretary

Appendix C

Sample Investment Policy Statement–Health & Welfare Fund

Provided by Terrence S. Moloznik
National Electrical Benefit Fund (NEBF)

Investment Policy Statement of Health & Welfare Fund

I. PURPOSES OF THIS STATEMENT OF GOALS AND OBJECTIVES

The purposes of this Statement of Investment Policy are to:

a. Articulate the Trustees' views of the Fund's investment objectives and tolerance for risk.

b. Formulate policies to assist the Trustees with selecting appropriate one or more investment managers and prudently monitoring and evaluating the performance of such managers.

II. INVESTMENT OBJECTIVES

1. Assets of the Fund shall be invested in a manner consistent with the fiduciary standards of the Employee Retirement Income Security Act of 1974, as amended ("ERISA").
2. The investment objectives of the Fund are, in order of importance:
   a. Preservation of capital
   b. Payment of benefits and expenses in timely fashion
   c. Favorable net return on investment at a prudent level of risk.

III. POLICY

The Board will select one or more investment managers consistent with the investment objectives. The assets subject to each such manager will constitute an "account" or "investment account." The Board may establish guidelines for each asset class and for each investment account, specifying (as applicable) acceptable and/or prohibited investments, limits on asset and asset class exposures, risk constraints and investment return objectives. In developing such guidelines, the Board shall take into account, among possible other factors, the above-stated objectives, current and projected actuarial factors, industry trends, current and expected benefit levels, liquidity needs, risk tolerances, desired levels of income and capital growth, diversification standards and other matters.

The Board will cause the activity and performance of each investment account and the Fund as a whole to be reviewed not less often than quarterly to assure continued compliance with this Statement.

A. Generally

The Fund's investments shall be limited to fixed income investments, including cash.

B. Specific Guidelines

1. Investment Objective

Fixed income investments are intended to provide a positive real rate of return over a full market cycle, (i.e., a period of both economic recession and recovery, of at least 3 years) and to provide a regular supply of cash flow.

2. Diversification

Because the Fund is of a very limited size, the fixed income portion of the Plan's portfolio may include only some of the instruments available in the market and in different proportions than they are available in the market. However, to assure a prudent degree of diversification and avoid excessive risk, the fixed income or balanced manager shall not exceed the following limits without prior written approval of the Board:

a. No more than 5% of the fixed income portion of the account shall be committed to the securities of any one issuer or affiliated group at the time of purchase, with the exception of securities issued or guaranteed by the full faith and credit of the United States or AAA-rated securities issued by federal government-sponsored enterprises (as to which there is no limit).

b. No more than 10% of the fixed income portion of the account shall be committed to any one industry (pursuant to a classification system to be agreed upon with each fixed income or balanced manager) at the time of the purchase.
c. No more than 5% of the outstanding principal value of the account shall be committed to any one bond issue.

3. Permitted Activity
Unless specifically restricted in writing by the Board, selection of fixed income securities shall not be subject to restrictions or requirements (beyond those imposed by law or prudence) pertaining to:
   a. Turnover
   b. Realized gains and losses
   c. Maturity and coupon
4. Prohibited Activity
Unless specifically exempted by the Board, investments in fixed income securities shall not include any of the following:
   a. Repurchase agreements against securities which are not permitted to be held in the portfolio
   b. Short sales
   c. Futures contracts or naked options
   d. Commodities
   e. Non-marketable securities
   f. Margin transactions or any other borrowing of money
   g. Securities whose interest or principal is denominated in a currency other than U.S. Dollars
   h. Securities not traded in and able to be custodied in the United States
   i. Commercial paper of issuers who have not maintained an average outstanding of at least $50 million over the prior 12 months
   j. Securities with a lesser rating than AA by Moodys or S&P
   k. Commercial paper which is not rated or is rated below Al, P1, or the equivalent by a recognized rating agency

5. Performance
   Specific performance objectives will be established for each investment account. Performance will be measured against both a market index and on an absolute basis, for quarterly and multiple quarter periods. Among other possible grounds, consistent failure to meet objectives over a three-year period will constitute grounds for dismissal.

BOARD OF TRUSTEES
HEALTH & WELFARE FUND

BY: ______________________________
Chairman

BY: ______________________________
Secretary

Appendix D

Checklist of Elements for Inclusion in Investment Policy Statement

A great deal of time and effort by the trustees and their professional advisors must precede the formalization of an investment policy statement. Hopefully, whatever is included in the statement will be *productive* toward and *facilitate* the successful attainment of the agreed upon goals.

The following is a checklist that can be used as an initial step in the preparation of the statement. Those involved in the process can use the checklist to indicate their opinion as to the advisability of including, or not including, the various items shown in the listing.

	Include	Not to be Included
Definition and Function		
Explanation of relationship between plan and collective bargaining agreement	☐	☐
Purpose for creation of the statement of investment objectives, policies and guidelines	☐	☐
Definition of terminology (as an attachment)	☐	☐
Acknowledgment by manager that he is a qualified fiduciary as defined in ERISA	☐	☐

	Include	Not to be Included
Summary description (as an attachment) describing characteristics and constraints of the plan fundamental to the development of funding policy (i.e., liability structure, actuarial funding techniques, pace of funding, etc.)	☐	☐
Methodology for periodic review and modification of statement	☐	☐
Objectives and Goals		
Compliance with fiduciary standards of ERISA	☐	☐
Preservation of principal value	☐	☐
Preservation of purchasing power	☐	☐
Control and stability of contributions required	☐	☐
Anticipated net cash flow schedule for liquidity needs assessment (as an attachment)	☐	☐
Income goal (yield requirement)		
Absolute	☐	☐
Relative	☐	☐
Potential seen for continuity or termination of the plan	☐	☐
Standards of Investment Performance		
Time-horizon to be used in evaluation process		
Stated in number of years	☐	☐
Stated in market cycle(s)	☐	☐
Willingness to extend horizon as "contrarian" investor	☐	☐
Performance to be calculated		
Including management fee	☐	☐
Excluding management fee	☐	☐

	Include	Not to be Included
Investment return objective stated in *absolute* terms:		
Minimum target to match actuarial investment return assumption	☐	☐
___% return target	☐	☐
Stated in *relative* terms		
Relative to other accounts having similar objectives managed by the manager	☐	☐
Minimum of ___% above annualized rate of inflation (stated separately for each class of assets)	☐	☐
___% above a published or privately produced index	☐	☐
___% above a database of other funds	☐	☐
___% above a market index in falling/ rising markets	☐	☐
___% above the actuarial investment return assumption	☐	☐
Conditions that could provoke termination of account relationship	☐	☐
Policy and Guidelines		
Conversion period allowed (upon transfer of assets) to position account in accordance with guidelines	☐	☐
Indifference to composition of investment return realized	☐	☐
Classes of investments authorized	☐	☐
Diversification of portfolio		
Variable posture with parameters	☐	☐
Variable posture without parameters	☐	☐
Restriction on use of cash reserves	☐	☐
Fixed posture	☐	☐

	Include	Not to be Included
Diversification within classes		
Industries	☐	☐
Companies	☐	☐
Sectors	☐	☐
Geographic areas	☐	☐
Homogeneous groups	☐	☐
Activity of portfolio		
Turnover parameters		
Bonds	☐	☐
Stocks	☐	☐
Designation of brokerage business	☐	☐
To seek "best execution"	☐	☐
Periodic reports on commissions activity	☐	☐
Authority to vote shares of stock	☐	☐
Restrictions:		
Use of commodities	☐	☐
Lending of securities	☐	☐
Realizing of capital losses	☐	☐
Prohibited transactions	☐	☐
Investments in securities of contributing employers	☐	☐
Specific industry investments	☐	☐
Investment manager's own "approved list"	☐	☐
Delegation of authority to exercise rights, warrants, conversion and redemption privileges	☐	☐

	Include	Not to be Included
Guidelines–*Bonds*		
___% limitation on the securities held representing exposure to any one industry	☐	☐
___% limitation on the securities held representing exposure to any one company	☐	☐
___% limitation on exposure to any one issue	☐	☐
Use of foreign securities	☐	☐
Use of convertibles	☐	☐
Minimum quality rate		
S&P (absolute on each security)	☐	☐
Moody's (absolute on each security)	☐	☐
Weighted average of portfolio	☐	☐
Use of private placements	☐	☐
Use of commingled funds	☐	☐
Use of mutual funds	☐	☐
Use of insurance company separate accounts	☐	☐
Use of commercial paper	☐	☐
Use of short sales	☐	☐
Use of certificates of deposit	☐	☐
Scheduling of maturities to meet benefit payment stream	☐	☐
Guidelines–*Common Stock*		
Minimum diversification requirements		
___% limitation on the securities held to any one issue		
Expressed as % of cost	☐	☐
Expressed as % at market	☐	☐
___% limitation on the securities held representing exposure to any one company		
Expressed as % of cost	☐	☐
Expressed as % at market	☐	☐

	Include	Not to be Included
Minimum S&P rating of ___		
Of each security	☐	☐
Weighted average of portfolio	☐	☐
Use of stock options, puts, calls, straddles or hedging	☐	☐
Use of foreign securities	☐	☐
Use of letter stock	☐	☐
Use of mutual funds	☐	☐
Use of insurance company separate accounts	☐	☐
Use of short sales	☐	☐
Use of commingled funds	☐	☐
Use of convertibles	☐	☐
Use of preferred stock	☐	☐
Market capitalizations	☐	☐
Projected growth rates	☐	☐
Marketability	☐	☐
Minimum cash dividends payers	☐	☐
Listed on exchanges	☐	☐

Guidelines–*Mortgages and/or Real Estate*

	Include	Not to be Included
Type	☐	☐
Geographical distribution	☐	☐
___% limitation in any one loan (property)	☐	☐
Restrictions		
Interim loans	☐	☐
Construction loans	☐	☐
Notification to trustees of mortgage commitments	☐	☐
Review of documentation by fund's real estate counsel	☐	☐

	Include	Not to be Included
Contact and Communication		
Frequency of meetings	☐	☐
Agenda items	☐	☐
Attendees	☐	☐
Periodic reporting		
Appraisal	☐	☐
Performance measurement	☐	☐
Compliance with guidelines	☐	☐
Transactions analysis	☐	☐
Documentation in support of manager's buy, sell, hold decisions	☐	☐

Appendix E

Following are AFL-CIO Pension Guidelines for Domestic and International Investments, as adopted by the AFL-CIO Executive Council, February 1993. The guidelines are reproduced herein without comment and with the AFL-CIO's expressed permission.

AFL-CIO PENSION GUIDELINES FOR DOMESTIC AND INTERNATIONAL INVESTMENTS

Adopted by the AFL-CIO Executive Council
February 18, 1993
Bal Harbour, Florida

Expanding Domestic Investment

The past several years have seen numerous proposals to encourage pension investment in traditional infrastructure projects such as roads and bridges. More recently, these proposals have been expanded to include housing, education and training, child care and other services essential to local economic growth. Organized labor's experience with Economically Targeted Investments (ETIs) suggests that so long as trustees make voluntary decisions about whether to invest in these vehicles, pension assets can be a source of long-term financing for these critical projects and serve to leverage federal and state dollars back to communities. This is not an area where government should mandate trustee action.

As trustees consider new investment opportunities at the federal and state level, they are urged to consider the following:

SAFETY AND PRUDENCE OF ECONOMICALLY TARGETED INVESTMENT: ETIs should provide a prudent rate-of-return. In any initiative for pension investment, trustees should consider the importance of investment guarantees and other credit enhancements that lower investment risk. These guarantees can be provided by governments or private sector financial institutions.

PROTECTIONS AGAINST THE PRIVATIZATION OF PUBLIC SERVICES: ETIs create new partnerships among state and local governments, private investors and pension funds. Union trustees should take steps to ensure that these new financial partnerships do not alter the traditional roles and responsibilities of the public sector by selling public assets or contracting out services to private sector entrepreneurs.

FINANCING OF PUBLIC SECTOR INFRASTRUCTURE PROJECTS: Recognizing that pension funds bring a long-term perspective to financing, trustees should consider participation in any national program of investment in public infrastructure projects that is (a) combined with direct federal subsidies to state and local governments; (b) contains federal authority to finance and administer the program, provides public oversight with adequate funding raised in a manner that is fair to working people, and contains federal, state, or private sector investment guarantees.

MAINTAINING LABOR PROTECTIONS: Union trustees should take steps to ensure that any investments do not rely on financing or contract mechanisms that undermine prevailing local standards for wages and employment practices or worker protections.

BROADENING ETI STRATEGIES: In addition to investing in real estate and construction trusts that use union-only labor, trustees should consider broadening the scope of ETIs by utilizing innovative mechanisms to prudently target pension assets for job creation, economic stimulus, and the generation of other economic benefits. Such mechanisms should include joining with state and local agencies to fund local economic projects, linking bank deposits with pension-sponsored economic renewal projects, and programs to use pension assets to leverage a range of member benefits (e.g., mortgage-origination programs) with local financial institutions.

Clarifying Guidelines for Pensions and Foreign Investments

Trustees should review their funds' written investment and proxy voting guidelines to determine if any direction is given to money managers on foreign investing. The focus of this review should be to determine whether the money manager's practices have been consistent with the fund's policies, *and whether those policies are serving the interests of plan participants and beneficiaries.* In the course of this review, trustees may find that their funds are direct foreign investors (e.g., investors in foreign securities or pooled global index funds, including American Depository Receipts), indirect foreign investors (e.g., through holdings in American multinationals) or targeted foreign investors (e.g., investment designed to benefit a certain population, industry, or geographic location), or devoid of foreign investment as a matter of either policy or circumstance.

AVOID UNRESTRICTED DIRECT FOREIGN INVESTMENTS: Funds should not knowingly make direct foreign investments that are not targeted or screened for their economic, social or environmental impacts.

- ◆ Screening should include an assessment of whether investments in business enterprises are likely to displace American products or employment.
- ◆ Screening should include an investigation of company violations of internationally recognized standards of employment, health and safety, labor and environmental standards. Existing codes of conduct, including broad standards developed by the ILO and the OECD, as well as the Standards of Conduct developed by the Coalition for Justice in the Maquiladora, should serve as models. Observance of the Statement of Principles For Corporate Activity in South Africa (formerly the Sullivan Principles), MacBride and Ceres Principles (formerly the Valdez Principles) should also be considered when evaluating corporate citizenship.
- ◆ Targeting may include specific investments that expand U.S. export markets and hence U.S. jobs, assist emerging democracies, or provide the host country with benefits at no economic costs to the U.S.

SCRUTINIZE INVESTMENTS IN AMERICAN MULTINATIONALS WITH FOREIGN INVESTMENT ACTIVITIES: Since 52% of Standard & Poors (S&P) companies report international activity (e.g., ownership of foreign assets or through revenues), pension funds investing in these multinationals are indirectly exposed to international capital markets. As a result, data should be compiled and tracked on overseas investment activities of portfolio multinationals for use in future investment decisions and in shareholder actions. Trustees should develop indicators or "flags" which will alert them to the need to seek more specific information from American multinationals in their portfolios.[1] Trustees or their investment managers should consider building profiles of American multinational activities that include such data as:

- Trends of increasing revenues from foreign sales and increasing foreign assets.
- Trends of increasing employment abroad of both American citizens and foreign nationals. This data should include wage levels and whether portfolio companies are paying less than American wages for the same jobs performed in other countries. This could serve as an indication that portfolio companies are engaging in "runaway" practices and thus, are displacing American products and employment.
- Whether engaged in "runaway" practices or seeking to legitimately open access to foreign markets, wage levels should be scrutinized to determine whether portfolio companies set wage levels that tend to elevate wages within the host country or at levels that will perpetuate low standards or undermine local wage norms.
- As with direct investments, investments in American-based multinationals should be screened for any record of company violation of internationally recognized standards of employment, health and safety, labor relations and environmental compliance. (See **"Avoid Unrestricted Direct Foreign Investments"** above, for investment screens and codes of conduct.)

PROHIBIT INVESTMENTS IN COUNTRIES WITH SYSTEMATIC WORKER AND HUMAN RIGHTS ABUSES: Funds should not knowingly make investments in countries that are known to violate internationally recognized worker and human rights. It is suggested that the reader contact the AFL-CIO Department of International Affairs for a current list of those nations with systematic

---

1. For example, if an examination of the company's balance sheets indicates an increase in foreign assets relative to domestic assets, trustees as shareholders should seek explanations for such a trend from the company's board. They may find that the numbers indicate the board's intention to develop a presence in a particular region of the world in order to tap a foreign market for either U.S. produced goods and services or ones produced within the market for that market–both good corporate policy goals. However, if the trend indicates that there is a decline in U.S. based assets that seems to correspond to the increase in foreign assets, they may find that this is a result of a program to shift productive capacity from a relative high wage and stringent regulatory environment to a lower wage and lax regulatory environment. This is clearly a bad corporate policy, one that would qualify the company for further shareholder or investment activity.

worker rights abuses, as well as nations with governments which prohibit independent trade unions.

MAINTAIN SCORECARD ON PORTFOLIO INVESTMENTS IN FOREIGN OWNED COMPANIES OPERATING IN THE U.S.: Compile and maintain records on compliance with U.S. standards for employment, health and safety, and the environment.

EXERCISE SHAREHOLDER RIGHTS: Proxy voting and the ability to initiate shareholder proposals are valuable assets of plan management, whether the company is domestic or foreign-based. Trustees should extend the principles of the AFL-CIO Proxy Voting Guidelines to international shareholder issues and ensure they are heeded by the custodian or manager with delegated voting authority.

INTERNATIONAL PENSION SOLIDARITY: American trade unionists should explore new ways to work with their counterparts abroad to adopt investment guidelines that reflect the principles stated above.

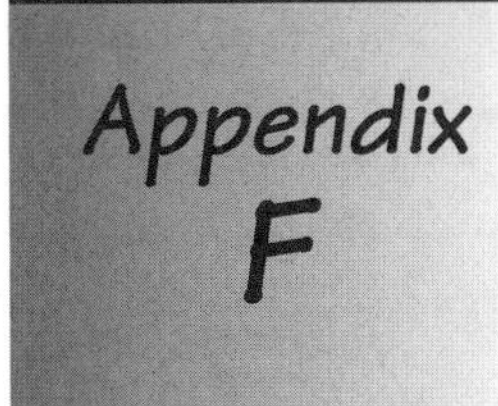

Department of Labor Interpretive Bulletin 94.1

Economically Targeted Investing

32606 Federal Register / Vol. 59, No. 120 / Thursday, June 23, 1994 / Rules and Regulations

DEPARTMENT OF LABOR

Pension and Welfare Benefits Administration

29 CFR Part 2509

[Interpretive Bulletin 94-1]

Interpretive Bulletin Relating to the Employee Retirement Income Security Act of 1974

AGENCY: Pension and Welfare Benefits Administration, Labor.

ACTION: Interpretive bulletin.

SUMMARY: This document sets forth the view of the Department of Labor (the Department) concerning the legal standard imposed by sections 403 and 404 of Part 4 of Title I of the Employee Retirement Income Security Act of 1974 (ERISA) with respect to a plan fiduciary's decision to invest plan assets in "economically targeted investments" (ETIs). ETIs are generally defined as investments that are selected for the economic benefits they create in addition to the investment return to the employee benefit plan investor. In this document, the Department states that the requirements of sections 403 and 404 do not prevent plan fiduciaries from deciding to invest plan assets in an ETI if the ETI has an expected rate of return that is commensurate to rates of return of alternative investments with similar risk characteristics that are available to the plan, and if the ETI is otherwise an appropriate investment for the plan in terms of such factors as diversification and the investment policy of the plan.

SUPPLEMENTARY INFORMATION: In order to provide a concise and ready reference to its interpretations of ERISA, the Department publishes its interpretive bulletins in the Rules and Regulations section of the Federal Register. Published in this issue of the Federal Register is ERISA Interpretive Bulletin 94-1, which clarifies that under ERISA a plan fiduciary may invest plan assets in an "economically targeted investment" (ETI) provided the fiduciary determines that such investment is appropriate for the plan in terms of the same factors that a prudent fiduciary would use in determining whether any other type of investment is appropriate for the plan. The Department is publishing this interpretive bulletin because it believes there is a need to summarize and clarify the guidance which it has provided regarding the fiduciary standards applicable to plan investments generally and to investments in ETIs specifically.

(Sec. 505, Pub. L. 93-406, 88 Stat. 894 (29 U.S.C. 1135))

Background

Several recent articles and reports have indicated that a perception exists within the investment community that investments in ETIs are incompatible with ERISA's fiduciary obligations.[1] In order to eliminate this misperception, the Department is issuing this interpretive bulletin to set forth its understanding of the term ETI, and to clarify its position regarding the application of the fiduciary provisions of Part 4 of Title I of ERISA to a decision to invest in an ETI.

As used in this interpretive bulletin, an ETI is an investment that is selected for the economic benefit it creates, in addition to the investment return to the employee benefit plan investor. ETIs fall within a wide variety of asset categories, including real estate, venture capital and small business investments. Although some of these asset categories may require a longer time to generate significant investment

1. *Financing the Future,* Report of the Commission to Promote Investment in America's Infrastructure, Feb. 1993; *Report of the Work Group on Pension Investments,* Advisory Council on Employee Welfare and Pension Benefit Plans, Nov. 1992, p.19; Maria O'Brien Hylton, *Socially Responsible Investing: Doing Good Versus Doing Well in an Inefficient Market,* 42 Am. U.L. Rev. 1 (1992).

returns, may be less liquid and may not have as much readily available information on their risks and returns as other asset categories, nothing in ERISA precludes trustees and investment managers from considering ETIs in constructing plan portfolios. While some of these asset categories may require special expertise to evaluate, they may be attractive to sophisticated, long-term investors, including many pension plans.

The Department has issued a number of letters concerning a fiduciary's ability to consider the collateral effects of an investment.[2] The Department has also granted a variety of prohibited transaction exemptions to both individual plans and pooled investment vehicles involving investments which produce collateral benefits.[3] These letters and exemptions illustrate circumstances under which fiduciaries may consider collateral benefits when investing plan assets.

In responding to these various opinion requests, the Department has established certain broad principles. The Department has stated that arrangements designed to bring areas of investment opportunity which provide collateral benefits to the attention of plan fiduciaries will not in and of themselves violate sections 403 or 404, where the arrangements do not restrict the exercise of the fiduciary's investment discretion. For example, in Advisory Opinion 88-16A, the Department considered an arrangement whereby a company and union proposed to make recommendations, for up to 5% of the annual contributions, of investments with the potential for providing collateral benefits to union members. The Department concluded

2. See, letters from the Department of Labor to Mr. John Kenney, dated June 3, 1980 (A.O. 80-33A); to Mr. George Cox, dated January 16, 1981; to Mr. Theodore Groom, dated January 16, 1981; to The Trustees of the Twin City Carpenters and Joiners Pension Plan, dated May 19,1981; to Mr. William Chadwick, dated July 21,1982; to Mr. Daniel O'Sullivan, dated August 2,1982; to Mr. Ralph Katz; dated March 15,1982 and October 23,1985 (A.O. 85-36A); to Mr. William Ecklund, dated December 18, 1985 and January 16, 1986; to Mr. Reed Larson, dated July 14, 1986; to Mr. James Ray, dated July 8, 1988; to Mr. Gregory Ridella, dated December 19, 1988 (A.O. 88-16A); to the Honorable Jack Kemp, dated November 23, 1990; and to Mr. Stuart Cohen, dated May 14, 1993.

3. See, PTE 76-1, part B, concerning construction loans by multiemployer plans; PTE 84-25, issued to the Pacific Coast Roofers Pension Plan; PTE 85-58, issued to the Northwestern Ohio Building Trades and Employer Construction Industry Investment Plan; PTE 87-20, issued to the Racine Construction Industry Pension Fund; PTE 87-70, issued to the Dayton Area Building and Construction Industry Investment Plan; PTE 88-96, issued to the Real Estate for American Labor A Balcor Group Trust; PTE 89-37, issued to the Union Bank; PTE 93-16, issued to the Toledo Roofers Local No. 134 Pension Plan and Trust et al.

that the arrangement would not be inconsistent with the requirements of sections 403(c) and 404(a)(1) of ERISA, where the investment managers having responsibility with respect to these recommendations retained exclusive investment discretion, and were required to secure, over the long term, the maximum attainable total return on investments consistent with the principles of sound pension fund management.[4] Moreover, the Department stated that in considering such investments plan fiduciaries could be influenced by factors that were not related to the plan's expected investment return, only if such investments were equal or superior to alternative available investments.

Similarly, in a case involving the financing of construction projects, the Department concluded that participation in an organization which presents investment opportunities but does not limit the investment alternatives available to the plans, and does not obligate the plans to invest in any project presented for consideration, does not, in itself, violate any of ERISA's fiduciary standards. Moreover, the Department concluded that in enforcing the plan's rights after making an investment, the fiduciary could consider factors unrelated to the plan's investment return only if, in the fiduciary's judgment, the course of action taken would be at least as economically advantageous to the plan as any alternative course of action.[5] In other letters, the Department concluded that the requirements of sections 403 and 404 do not exclude the consideration of collateral benefits in a fiduciary's evaluation of a particular investment opportunity. However, existence of such collateral benefits may be decisive in evaluating an investment only if the fiduciary determines that the investment containing the collateral benefits is expected to provide an investment return to the plan commensurate to alternative investments having similar risks.[6]

While the Department has stated that a plan fiduciary may consider collateral benefits in choosing between investments that have comparable risks and rates of return, it has consistently held that fiduciaries who are willing to accept expected reduced returns or

---

4. See, letter from the Department of Labor to Mr. Gregory Ridella, dated December 19, 1988 (A.O. 88-16A); see also, letters to Mr. John Kenney, dated June 3, 1980 (A.O. 80-33A); and to Mr. Stuart Cohen, dated May 14, 1993.

5. See, letter from the Department to Mr. George Cox, dated January 16, 1981.

6. See, letters from the Department of Labor to Mr. Theodore Groom, dated January 16, 1981; to Mr. Daniel O'Sullivan, dated August 2, 1982; to Mr. James Ray, dated July 8, 1988; and to Mr. Stuart Cohen, dated May 14, 1993.

greater risks to secure collateral benefits are in violation of ERISA.[7] It follows that, because every investment necessarily causes a plan to forgo other investment opportunities, an investment will not be prudent if it would provide a plan with a lower expected rate of return than available alternative investments with commensurate degrees of risk or is riskier than alternative available investments with commensurate rates of return.

The following interpretive bulletin deals solely with the applicability of the prudence and exclusive purpose requirements of ERISA as applied to fiduciary decisions to invest plan assets in ETIs. The bulletin does not supersede the regulatory standard contained at 29 CFR 2550.404a-1, nor does it address any issues which may arise in connection with the prohibited transaction provisions or the statutory exemptions from those provisions.

List of Subjects in 29 CFR Part 2509

Employee benefit plans, Pensions.

For the reasons set forth in the preamble, Part 2509 of Title 29 of the Code of Federal Regulations is amended as follows:

PART 2509-INTERPRETIVE BULLETINS RELATING TO THE EMPLOYEE RETIREMENT INCOME SECURITY ACT OF 1974

1. The authority citation for Part 2509 is revised to read as follows:

Authority: 29 U.S.C. 1135. Section 2509.75-1 is also issued under 29 U.S.C. 1114. Sections 2509.75-10 and 2509.75-2 also issued under 29 U.S.C. 1052, 1053, 1054. Secretary of Labor's Order No. 1-87 (52 FR 13139).

2. Part 2509 is amended by adding a new Sec. 2509.94-1 to read as follows:

Sec. 2509.94-1–Interpretive Bulletin relating to the fiduciary standard under ERISA in considering economically targeted investments.

---

7. See, letters from the Department of Labor to the Trustees of the Twin City Carpenters and Joiners Pension Plan, dated May 19, 1981; to Mr. William Ecklund, dated December 18, 1985 and January 16, 1986; to Mr. Reed Larson, dated July 14, 1986; and to the Honorable Jack Kemp, dated November 23, 1990. Also note, that in letters to Mr. Ralph Katz, dated March 15, 1982 and October 23, 1985 (A.O. 85-36A), the Department held that increases to plan assets obtained from an increased contribution level, or other collateral benefits could not be added to the investment return of the plan's investment. Thus, for comparison purposes, the economic evaluation of the investment is limited to its actual return.

This Interpretive Bulletin sets forth the Department of Labor's interpretation of sections 403 and 404 of the Employee Retirement Income Security Act of 1974 (ERISA), as applied to employee benefit plan investments in "economically targeted investments" (ETIs), that is, investments selected for the economic benefits they create apart from their investment return to the employee benefit plan. Sections 403 and 404, in part, require that a fiduciary of a plan act prudently, and to diversify plan investments so as to minimize the risk of large losses, unless under the circumstances it is clearly prudent not to do so. In addition, these sections require that a fiduciary act solely in the interest of the plan's participants and beneficiaries and for the exclusive purpose of providing benefits to their participants and beneficiaries. The Department has construed the requirements that a fiduciary act solely in the interest of, and for the exclusive purpose of providing benefits to, participants and beneficiaries as prohibiting a fiduciary from subordinating the interests of participants and beneficiaries in their retirement income to unrelated objectives.

With regard to investing plan assets, the Department has issued a regulation, at 29 CFR 2550.404a-1, interpreting the prudence requirements of ERISA as they apply to the investment duties of fiduciaries of employee benefit plans. The regulation provides that the prudence requirements of section 404(a)(1)(B) are satisfied if (1) the fiduciary making an investment or engaging in an investment course of action has given appropriate consideration to those facts and circumstances that, given the scope of the fiduciary's investment duties, the fiduciary knows or should know are relevant, and (2) the fiduciary acts accordingly. This includes giving appropriate consideration to the role that the investment or investment course of action plays (in terms of such factors as diversification, liquidity and risk/return characteristics) with respect to that portion of the plan's investment portfolio within the scope of the fiduciary's responsibility.

Other facts and circumstances relevant to an investment or investment course of action would, in the view of the Department, include consideration of the expected return on alternative investments with similar risks available to the plan. It follows that, because every investment necessarily causes a plan to forgo other investment opportunities, an investment will not be prudent if it would be expected to provide a plan with a lower rate of return than available alternative investments with commensurate degrees of risk or is riskier than alternative available investments with commensurate rates of return.

The fiduciary standards applicable to ETIs are no different than the standards applicable to plan investments generally. Therefore, if the above requirements are met, the selection of an ETI, or the engaging in an investment course of action intended to result in the selection of ETIs, will not violate section 404(a)(1)(A) and (B) and the exclusive purpose requirements of section 403.

Signed at Washington, DC, this 17th day of June 1994.

Olena Berg
Assistant Secretary,
Pension and Welfare Benefit Administration
U.S. Department of Labor.

Appendix G

Following are AFL-CIO Product Criteria from the Investment Product Review, as published by the AFL-CIO, October 1999. The criteria are reproduced herein without comment and with the AFL-CIO's expressed permission.

AFL-CIO PRODUCT CRITERIA FROM THE INVESTMENT PRODUCT REVIEW

Published by the AFL-CIO
October 1999

Appendix III. Product Criteria

CRITERIA FOR REAL ESTATE AND MORTGAGE INVESTMENTS

A. Introduction

The Real Estate Committee of the Investment Product Review Working Group will evaluate real estate and mortgage investment vehicles to see if they provide appropriate collateral benefits of work for unionized contractors and job creation in regions where pension plan beneficiaries live and work. The primary criteria for employee benefit funds is a competitive rate of return in the best interest of pension fund beneficiaries. Therefore, these criteria are not meant, nor should be used to evaluate, the investment performance, risk, diversification characteristics or other financial characteristics of investment products. Trustees should seek advice from qualified investment advisors on the financial merits of investment products. The committee will consider the collateral benefits of equity and debt investment products that own and finance real estate projects.* The committee will review products and investment firms that claim to offer collateral benefits to workers in addition to providing competitive rates of return. (For an updated investment product review focusing exclusively on private capital the reader is referred to the AFL-CIO publication *Private Capital 2002.)*

B. General Criteria

1) Collective Bargaining Agreement:
   All infrastructure, industrial, commercial and residential general contractors and subcontractors, including building service, information technology installation and maintenance providers, shall (1) be parties to a collective bargaining agreement with a labor organization affiliated with the AFL-CIO or, in the case of construction, with the Building and Construction Trades Department of the AFL-CIO; and (2) employ the workers of only such organizations to perform work within their respective jurisdictions.
   1.1) *Definition:* For the purpose of these proposed criteria, "contractors" and "subcontractors" shall include all of the work of developers; construction firms, including highway and other infrastructure; property managers; and providers of building services, maintenance, retrofitting, installation and improvements, including tenant improvements.
2) Project Labor Agreements:
   Project labor agreements between developers, contractors and AFL-CIO affiliate unions must be approved by the Building and Construction Trades Department of the AFL-CIO.
3) Responsible Contractor Policy:
   Direct investment and mortgage vehicles should include a Responsible Contractor Policy (RCP) covering real estate. The RCP should establish a preference for the selection of construction and building operations, service and maintenance contractors who pay their workers a fair wage, obey

*The subcommittee will not review individual real estate investments.

the law, and provide employer-paid family health insurance, pension benefits and training opportunities. RCPs are particularly relevant for vehicles investing in markets with historically lower rates of unionization. (See Section C below.)

4) Collateral Benefits:
The Working Group encourages investment firms and their products to contribute to economic development in a manner appropriate to particular asset classes. Vehicles engaging in commercial development should look to participate in community economic development efforts in working families' communities. Vehicles developing residential housing should participate in projects that benefit participants by investing in low- and moderate-income communities and housing for working people. Those firms creating collateral benefits while also adopting the criteria of this document will receive recognition for their efforts.

C. Additional Criteria for Certain Labor Market Conditions

1) Best Efforts:
The subcommittee recognizes that there are regions and markets with historically lower rates of unionization. In these situations, the subcommittee will give credit to vehicles that provide equity and mortgage financing to developers/owners who have made their best efforts to hire general contractors and subcontractors who are parties to a collective bargaining agreement with a labor organization affiliated with the AFL-CIO in the markets in which they operate, and who employ only workers represented by such organizations to perform work within their respective jurisdictions.

2) Firmwide Policies:
Investment firms that adopt consistent firmwide policies toward a goal of improving the quality of the construction, building operations and other relevant services received, including 100 percent union objectives on every project that the firm as a whole undertakes, will receive higher marks.

3) Neutrality and Card-Check:
Best efforts should also be made such that the maintenance and service work on properties owned or financed by the investment vehicle is performed by subcontractors with collective bargaining agreements with labor organizations affiliated with the AFL-CIO. In the event that there are no union contractors or subcontractors, the developer, contractor and sub-

contractors should adopt a stance of neutrality and card-check recognition should workers seek unionization in the markets in which they operate.

4) General Impact:
In addition to the policy stated above, investment vehicles should strive to increase employment and improve labor standards in the construction, building operations, maintenance and other relevant industries.

CRITERIA FOR U.S. PUBLIC EQUITIES INVESTMENTS

A. Introduction

Investment products that invest in public equities invest in stocks of companies that are traded on public market, primarily the New York and American Stock Exchanges and NASDAQ. Investment managers can choose among thousands of stocks and do so using a variety of strategies. Investment products that define themselves as worker-friendly in this area seek to persuade companies to pursue worker-friendly business strategies. Some actively managed funds also aim to change company behavior by only investing in companies that themselves are committed to worker-friendly business strategies. These criteria presume such funds will use all their rights as shareholders to persuade management to adopt such strategies.

The primary criteria for benefit fund investors is a competitive rate of return in the best interest of pension fund beneficiaries. Therefore, these criteria are not meant, nor should be used to, evaluate the investment performance, risk, diversification characteristics or other financial characteristics of investment products. Trustees should seek advice from qualified investment advisors on the financial merits of investment products. The purpose of these criteria is to provide general information as to the extent to which investment products that market themselves based in part on collateral benefits to worker beneficiaries provide such benefits.

B. General Criteria

1) Active Ownership:
Regardless of a particular product's investment philosophy, managers of investment products should make appropriate use of the rights that accrue to them as a result of their share

ownership when the authority to do so rests with the investment manager. Those rights include

- right to vote proxies;
- right to request and receive information from the company;
- right to communicate with and meet with company management and outside directors;
- right to propose shareholder resolutions;
- right to run proxy contests, including consent solicitations;
- right to nominate directors; and
- right to bring securities and derivative litigation either individually or as a lead plaintiff in a class action or a named plaintiff in derivative litigation.

2) Reporting:
Investment product managers should report regularly to their clients on their proxy voting and other active ownership activity, including the activity undertaken on the part of their larger portfolio, when relevant. Investment product managers should report regularly on proxy voting and other active ownership activity to the AFL-CIO.

3) Public Policy Positions:
Investment product managers and their parent institutions should not take public policy positions harmful to the retirement security of working families.

C. Additional Criteria

1) Screening Criteria:
Those investment products that seek to provide a pro-worker orientation through active investment management should develop screening criteria that assess companies' commitment to the high road to value that include the following factors:

- employer respect for human rights (including the right to organize and right to a living wage) of both U.S. and non-U.S. workers;
- company legal and regulatory compliance, including compliance with relevant labor and employment law;
- unionization level and state of labor-management relations, including commitment to prevailing wages in any given industry;

- employer commitment to and investment in workforce training and development;
- employer commitment to and investment in workforce diversity at all levels of the organization; and
- general company relations with stakeholders, with particular reference to communities, supporting a healthy public sector, environmental issues and downsizing.

2) Portfolio Review Process:
Screened investment products should have a portfolio review process that has the following elements:
    - process for consulting with worker representatives on both the investment product's general criteria and its specific holdings;
    - process for periodic review of portfolios in light of company behavior; and
    - process for gathering information from firms the investment product manager invests in or is considering investing in.

3) Company Communication:
Screened investment products should have a process for communicating with companies they invest in or divest from as to the reasons for including or excluding that company in their portfolio.

CRITERIA FOR PRIVATE CAPITAL INVESTMENTS

A. Introduction

The Private Capital Committee of the Investment Product Review Working Group will evaluate private capital investment vehicles to determine whether they provide advertised collateral benefits to workers. The primary criteria for employee benefit funds is a competitive rate of return in the best interests of pension fund beneficiaries. Therefore, these criteria are not meant, nor should they be used to evaluate the investment performance, risk, diversification characteristics or other financial characteristics of investment products. Trustees should seek advice from qualified investment advisors on the financial merits of investment products. The committee will consider equity and debt investment products. The committee will not review prospective private capital investments that may become components of private capital investment vehicles.

All funds must comply with all aspects of ERISA.

B. General Criteria

1) Principal History:
   Principals of the fund should have experience in the labor community and have a good track record with respect to workers' concerns. There is an additional benefit if the potential exists for a long-term strategic relationship with the principals.
2) Philosophy:
   The fund philosophy should include respect for workers' rights and a commitment to partnering with workers.
3) Advisory Board:
   The fund should have an advisory board with labor representation. This representation could include an invested Taft-Hartley fund designee.
4) Co-Investment:
   Where applicable, the fund should make co-investment opportunities available to fund investors.
5) Strategic Impact:
   If the fund operates in industries or geographical regions that would provide particular collateral benefits to workers, this will be considered a plus.
6) Monitoring and Verification:
   There should be an explicit mechanism for monitoring and verifying the fund's progress in meeting its objectives.
7) Dispute Resolution:
   There should be a mechanism for dispute resolution between the general partner and limited partners.
8) Governance and Control:
   A preference will be given to funds that have mechanisms for greater influence by the limited partners, such as a "no-fault divorce" or "opt-out" provision.

C. Criteria for Investments

1) Management History:
   Company management should have a positive track record with respect to partnership with workers or should be committed to a positive change in the company's approach to its employees.

2) Job Impact:
Investments should look to preserving or creating jobs. At a minimum, the investment or transaction should not result in job losses.*

3) Card-Check:
To the extent company employees are not represented by a union, card-check and neutrality agreements must be executed, with reasonable access to employees given.

CRITERIA FOR INTERNATIONAL INVESTMENT VEHICLES

A. Introduction

The International Committee of the Investment Product Review Working Group will evaluate international investment vehicles for screened products and direct targeted investments. These criteria, where applicable, should be read in conjunction with criteria for other product types, including public equities, private capital and real estate. The primary goal for employee benefit fund investment is a competitive rate of return in the best interest of pension fund beneficiaries. These criteria are not meant, and should not be used, to evaluate the investment performance, risk, diversification characteristics or other financial characteristics of investment products, as to which fiduciaries should seek advice from qualified investment advisors.

Moreover, these criteria are not designed to advise benefit funds as to whether to invest internationally. There are a variety of views on this question among benefit funds. The AFL-CIO's publication *"Pensions in Changing Capital Markets"* provides a broader discussion of the issues that benefit funds face in considering whether to invest internationally.

While these criteria take no positions on particular investment strategies, they do proceed from an assumption that there may be countries where labor rights are so systematically violated that no investment vehicle evaluating itself as worker-friendly could as a general matter invest in such countries. Even in such countries there might be specific situations in which investments

*This provision should not be used to penalize a fund involved in special situations, such as restructuring a troubled organized company, that may cause a temporary loss of jobs in order to turn the company around.

clearly support workers' rights and would be appropriate for a worker-friendly investment vehicle.

Globally, there are many types of corporate governance systems. This document does not promote nor advocate any one model of corporate governance. Rather, for holders of foreign equity and debt, it encourages active ownership as appropriate with each system.

B. Principal History

Principals of the investment vehicle should have experience in the labor community and have a good track record with respect to workers' concerns. There is an additional benefit if the potential exists for a long-term strategic relationship with the principals.

C. Criteria for Active Ownership and Client Reporting

1) Active Ownership:
   All international investment vehicles, regardless of their investment strategy, should make appropriate use of the rights that accrue to them as a result of share ownership or standing as a lender or other investor. It is understood that those rights will depend on the corporate and securities laws and practices in the relevant countries. There may be countries where the ability of investors to engage in active ownership is so limited as to require that worker-friendly investment vehicles engage in screening as discussed in section D.
2) Client Reporting:
   The investment vehicle should report at least annually on their active ownership activity to their clients.

D. Criteria for Country Selection

1) Selecting Countries to Invest In:
   The decision whether and how to invest in particular countries should be made in consultation with international organizations and trade unions that investigate and monitor fundamental workers' and human rights and global economic conditions to determine whether the country complies with (or violates) internationally recognized standards for workers' rights. At a minimum, these standards include the ILO Core Conventions that address
   - freedom of association,
   - the right to organize and bargain collectively,

- prohibition on the use of any form of forced or compulsory labor,
- a minimum age for the employment of children, and
- prohibition on discrimination in employment

as well as the UN Universal Declaration of Human Rights. To assist investment vehicles, the AFL-CIO maintains a Country Watch List identifying jurisdictions that do not have labor laws recognizing fundamental workers' rights, or that do not enforce fundamental workers' rights purportedly embodied in existing law.

2) Company Selection:

In countries that comply with internationally recognized workers' rights standards such as freedom of association, the right to organize and bargain collectively, prohibition on the use of any form of forced or compulsory labor, a minimum age for the employment of children and prohibition on discrimination in employment, certain companies may nonetheless be in gross violation of these standards. When the investment vehicle has reason to believe that a portfolio company violates internationally recognized workers' rights, it should (a) request the company to comply with the internationally recognized standards, (b) notify its clients about the potential violation and (c) work with the AFL-CIO to advance the passage of a resolution on ILO conventions on workplace rights at the next annual meeting of the portfolio company.

The investment vehicle should also regularly review the *U.S. Federal Register* to determine the list of products that the U.S. Departments of Labor, Treasury and State have a reasonable basis to believe might have been mined, produced or manufactured by forced or indentured child labor. When the investment vehicle has reason to believe that a portfolio company violates internationally recognized child labor standards, it should bring a potential violation of these standards for investigation to the U.S. Attorney General and Secretary of the Treasury based on the Executive Order "Prohibition of Acquisition of Products Produced by Forced or Indentured Child Labor."

3) Involvement of Organized Labor:

The investment vehicle should (a) consult with free and independent trade unions in the country at issue and in the U.S. to determine whether and how to invest in particular countries and (b) ensure that organized labor can actively participate in effectively monitoring and enforcing conditions and criteria associated with the investment in such country.

E. Criteria for Company-Specific Exclusionary Screening and Targeting Investments within Particular Countries

Those investment vehicles that seek to provide a pro-worker orientation through active investment management within particular countries, such as through screening or through direct foreign investment, should assess the following issues with respect to particular companies they invest in.

1) International Standards:
   Is the company in compliance with appropriate standards (not merely the bare minimum) for workers' rights? At a minimum, these standards include the ILO Core Conventions that address
   - freedom of association,
   - the right to organize and bargain collectively,
   - prohibition on the use of any form of forced or compulsory labor,
   - a minimum age for the employment of children, and
   - prohibition on discrimination in employment

   as well as the UN Universal Declaration of Human Rights. Is the company domiciled or operating in a country on the AFL-CIO Country Watch List, i.e., in a country that (a) does not recognize fundamental workers' rights in labor laws or (b) does not protect or enforce fundamental workers' rights existing in the law?
2) Impact on Beneficiaries and Participants:
   To what extent do business strategies of a potential portfolio company rely on either raising or lowering global labor standards within its industry? What are the consequences of a company's operations for the interests of workers whose pension assets or other assets are to be invested in the vehicle?
3) High Road to Value:
   To what extent does a company show a commitment to the high road to value that includes the following factors:
   - employer respect for human rights, including the right to organize and bargain collectively;
   - general company relations with stakeholders;

- employer compliance with relevant labor and employment law;
- unionization level and the state of labor-management relations;
- employer commitment to and investment in workforce training and development; and
- employer commitment to and investment in workforce diversity at all levels of the organization?

4) Effective Communication:
Screened investment vehicles should have a process for communicating with companies and countries they invest in or divest from as to the reasons for including or excluding that country or company in their portfolios.
5) Economic Progress:
The investment vehicle should maintain and follow systematic mechanisms (including transparency and communication of data) for ensuring that its investments in a particular industry or enterprise do not have any adverse economic impact on plan participants investing in the vehicle or on worker interests and organized labor in the jurisdiction where the investment is made, as well as in the United States. Investments should lead to sustainable economic progress that benefits (a) the target country and (b) the U.S. economy and U.S. workers.
6) Portfolio Review Process for Consulting with Organized Labor:
The investment vehicle should conduct a periodic review of the portfolio evaluating company behavior. Participants in the review process should include representatives of free and independent trade unions. Participants could also include union-designated worker representatives on both supervisory boards and work councils of portfolio companies if this is possible under country-specific labor and corporate laws.

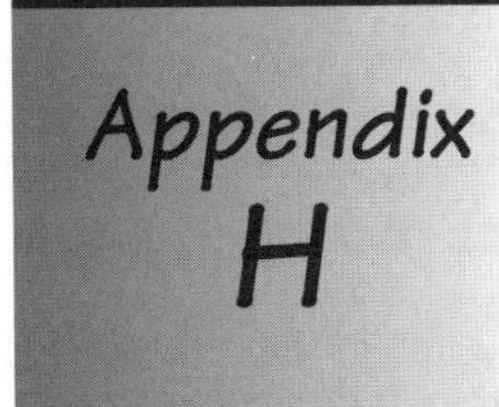

Department of Labor Interpretive Bulletin 94.2

Proxy Voting, dated July 21, 1994

38860 Federal Register/Vol. 59, No.145/Friday, July 29, 1994/Rules and Regulations

DEPARTMENT OF LABOR

Pension and Welfare Benefits Administration

29 CFR Part 2509

[Interpretive Bulletin 94.2]

Interpretive Bulletins Relating to the Employee Retirement Income Security Act of 1974

AGENCY: Department of Labor.

ACTION: Interpretive Bulletin.

SUMMARY: This document summarizes the Department of Labor's (the Department) statements with respect to the duty of employee benefit plan fiduciaries to vote proxies appurtenant to shares of corporate stock held by their plans. In these statements, the Department has explained, among other things, that the voting of proxies is a fiduciary act of plan asset management. This document also describes the Department's view of the legal standards imposed by sections 402(c)(3), 403(a) and 404(a)(1)(B) of part 4 of title I of the Employee Retirement Income Security Act of 1974 (ERISA) on the use of written statements of investment policy, including statements of proxy voting policy or guidelines. The bulletin makes clear that a named fiduciary who appoints an investment manager may, consistent with its fiduciary obligations, issue written statements of investment policy, including guidelines as to the voting of proxies by the investment manager. Moreover, an investment manager may be required to comply with such investment policies to the extent that any given investment decision (including a proxy voting decision) is consistent with the provisions of title I or title IV of ERISA. Finally, this document provides guidance concerning the appropriateness under ERISA of more active monitoring of corporate management by fiduciaries of plans that own corporate securities.

SUPPLEMENTARY INFORMATION: In order to provide a concise and ready reference to its interpretations of ERISA, the Department publishes its Interpretive Bulletins in the Rules and Regulations section of the Federal Register.

Published in this issue of the Federal Register is ERISA Interpretive Bulletin 94-2, which consolidates information contained in previous statements issued by the Department on the duty of employee benefit plan fiduciaries to vote proxies appurtenant to shares of corporate stock held by their plans. This document also explains that the maintenance of written statements of investment policy, including guidelines on voting proxies on securities held in plan investment portfolios is consistent with title I of ERISA and that compliance with such a policy would be required under ERISA to the extent that such compliance with respect to any given investment decision is consistent with the provisions of title I or title IV of ERISA. Finally, this document provides guidance concerning the appropriateness under ERISA of more active monitoring of corporate management by fiduciaries of plans that own corporate securities.

The Department is publishing this interpretive bulletin because it believes there is a need to publish in the Federal Register guidance that the Department has previously provided through letters regarding responsibilities of named fiduciaries, trustees and investment managers with respect to the voting of proxies. In addition, the Department believes that there is a need to publish further guidance on the maintenance of and compliance with written statements of investment policy issued by named fiduciaries to trustees and investment managers, and on the appropriateness of more active monitoring of corporate management by plan fiduciaries.

(Sec. 505, Pub. L. 93-406, 88 Stat. 894 (29 U.S.C. 1135).)

Background

(1) Department Letters on Proxy Voting

The Department has issued two letters publicly addressing questions that have arisen concerning the voting of proxies on shares of corporate stock held by plans. In the first of these letters, addressed to Helmuth Fandl, the Chairman of the Retirement Board of Avon Products, Inc. and dated Feb. 23, 1988 (hereinafter referred to as the "Avon letter"), the Department stated that the fiduciary act of managing plan assets that are shares of corporate stock includes the voting of proxies appurtenant to those shares of stock. As a result, the Department stated, the responsibility for voting proxies lies exclusively with the plan trustee unless either (1) the trustee is subject to the directions of a named fiduciary pursuant to ERISA Sec. 403(a)(1);[1] or (2) the power to manage, acquire or dispose of the relevant assets has been delegated by a named fiduciary to one or more investment managers pursuant to ERISA Sec. 403(a)(2).[2] Where the authority to manage plan assets has been delegated to an investment manager pursuant to ERISA Sec. 403(a)(2), no person other than the investment

---

1. ERISA Sec. 403(a)(1) provides that if the plan expressly provides that the trustee is subject to the direction of a named fiduciary who is not a trustee, the trustee shall be subject to proper directions which are made in accordance with the terms of the plan and which are not contrary to ERISA.

2. ERISA Sec. 403(a)(2) provides that if the authority to manage, acquire or dispose of assets of the plan is delegated to one or more investment managers pursuant to ERISA Sec. 402(c)(3), the trustee shall not have exclusive authority with respect to such assets. Coincident with the trustee's lack of exclusive authority, ERISA Sec. 405(d) relieves the trustee of the obligation to manage such assets and also limits the trustee's liability for acts and omissions of such investment managers.

ERISA Sec. 402(c)(3) provides:

(c) Any employee benefit plan may provide-

***

(3) that a person who is a named fiduciary with respect to control or management of the assets of the plan may appoint an investment manager or managers to manage (including the power to acquire and dispose of) any assets of a plan.

ERISA Sec. 3(38) defines "investment manager" as: any fiduciary (other than a trustee or named fiduciary, as defined in section 402(a)(2))–

(A) who has the power to manage, acquire, or dispose of any asset of the plan;

(B) who is (i) registered as an investment adviser under the Investment Advisers Act of 1940; (ii) is a bank, as defined in that Act; or (iii) is an insurance company qualified to perform services described in subparagraph (A) under the laws of more than one State; and

(C) has acknowledged in writing that he is a fiduciary with respect to the plan.

manager has authority to vote proxies appurtenant to such plan assets, except to the extent the named fiduciary has reserved to itself the right to direct a plan trustee regarding the voting of proxies. Although not specifically mentioned in the Avon letter, it follows that, in delegating investment management authority to an investment manager, the named fiduciary may reserve the right to direct a trustee regarding the voting of proxies relating to specified shares of stock or issues. Moreover, in delegating investment management authority to an investment manager, a named fiduciary may also reserve to another named fiduciary the right to direct the trustee regarding the voting of proxies, if the plan document provides for procedures for allocating fiduciary responsibilities among named fiduciaries. ERISA Sec. 405(c)(1).

In the Avon letter, the Department indicated that an investment manager would not be relieved of its fiduciary responsibility merely because it follows directions of some other person as to the voting of proxies, or delegates such responsibility to another person. The Department also indicated that ERISA Sec. 404(a)(1)(B) requires the named fiduciary appointing an investment manager to periodically monitor the activities of the investment manager with respect to the management of plan assets.[3] These activities would include, according to the Avon letter, decisions made and actions taken with regard to proxy voting. The letter pointed out that compliance with this requirement would in turn require proper documentation of the activities that are subject to monitoring, including accurate records as to the voting of proxies.

In a subsequent letter, addressed to Robert A.G. Monks of Institutional Shareholder Services, Inc. and dated January 23, 1990 (hereinafter referred to as the "ISSI letter"), the Department stated that an ERISA violation would occur if the investment manager is explicitly or implicitly assigned the authority to vote proxies appurtenant to certain plan-owned stock and the named fiduciary, trustee or any person other than the investment manager makes the decision on how to vote the same proxies. Thus, according to the letter, if the investment management contract expressly provides that the investment manager is not required to vote proxies, but does not expressly pre-

3. A named fiduciary who appoints an investment manager in accordance with ERISA Sec. 402(c)(3) may be liable for an act or omission of the investment manager to the extent that the named fiduciary violated ERISA Sec. 404(a)(1) in continuing the appointment. See 29 CFR Sec. 2509.75-8 (FR-17); *Brock v. Berman,* 673 F.Supp. 634, 637 (D. Mass. 1987).

clude the investment manager from voting the relevant proxies, the investment manager would nevertheless have the exclusive fiduciary responsibility for voting the proxies. In contrast, the letter points out, if either the plan document or the investment management contract expressly precludes the investment manager from voting proxies, the responsibility for voting proxies lies exclusively with the trustee. Consistent with the requirements of ERISA Sec. 403(a)(1), the trustee may, however, be subject to the directions of a named fiduciary if the plan so provides.

In the ISSI letter, the Department also stated that the fiduciary who has the authority to vote proxies has an obligation under ERISA to take reasonable steps under the circumstances to ensure that the proxies for which it is responsible are received. With respect to the named fiduciary's duty to monitor the proxy voting activities of an investment manager, the Department stated that the named fiduciary must be able to review not only the investment manager's proxy voting procedure, but also the actions taken in individual situations. Without such information, the named fiduciary would not be able to determine if the investment manager had fulfilled its fiduciary obligations in a manner that justified continuation of the appointment.

Although the Avon and ISSI letters were almost entirely concerned with procedural issues, the Department also reiterated its long-standing interpretation of ERISA Sec. 404(a)(1) that fiduciaries must act prudently and must not subordinate the interests of the participants and beneficiaries to unrelated objectives. In the context of proxy voting, the Department in the Avon letter noted that prudence requires that the fiduciary consider those factors that may affect the value of the plan's investment. Regarding the named fiduciary's obligation to monitor the activities of investment managers, the Department in the ISSI letter stated that the named fiduciary must act solely in the interest of the participants and beneficiaries and without regard to its relationship to the plan sponsor.

The statements in the document published today are intended to reiterate and supplement, rather than supersede, the contents of the Avon and ISSI letters.

The Avon and ISSI letters did not specifically address the voting of proxies on shares of foreign corporations, but it is the Department's view that the same principles apply. Namely, plan fiduciaries have a responsibility to vote proxies on issues that may affect the value of the shares in the plan's portfolio. There may, however, be additional costs to the plan in voting shares of foreign corporations, due to the variety of regulatory schemes and corporate practices in foreign countries with respect to proxy voting. The Department recognizes that the cost of exercising a vote on a particular proxy proposal could exceed any benefit that the plan could expect to gain in voting on the proposal. In this regard, the Department interprets ERISA Sec. 404(a)(1) to require the responsible plan fiduciary to weigh the costs and benefits of voting on proxy proposals relating to foreign securities and make an informed decision with respect to whether voting a given proxy proposal is prudent and solely in the interest of the plan's participants and beneficiaries. The fiduciary's decision should take into account the effect that the plan's vote, either by itself or together with other votes, is expected to have on the value of the plan's investment and whether this expected effect would outweigh the cost of voting. Moreover, a fiduciary, in deciding whether to purchase shares of a foreign corporation, should consider, among other things, whether the difficulty and expense of voting its shares is reflected in their market price.

(2) Written Statements of Investment Policy

A second purpose of this interpretive bulletin is to explain how positions taken by the Department in the Avon and ISSI letters apply to the use of written statements of investment policy, including statements of proxy voting policy. For purposes of this document, the term "statement of investment policy" means a written statement that provides the fiduciaries who are responsible for plan investments with guidelines or general instructions concerning various types or categories of investment management decisions, which may include proxy voting decisions. A statement of investment policy as discussed in this document would not encompass specific directions concerning the purchase or sale of a specific investment at a stated time or the voting of a specific proxy.

It is the Department's position that a named fiduciary's authority to issue statements of investment policy to investment managers is inherent in the named fiduciary's authority under the terms of the plan, pursuant to ERISA Sec. 402(c)(3), to appoint investment managers. The Department believes that statements of investment policy issued by a named fiduciary are part of the "documents and instruments governing the plan" within the meaning of ERISA Sec. 404(a)(1)(D). Thus, an investment manager to whom an investment policy applies would be required to comply with such policy to the extent permitted by ERISA Sec. 404(a)(1)(D). *See Dardaganis v. Grace Capital, Inc.*, 664 F.Supp. 105,108 (S.D.N.Y. 1987) (Noncompliance with investment guidelines by investment manager held to violate ERISA Sec.

404(a)(1)(D)); *Marshall v. Teamsters Local 282 Pension Trust Fund*, 458 F.Supp. 986, 990-991 (E.D.N.Y. 1978) (Investment made in excess of trust percentage restrictions held to violate ERISA Sec. 404(a)(1)(D).) Pursuant to this section, a fiduciary must discharge his or her duties with respect to the plan in accordance with the documents and instruments governing the plan insofar as such documents and instruments are consistent with the provisions of title I and title IV of ERISA.

It is the Department's view that statements of investment policy should, in general, be distinguished from directions made by a named fiduciary to a trustee pursuant to ERISA Sec. 403(a)(1). As used in this interpretive bulletin, a statement of investment policy provides general instructions or guidelines to be applied in all applicable situations, such as identification of acceptable classes or types of investments, limitations on investment categories as a percentage of the plan's portfolio, or generally applicable guidelines regarding voting positions in proxy contests (for example, criteria regarding the support of or opposition to recurring issues, such as proposals to create classified boards of directors or to provide for cumulative voting for board members), rather than specific instructions as to the purchase or sale of a specific investment at a specific time or specific instructions to vote specific plan proxies a certain way.

The plan document or trust agreement may expressly provide a statement of investment policy to guide the trustee or may authorize a named fiduciary to issue a statement of investment policy applicable to a trustee. Thus, in cases where the named fiduciary issues a statement of investment policy to the plan trustee, the trustee's obligation to follow the investment policy would also be analyzed under ERISA Sec. 404(a)(1)(D). Although, in the absence of proper directions under ERISA Sec. 403(a)(1) or of an investment manager appointed pursuant to ERISA Sec. 402(c)(3), the trustee or trustees of a plan have exclusive authority and discretion to manage and control plan assets, the trustees, like other fiduciaries, are also required to comply with the governing instruments of the plan insofar as such documents are consistent with titles I and IV of ERISA. Accordingly, a trustee to whom a statement of investment policy applies would be required to comply with such policy unless, for example, it would be imprudent to do so in a given instance.

Maintenance of statements of investment policy is not specifically required under ERISA. The Department, however, believes that such statements serve a legitimate purpose in many plans by helping to assure that investments are made in a rational manner and are designed to further the purposes of the plan and its funding policy.[4] A statement of investment policy that includes a statement of proxy voting policy may increase the likelihood that proxy voting decisions are consistent with other aspects of the investment policy. Moreover, in plans with multiple investment managers, a written proxy voting policy may also prevent (where such prevention is desirable) the managers from taking conflicting positions on a given voting decision. One purpose of this interpretive bulletin is to clarify that maintenance of a statement of investment policy, including a statement of proxy voting policy, is consistent with the fiduciary duty of prudence under ERISA Sec. 404(a)(1)(B).[5] In the view of the Department, a named fiduciary's determination of the terms of a statement of investment policy is an exercise of fiduciary responsibility and, as such, statements may need to take into account factors such as the plan's funding policy and its liquidity needs as well as issues of prudence, diversification and other fiduciary requirements of ERISA.

Another issue that has arisen with respect to statements of investment policy, including statements of proxy voting policy, concerns investment managers of pooled investment accounts holding the assets of more than one employee benefit plan. Such managers may be subject, for example, to a proxy voting policy from one plan that conflicts with the policy from another plan. It is the Department's view that investment managers of pooled accounts who are required to comply with multiple investment policies, including proxy voting policies, must to the extent possible, comply with each policy (assuming compliance with each policy would be consistent with ERISA Sec. 404(a)(1)(D)). If investment policies conflict, it may be necessary to

---

4. ERISA Sec. 402(b)(1) requires every plan to "provide a procedure for establishing and carrying out a funding policy and method consistent with the objectives of the plan and the requirements of title 1." The ERISA Conference Report indicates that the purpose of this requirement is to–

enable the plan fiduciaries to determine the plan's short- and long-run financial needs and communicate these requirements to the appropriate persons. For example, with a retirement plan it is expected that under this procedure the persons who manage the plan will determine whether the plan has a short-run need for liquidity, (e.g., to pay benefits) or whether liquidity is a long-run goal and investment growth is a more current need. This in turn is to be communicated to the persons responsible for investments so that investment policy can be appropriately coordinated with plan needs.

H.R. Rep. No. 93-1280, 93rd Cong., 2nd Sess. at 297 (1974).

5. ERISA Sec. 404(a)(1)(B) provides that a plan fiduciary shall discharge his or her duties "with the care, skill, prudence and diligence under the circumstances then prevailing that a prudent man acting in a like capacity and familiar with such matters would use in the conduct of an enterprise of a like character and with like aims."

vote proxies to reflect each policy in proportion to the respective plan's interest in the pooled account, unless in the particular situation voting in such a manner would be imprudent or otherwise inconsistent with applicable law. Nothing in ERISA, however, prevents such an investment manager from maintaining a single investment policy, including a proxy voting policy, and requiring all participating investors to give their assent to such policy as a condition of investing in the pooled account. As with policies originated by named fiduciaries, a statement of investment policy issued by an investment manager and adopted by the participating plans would be regarded as an instrument governing the participating plans, and compliance with such a policy would be governed by ERISA Sec. 404(a)(1)(D).

(3) Shareholder Activism

The Department believes that, where proxy voting decisions may have an effect on the value of the plan's underlying investment, plan fiduciaries should make proxy voting decisions with a view to enhancing the value of the shares of stock, taking into account the period over which the plan expects to hold such shares. Similarly, in certain situations it may be appropriate for a fiduciary to engage in activities intended to monitor or influence corporate management if the fiduciary expects that such activities are likely to enhance the value of the plan's investment.

Although, within the corporate structure, the primary responsibility to oversee corporate management falls on the corporation's board of directors, the Department believes that active monitoring and communication with corporate management is consistent with a fiduciary's obligations under ERISA where the responsible fiduciary concludes that there is a reasonable expectation that such activities by the plan alone, or together with other shareholders, are likely to enhance the value of the plan's investment, after taking into account the costs involved. Such a reasonable expectation may exist in various circumstances, for example, where plan investments in corporate stock are held as long-term investments or where a plan may not be able to easily dispose such an investment.[6]

---

6. In this regard, the Department believes that this standard would not be different for portfolios designed to match the performance of market indexes (sometimes referred to as "index funds"). In such funds, the investments are often held on a long-term basis and the prudent exercise of proxy voting rights or other forms of corporate monitoring of communication may be the only method available for attempting to enhance the value of the portfolio.

Active monitoring and communication activities may concern a variety of issues, such as the independence and expertise of candidates for the corporation's board of directors or assuring that the board has sufficient information to carry out its responsibility to monitor management. Other issues might include consideration of the appropriateness of executive compensation, the corporation's policy regarding mergers and the extent of debt financing and capitalization, the nature of long-term business plans, the corporation's investment in training to develop its work force, other workplace practices and financial and non-financial measures of corporate performance. Active monitoring and communication may be carried out through a variety of methods including by means of correspondence and meetings with corporate management as well as by exercising the legal rights of a shareholder.

Given the absence of guidance published by the Department on statements of investment policy in general and on proxy voting guidelines in particular, the Department has determined that publication of this document would be beneficial to practitioners in the field of employee benefit plan investments.

List of Subjects in 29 CFR Part 2509

Employee benefit plans, Pensions.

For the reasons set forth in the preamble, Part 2509 of Title 29 of the Code of Federal Regulations is amended as follows:

Part 2509–INTERPRETIVE BULLETINS RELATING TO THE EMPLOYEE RETIREMENT INCOME SECURITY ACT OF 1974

1. The authority citation for Part 2509 continues to read as follows:

Authority: 29 U.S.C. 1135. Section 2509.75-1 is also issued under 29 U.S.C. 1114. Sections 2509.75-10 and 2509.75-2 are also issued under 29 U.S.C. 1052, 1053, 1054. Secretary of Labor's Order No. 1-87 (52 FR 13139).

2. Part 2509 is amended by adding a new Sec. 2509.94-2 to read as follows:

Sec. 2509.94-2–Interpretive Bulletin relating to written statements of investment policy, including proxy voting policy or guidelines.

This interpretive bulletin sets forth the Department of Labor's (the Department) interpretation of sections 402, 403 and 404 of the Employee Retirement Income Security Act of 1974 (ERISA) as those sections apply to voting of proxies on securities held in employee benefit plan investment portfolios and the maintenance of and compliance with statements of investment policy, including proxy voting policy. In addition, this interpretive bulletin provides guidance on the appropriateness under ERISA of active monitoring of corporate management by plan fiduciaries.

(1) Proxy Voting

The fiduciary act of managing plan assets that are shares of corporate stock includes the voting of proxies appurtenant to those shares of stock. As a result, the responsibility for voting proxies lies exclusively with the plan trustee except to the extent that either (1) the trustee is subject to the directions of a named fiduciary pursuant to ERISA Sec. 403(a)(1); or (2) the power to manage, acquire or dispose of the relevant assets has been delegated by a named fiduciary to one or more investment managers pursuant to ERISA Sec. 403(a)(2). Where the authority to manage plan assets has been delegated to an investment manager pursuant to Sec. 403(a)(2), no person other than the investment manager has authority to vote proxies appurtenant to such plan assets except to the extent that the named fiduciary has reserved to itself (or to another named fiduciary so authorized by the plan document) the right to direct a plan trustee regarding the voting of proxies. In this regard, a named fiduciary, in delegating investment management authority to an investment manager, could reserve to itself the right to direct a trustee with respect to the voting of all proxies or reserve to itself the right to direct a trustee as to the voting of only those proxies relating to specified assets or issues.

If the plan document or investment management agreement provides that the investment manager is not required to vote proxies, but does not expressly preclude the investment manager from voting proxies, the investment manager would have exclusive responsibility for voting proxies. Moreover, an investment manager would not be relieved of its own fiduciary responsibilities by following directions of some other person regarding the voting of proxies, or by delegating such responsibility to another person. If, however, the plan document or the investment management contract expressly precludes the investment manager from voting proxies, the responsibility for voting proxies would lie exclusively with the trustee. The trustee, however, consistent with the requirements of ERISA Sec. 403(a)(1), may be subject to the directions of a named fiduciary if the plan so provides.

The fiduciary duties described at ERISA Sec. 404(a)(1)(A) and (B), require that, in voting proxies, the responsible fiduciary consider those factors that may affect the value of the plan's investment and not subordinate the interests of the participants and beneficiaries in their retirement income to unrelated objectives. These duties also require that the named fiduciary appointing an investment manager periodically monitor the activities of the investment manager with respect to the management of plan assets, including decisions made and actions taken by the investment manager with regard to proxy voting decisions. The named fiduciary must carry out this responsibility solely in the interest of the participants and beneficiaries and without regard to its relationship to the plan sponsor.

It is the view of the Department that compliance with the duty to monitor necessitates proper documentation of the activities that are subject to monitoring. Thus, the investment manager or other responsible fiduciary would be required to maintain accurate records as to proxy voting. Moreover, if the named fiduciary is to be able to carry out its responsibilities under ERISA Sec. 404(a) in determining whether the investment manager is fulfilling its fiduciary obligations in investing plans assets in a manner that justifies the continuation of the management appointment, the proxy voting records must enable the named fiduciary to review not only the investment manager's voting procedure with respect to plan-owned stock, but also to review the actions taken in individual proxy voting situations.

The fiduciary obligations of prudence and loyalty to plan participants and beneficiaries require the responsible fiduciary to vote proxies on issues that may affect the value of the plan's investment. Although the same principles apply for proxies appurtenant to shares of foreign corporations, the Department recognizes that in voting such proxies, plans may, in some cases, incur additional costs. Thus, a fiduciary should consider whether the plan's vote, either by itself or together with the votes of other shareholders, is expected to have an effect on the value of the plan's investment that will outweigh the cost of voting. Moreover, a fiduciary, in deciding whether to purchase shares of a foreign corporation, should consider whether the difficulty and expense in voting the shares is reflected in their market price.

(2) Statements of Investment Policy

The maintenance by an employee benefit plan of a statement of investment policy designed to further the purposes of the plan and its funding policy is consistent with the fiduciary obligations set forth in ERISA Sec. 404(a)(1)(A) and (B). Since the fiduciary act of managing plan assets that are shares of corporate stock includes the voting of proxies appurtenant to those shares of stock, a statement of proxy voting policy would be an important part of any comprehensive statement of investment policy. For purposes of this document, the term "statement of investment policy" means a written statement that provides the fiduciaries who are responsible for plan investments with guidelines or general instructions concerning various types or categories of investment management decisions, which may include proxy voting decisions. A statement of investment policy is distinguished from directions as to the purchase or sale of a specific investment at a specific time or as to voting specific plan proxies.

In plans where investment management responsibility is delegated to one or more investment managers appointed by the named fiduciary pursuant to ERISA Sec. 402(c)(3), inherent in the authority to appoint an investment manager, the named fiduciary responsible for appointment of investment managers has the authority to condition the appointment on acceptance of a statement of investment policy. Thus, such a named fiduciary may expressly require, as a condition of the investment management agreement, that an investment manager comply with the terms of a statement of investment policy which sets forth guidelines concerning investments and investment courses of action which the investment manager is authorized or is not authorized to make. Such investment policy may include a policy or guidelines on the voting of proxies on shares of stock for which the investment manager is responsible. In the absence of such an express requirement to comply with an investment policy, the authority to manage the plan assets placed under the control of the investment manager would lie exclusively with the investment manager. Although a trustee may be subject to the directions of a named fiduciary pursuant to ERISA Sec. 403(a)(1), an investment manager who has authority to make investment decisions, including proxy voting decisions, would never be relieved of its fiduciary responsibility if it followed directions as to specific investment decisions from the named fiduciary or any other person.

Statements of investment policy issued by a named fiduciary authorized to appoint investment managers would be part of the "documents and instruments governing the plan" within the meaning of ERISA Sec. 404(a)(1)(D). An investment manager to whom such investment policy applies would be required to comply with such policy, pursuant to ERISA Sec. 404(a)(1)(D) insofar as the policy directives or guidelines are consistent with titles I and IV of ERISA. Therefore, if, for example, compliance with the guidelines in a given instance would be imprudent, then the investment manager's failure to follow the guidelines would not violate ERISA Sec. 404(a)(1)(D). Moreover, ERISA Sec. 404(a)(1)(D) does not shield the investment manager from liability for imprudent actions taken in compliance with a statement of investment policy.

The plan document or trust agreement may expressly provide a statement of investment policy to guide the trustee or may authorize a named fiduciary to issue a statement of investment policy applicable to a trustee. Where a plan trustee is subject to an investment policy, the trustee's duty to comply with such investment policy would also be analyzed under ERISA Sec. 404(a)(1)(D). Thus, the trustee would be required to comply with the statement of investment policy unless, for example, it would be imprudent to do so in a given instance.

Maintenance of a statement of investment policy by a named fiduciary does not relieve the named fiduciary of its obligations under ERISA Sec. 404(a) with respect to the appointment and monitoring of an investment manager or trustee. In this regard, the named fiduciary appointing an investment manager must periodically monitor the investment manager's activities with respect to management of the plan assets. Moreover, compliance with ERISA Sec. 404(a)(1)(B) would require maintenance of proper documentation of the activities of the investment manager and of the named fiduciary of the plan in monitoring the activities of the investment manager. In addition, in the view of the Department, a named fiduciary's determination of the terms of a statement of investment policy is an exercise of fiduciary responsibility and, as such, statements may need to take into account factors such as the plan's funding policy and its liquidity needs as well as issues of prudence, diversification and other fiduciary requirements of ERISA.

An investment manager of a pooled investment vehicle that holds assets of more than one employee benefit plan may be subject to a proxy voting policy of one plan that conflicts with the proxy voting policy of another plan. Compliance with ERISA Sec. 404(a)(1)(D) would require such investment manager to reconcile, insofar as possible, the conflicting policies (assuming compliance with each policy would be consistent with ERISA Sec. 404(a)(1)(D)) and, if necessary and to the extent permitted by applicable law, vote the relevant proxies to reflect such policies in proportion to each plan's interest in the pooled investment vehicle. If, however, the investment manager determines that compliance with conflicting voting policies would violate ERISA Sec. 404(a)(1)(D) in a particular instance, for example, by being imprudent or not solely in the interest of plan participants, the investment manager would be required to ignore the voting policy that would violate ERISA Sec. 404(a)(1)(D) in that instance. Such an investment manager may, however, require participating investors to accept the investment manager's own investment policy statement, including any statement of proxy voting policy, before they are allowed to invest. As with investment policies originating from named fiduciaries, a policy initiated by an investment manager and adopted by the participating plans would be regarded as an instrument governing the participating plans, and the investment manager's compliance with such a policy would be governed by ERISA Sec. 404(a)(1)(D).

(3) Shareholder Activism

An investment policy that contemplates activities intended to monitor or influence the management of corporations in which the plan owns stock is consistent with a fiduciary's obligations under ERISA where the responsible fiduciary concludes that there is a reasonable expectation that such monitoring or communication with management, by the plan alone or together with other shareholders, is likely to enhance the value of the plan's investment in the corporation, after taking into account the costs involved. Such a reasonable expectation may exist in various circumstances, for example, where plan investments in corporate stock are held as long-term investments or where a plan may not be able to easily dispose such an investment. Active monitoring and communication activities would generally concern such issues as the independence and expertise of candidates for the corporation's board of directors and assuring that the board has sufficient information to carry out its responsibility to monitor management. Other issues may include such matters as consideration of the appropriateness of executive compensation, the corporation's policy regarding mergers and acquisitions, the extent of debt financing and capitalization, the nature of long-term business plans, the corporation's investment in training to develop its work force, other workplace practices and financial and non-financial measures of corporate performance. Active monitoring and communication may be carried out through a variety of methods including by means of correspondence and meetings with corporate management as well as by exercising the legal rights of a shareholder.

Signed at Washington, DC, this 21st day of July, 1994.

E. Olena Berg
Assistant Secretary
Pension and Welfare Benefits Administration
U.S. Department of Labor.

Appendix I

ERISA Fiduciary Duty, Proxy Voting Guidelines and Shareholder Activism: An Overview

Provided by Ian D. Lanoff and Susan I. Brown
Groom Law Group, Chartered

General Fiduciary Duties Under ERISA

The Duty of Loyalty

Section 404(a)(1)(A) of ERISA requires a fiduciary to discharge its duties with respect to a plan "solely in the interest" of plan participants and beneficiaries and for the "exclusive purpose" of providing plan benefits and defraying reasonable expenses of the plan administration. See 29 U.S.C. §1104(a)(1)(A). The Second Circuit interprets this duty of loyalty to require that a fiduciary's decision be made "with an eye single to the interests of the participants and beneficiaries." *Donovan v. Bierwirth,* 680 F.2d 263, 271 (2nd Cir. 1982). Thus, the court says fiduciaries must avoid placing themselves in a position where their acts in another official capacity will impede their functioning with the total loyalty required of them as pension plan fiduciaries. Id. at 271. In determining whether a plan fiduciary has breached its duty of loyalty due to an alleged conflict of interest, the courts have suggested that a conflict may be so substantial that "it [is] virtually impossible for fiduciaries to discharge their duties with an 'eye single' to the interests of the beneficiaries, and the fiduciaries may need to step aside, at least temporarily [.]" *Leigh v. Engle,* 727 F.2d 113, 125 (7th Cir. 1984); see also *Donovan v. Bierwirth,* 680 F.2nd 263, 271 (2nd Cir. 1982).

The Department of Labor (DOL) has construed the requirements of the duty of loyalty as "prohibiting a fiduciary from subordinating the interests of participants and beneficiaries in their retirement income to unrelated objectives." See, e.g., Interpretive Bulletin 94-2 (IB 94-2), 29 CFR §2509.94-2 (July 29, 1994). A fiduciary may pursue other secondary or incidental objectives so long as they do not take precedence over the interests of participants and beneficiaries in their retirement income. See, e.g., Department of Labor Opinion Letter (July 8, 1988) (ULLICO letter). See also *Donovan v. Walton,* 609 F.Supp. 1221 (S.D.Fla. 1985), *aff'd per curiam sub nom Brock v. Walton,* 794 F.2d 586 (11th Cir. 1986), *rehearing denied without opinion,* 802 F.2d 1399 (11th Cir. 1986).

Where a fiduciary's actions are challenged as breaching its duty of loyalty, "[g]ood faith is not a defense." *Leigh v. Engle,* 727 F.2d at 124. Rather, as a threshold matter, courts require that the fiduciary demonstrate that the actions were taken only after a thorough and independent examination of the alternatives. See *Metzler v. Graham,* 112 F.3d 207, 213 (5th Cir. 1997); *Leigh v. Engle,* 727 F.2d 113, 125-6 (7th Cir. 1984); *Donovan v. Bierwirth,* 538 F.Supp. 463 (E.D.N.Y 1981), *aff'd as modified,* 680 F.2d 263, 272-275 (2nd Cir. 1982), *cert. denied,* 459 U.S. 1069. Therefore, a fiduciary's decision to take an action that it believes to be in the best interests of participants and beneficiaries, but which also benefits the company, will not violate the fiduciary's duty of loyalty if a prudent investigation with regard to the decision was conducted. See *Bussian v. RJR Nabisco, Inc.,* 223 F.3d 286, 302 (5th Cir. 2000). The duty of loyalty thus overlaps with a second fiduciary duty under ERISA–the duty of prudence.

The Duty of Prudence

Section 404(a)(1)(B) requires that a fiduciary act with the "care, skill, prudence, and diligence" of a similarly situated prudent person knowledgeable in such matters. See 29 U.S.C. §1104(a)(1)(B). While modeled on the "prudent person" standard that has traditionally governed trusts under the common law, this prudent person standard is stricter in that the fiduciary is required to act as one "familiar with such matters," and is thus also called the "prudent expert" standard.

In determining whether a fiduciary has breached its duty of prudence, courts, as in *Donovan v. Bierwirth,* 538 F.Supp. 463 (E.D.N.Y. 1981), *aff'd as modified,* 680 F.2d 263 (2nd Cir. 1982), *cert. denied,* 459 U.S. 1069 (1982), will focus on whether a fiduciary has conducted a thorough and independent investigation of the merits of its action and of possible alternatives. In *Donovan v. Bierwirth,* trustees for the Grumman Corporation Pension Plan, who were also officers of Grumman, used plan funds to purchase a large block of Grumman stock during a control contest to help thwart a takeover by LTV. DOL brought an action against the trustees arguing that the trustees' purchase of the stock was a per se violation of their duty of loyalty because of their conflict of interest. The court rejected DOL's argument. Instead, applying the prudence standard, the court focused on the extent to which the fiduciaries followed procedures designed to ensure that the decisions they reached would be in the best interests of participants. Under this analysis, the court found the trustees had breached their fiduciary duty by failing to conduct an "independent," "intensive," and "scrupulous" examination both of whether the plan would have benefited more by tendering its stock to LTV and of how to protect the plan if the LTV tender offer succeeded. See *Bierwirth,* 538 F.Supp. at 470. Furthermore, the court's decision indicates that to comply with ERISA's "prudent expert" standard, a fiduciary that lacks the skill and knowledge necessary to make prudent investment decisions regarding plan assets has an affirmative duty to seek expert independent assistance. See *Bierwirth,* 680 F.2d at 272, 274.

A joint letter by DOL and the Department of the Treasury further clarifies a fiduciary's duty of prudence regarding the weighing of long-term versus short-term benefits in the context of making decisions about mergers and tender offers. See Joint Department of Labor/ Department of the Treasury Statement of Pension Investments Jan. 31, 1989, reprinted in 16 Pens. Rep. (BNA) 215. The joint announcement states that, even though a tender offer represents a premium over the prevailing market price for the target company's stock, a plan fiduciary is not automatically required to tender shares held by the plan. Instead, a fiduciary's duty to act prudently and in the "best economic interest" of the plan participants and beneficiaries requires evaluating the tender offer on its merits:

> [I]t would be appropriate to weigh a tender offer against the underlying intrinsic value of the target company and the likelihood of that value being realized by current management or by a possible subsequent tender offer. It would also be proper to weigh the long-term value of the company against the value presented by the tender offer and the ability to invest the proceeds elsewhere. In making these determinations, the long-term business plan of the target company's management would be relevant.
>
> Id. at 215.

The Duty to Act in Accordance With Plan Documents

Section 404(a)(1)(D) requires that a fiduciary act "in accordance with the documents and instruments governing the plan insofar as such documents and instruments are consistent with the provisions of [Title I and Title IV of ERISA]." 29 U.S.C. §1104(a)(1)(D). Thus, while in general a fiduciary must act in accordance with a provision of a plan document, the fiduciary breaches its fiduciary duty by acting in accordance with a provision that violates the requirements of ERISA. See *Central States Pension Fund v. Central Transport, Inc.*, 472 U.S. 559, 568 (1985); *Martin v. NationsBank of Georgia, N.A.*, 1993 WL 345606 (N.D.Ga. Apr. 6, 1993).

In some cases, courts have held that a fiduciary may in some circumstances decline to follow a plan provision that does not violate ERISA without violating its fiduciary duty under Section 404(a)(1)(D). For example, in *Central Trust Co. v. American Avents Corp.*, 771 F.Supp. 871 (S.D.Ohio 1989), the court upheld an employee stock ownership plan (ESOP) trustee's decision to ignore a plan provision requiring that plan participants vote on tender offers and to accept a tender offer based on the determination that acceptance was in the economic interest of plan participants. See also *Herman v. NationsBank Trust Co.*, 126 F.3d 1354 (11th Cir. 1997).

Prohibited Transactions

Section 406 of ERISA, 29 U.S.C. §1106, prohibits a plan fiduciary from engaging in transactions "in which the potential for misuse of plan assets is particularly great." *Leigh v. Engle*, 727 F.2d 113, 123 (7th Cir. 1984). These per se prohibited transaction rules are intended to simplify the enforcement of ERISA's more general fiduciary obligations by barring those transactions in which the conflicting interests of the parties dealing with the plan could lead to self-dealing. Id. at 123.

While Section 406 addresses a broad range of transactions, the provisions most relevant to ascertaining a fiduciary's duties in the proxy voting and shareholder activism contexts are:

(a) Except as provided in Section 408 of this title:

  (1) A fiduciary with respect to a plan shall not cause the plan to engage in a transaction, if he knows or should know that such a transaction constitutes a direct or indirect . . .

    (D) transfer to, or use by or for the benefits of, a party in interest, of any assets of the plan . . .

(b) A fiduciary with respect to a plan shall not–
   (1) deal with the assets of the plan in his own interest or for his own account;
   (2) in his individual or any other capacity act in any transaction involving the plan on behalf of a party (or represent a party) whose interests are adverse to the interests of the plan or the interests of its participants or beneficiaries, or
   (3) receive any consideration for his own personal account from any party dealing with such plan in connection with a transaction involving the assets of the plan . . .

Courts have differed in how broadly these provisions should be interpreted. As noted above in *Donovan v. Bierwirth,* the Second Circuit ruled that none of the above-mentioned "prohibited transaction" provisions applied to a plan fiduciary's use of an employee plan's assets to defend the employer corporation from a hostile tender offer even though the fiduciary was an executive officer of the employer corporation. The court reasoned:

> We see no reason to think Congress intended the expansive interpretation of the various specific provisions of §406 . . . in light of the inclusion of the sweeping requirements of prudence and loyalty contained in §404.

Donovan v. Bierwirth, 680 F.2d at 270. However, in other contexts, the Second Circuit has interpreted the requirements of Section 406 more broadly. See *Lowen v. Tower Asset Management, Inc.,* 829 F.2d 1209 (2d Cir. 1987).

In contrast to the Second Circuit's opinion in *Donovan v. Bierwirth,* the Seventh Circuit has ruled that at least some Section 406 requirements should be interpreted broadly:

> [W]e believe that the protective provisions of Section 406(a)(1)(D) and (b)(1) should be read broadly in light of Congress' concern with the welfare of plan beneficiaries. We read those provisions dealing with the use of plan assets for the benefit of "parties in interest" and plan fiduciaries as a gloss on the duty of loyalty required by Section 40. . . . We do not believe that Congress intended the language "use by or for the benefit of a party in interest," §406(a)(1)(D), and "deal . . . in his own interest." §406(b)(1) to be interpreted narrowly.

Leigh v. Engle, 727 F.2d 113, 126 (7th Cir. 1984). As a result, the court found that Section 406(a)(1)(D) could cover the actions of a plan fiduciary that bought shares in a target corporation to assist either the target's management or the raider in a control contest. See *Leigh,* 727 F.2d at 126 (citing *Dimond v. Retirement Plan,* 582 F.Supp. 892 (W.D.Pa. 1983)). The court also indicated that Section 406(b)(1) could cover a plan fiduciary's investment activities in a corporate control contest, particularly when the fiduciary is also an officer of the target or raider corporation or of a closely related entity. Id. at 127 (citing *Freund v. Marshall & Ilsley Bank,* 485 F.Supp. 629, 637 (W.D.Wis. 1979)). Moreover, the court read broadly the term "interest" in Section 406(b)(1) to include not only direct financial interest, but also such interests as holding onto one's job or maintaining good relations with a customer company. Id. at 127.

ERISA's Fiduciary Duties in the Proxy Voting Context

Introduction

While ERISA itself does not mention proxy voting, the Department of Labor has made clear that ERISA's fiduciary principles apply in the proxy voting context. DOL clearly stated this position in a 1994 interpretive bulletin– "the fiduciary act of managing plan assets that are shares of corporate stock includes the voting of proxies appurtenant to those shares of stock." See Interpretive Bulletin 94-2 (IB 94-2), 29 CFR §2509.94-2 (July 29, 1994) (restating positions taken in its Information Letter to H. Fandl (Feb. 23, 1988) (the Avon letter) and its Information Letter to R. Monks (Jan. 23, 1990) (the Monks letter)).

DOL also made clear in IB 94-2 that ERISA's general fiduciary standards of prudence and loyalty apply to proxy voting wherever such proxy votes have an impact on the value of shares held by a plan. See IB 94-2(1). This position reinforces statements by DOL representatives made prior to the release of IB 94-2:

> Proxy votes that can affect the economic value of plan investment unquestionably involve the exercise of fiduciary responsibility. As a result, a fiduciary who manages a portfolio has a duty to evaluate issues that can have an impact on the economic value of the stock in the portfolio and to vote on those issues. These votes must be prudent and consistent with the fiduciary standards of ERISA (solely in the interest of plan participants and their beneficiaries, and for the exclusive purpose of paying benefits . . .).

Speech by David M. Walker, former Assistant Secretary of Labor for Pension and Welfare Benefits, Corporate Governance and Related Issues (Feb. 17, 1988) at 3. Furthermore, "a fiduciary who fails to vote, or casts a vote without considering the impact of the question or votes blindly with management would appear to violate his duty [of loyalty.]" Speech of Assistant Secretary David Ball before the Financial Executives Institute (Jan. 23, 1990) at 14-15; see also, Department of Labor, Proxy Project Report (Mar. 2, 1989) at 8.

DOL further states in IB 94-2 that the proper analysis to be undertaken by a plan fiduciary in voting on proxy proposals is a cost/benefit analysis. See IB94-2(1). DOL provides an example of the cost/benefit prudence analysis as applied to the voting of proxies appurtenant to foreign securities. With regard to the voting of these proxies, DOL notes that it may be costly and time-consuming, and that those factors may be considered in deciding whether to vote such proxies. DOL has not, therefore, adopted an approach that necessarily requires a fiduciary to vote proxies in all cases regardless of cost, but instead focuses on whether the voting of proxies "may affect the value of the plan's investment." IB 94-2(1).

The Investment Manager Has the Fiduciary Duty to Vote Proxies Under the Investment Manager Exception

Section 403(a) of ERISA requires that all plan assets be held in trust by one or more trustees that are either named in the plan documents or appointed by a named fiduciary. See 29 U.S.C. §1103(a). These trustees shall have exclusive authority and discretion to manage and control these assets, with two exceptions: (1) when the plan expressly provides that they are subject to the direction of a named fiduciary who is not a trustee, in which case the trustees shall be subject to proper directions of such fiduciary which are made in accordance with the plan's terms and do not violate ERISA; or (2) when the authority to manage, acquire, or dispose of assets of the plan is delegated to one or more investment managers. See id. Section 3(38) of ERISA defines "investment manager" as any fiduciary, other than a trustee or named fiduciary, who (1) has the power to manage, acquire, or dispose of any asset of a plan; (2) is a registered investment advisor under the Investment Advisers Act of 1940, a bank, or an insurance company; and (3) has acknowledged in writing its fiduciary status with respect to the plan. See 29 U.S.C. §1002(38). The following explanation of fiduciary duties in the proxy voting context focuses on the investment manager exception.

IB 94-2 states that where a named fiduciary has delegated asset management authority to an investment advisor, as provided for by specific plan provisions and by ERISA, that advisor has the fiduciary responsibility and related liability for making the proxy voting decisions for all shares under its management, unless the named fiduciary, in delegating investment management responsibility, has reserved to itself the right to vote proxies. To the extent that a named fiduciary retains the right to direct the investment manager to vote proxies, the investment manager will not have fiduciary responsibility for voting. Instead the named fiduciary will have full fiduciary responsibility and related liability for voting the proxies. However, to the extent that the named fiduciary does not retain the voting rights, it would be a violation of Section 404(a)(1)(D) if either the trustee or named fiduciary, during the duration of the delegation, made or substantially influenced the investment manager's decision on how to vote any proxy appurtenant to the shares under the investment manager's authority because, under the plan's provisions, they have no such authority. See IB 94-2(1). Moreover, in such circumstances, the delegating trustees lose the liability protection afforded by having delegated the voting authority and become liable for the proxy voting decisions they make or direct the investment manager to make.

Once voting authority has been delegated to the investment manager, IB 94-2 makes clear that the investment manager has the fiduciary responsibility and the related liability for making proxy voting decisions, and therefore must discharge its proxy voting responsibilities in accordance with the duties of loyalty and prudence. The manager cannot relieve itself of fiduciary responsibility and related liability by accepting the directions of another or by delegating the authority to another, and furthermore, would breach its fiduciary responsibility if it permitted a named fiduciary or trustee to vote proxies when voting authority had been assigned to the manager. See IB 94-2(1).[1]

Other Specific Fiduciary Duties Imposed by ERISA With Respect to Proxy Voting

ERISA Section 405(c)(2) provides that where voting authority is

---

1. The Monks letter clarifies that an investment manager may avoid the responsibility and liability for proxy voting if either the plan document so states or, where the plan document is silent, if the investment management contract specifically forbids the investment manager from voting proxies.

delegated to an investment manager consistent with plan provisions and ERISA, the trustee or named fiduciary shall not be liable for an act or omission by the manager in the course of voting proxies. See 29 U.S.C. §1105(c)(2). Nevertheless, DOL has indicated that ERISA's fiduciary standards impose certain specific duties both on the named fiduciary or trustee that delegates voting authority and on the investment manager to which the authority is delegated.

According to DOL, the trustee or named fiduciary shall still be liable for acts or omissions to the extent that the fiduciary violated any of its 404(a)(1) duties (the duty of loyalty, the duty of prudence and the duty to act in accordance with the plan) in (1) establishing or implementing a procedure for delegating management responsibilities, (2) designating a particular investment manager or (3) in continuing the designation. See IB 94-2(1); Avon letter. Furthermore, DOL has construed the fiduciary standards of 404(a)(1) to require the named fiduciary or trustee "to periodically monitor . . . decisions made and actions taken [by investment managers] with regard to proxy voting" IB 94-2(1). Therefore, to ensure compliance with its 404(a)(1) duties, the named fiduciary should retain records, demonstrating its periodic review of the performance of the investment manager's proxy voting, so that a determination can be made whether the investment manager is fulfilling its fiduciary obligations and merits the continuation of its appointment. See id.

Corresponding with the above duties imposed upon named fiduciaries, DOL has interpreted the general fiduciary duties of loyalty and prudence as imposing certain more specific duties on the investment manager delegated with voting authority. Thus, the investment manager must keep accurate records of its proxy voting activities. Those records must be sufficient to enable the named fiduciary to carry out its fiduciary responsibility of periodically reviewing the investment manager's proxy voting and therefore should include not only the investment manager's voting procedures, but also the investment manager's actions in individual situations so that a determination can be made whether the manager is fulfilling his fiduciary obligations and merits the continuation of his appointment. See IB 94-2(1).

Finally, the investment manager has a fiduciary duty to match proxies received with the plan's holdings on a record date, and to make reasonable efforts to guarantee that the proxies for which the manager is responsible are received. While DOL has not specified what constitutes reasonable efforts, the department has recommended that the manager develop specific procedures for reconciling proxies and has indicated that a manager who makes no such effort has violated his fiduciary duties. See Monks letter.

Investment Managers Must Follow Proxy Voting Guidelines to the Extent They Are Consistent With the Fiduciary Standards of Loyalty and Prudence

"[A] named fiduciary's authority to issue statements of investment policy," including those that include proxy voting guidelines, "is inherent in the named fiduciary's authority under the terms of the plan . . . to appoint investment managers." See IB 94-2(2). A statement of investment policy, and any proxy voting guidelines contained therein, is not required by ERISA. See id.; but see *Liss v. Smith,* 991 F.Supp. 278 (S.D.N.Y. 1998). However, once issued by a named fiduciary, such statements and guidelines become part of the "documents and instruments governing the plan" under Section 404(a)(1)(D) and are binding on the investment manager unless contrary to the provisions of ERISA. See IB 94-2(2). In fact, a named fiduciary may condition the appointment of an investment manager on the investment manager agreeing to comply with a statement of investment policy or proxy voting guidelines. See id. However, the contents of proxy voting guidelines should not direct the investment manager how to vote on a particular matter. Rather, the guidelines should contain generally applicable advice for investment managers, such as factors to consider in making particular types of proxy voting decisions. See id.

As discussed earlier, an investment manager to which voting authority has been delegated is clearly bound under ERISA to exercise its authority in accordance with the fiduciary standards of loyalty and prudence. Thus, proxy voting guidelines need only be followed where they are based on and reflect a rigorous analysis founded on the standards of prudence and loyalty. See, e.g., *Herman v. NationsBank,* 126 F.3d 1354 (11th Cir. 1997). In a situation where the investment manager decides that following proxy voting guidelines would conflict with its fiduciary duties of loyalty and prudence and therefore does not follow the guidelines, the investment manager must be able to demonstrate a well-founded rationale for its decision. See DOL Information Letter to I. Lanoff (Sept. 28, 1995) (discussed in the context of trustees bound by pass-through voting provisions in a plan). In such situations, DOL recommends that the investment manager set forth its rationale in a "contemporaneous writing that can be made available to any party challenging" its decision. See id. Where, however, the investment manager can be confident that the views expressed in proxy voting guidelines are consistent with ERISA's standards of prudence and loyalty, the manager is bound by the guidelines in making proxy voting decisions.

With respect to investment managers of pooled investment funds, DOL guidance states that the manager of a pooled fund may issue its own investment policy statement and require all of the investing plans to adopt it as a prerequisite to investment. See IB 94-2(2). In the absence of such a uniform statement for the pooled fund, fund managers must attempt to harmonize the investment policies of the various participating plans, and in the case of conflicts among plan proxy voting policies, fund managers without uniform policies may be required to vote proxies in proportion to the interests held by the various plans. See id.

ERISA's Fiduciary Duties in the Shareholder Activism Context

Introduction

In addition to explaining a fiduciary's duties with regard to the voting of proxies, DOL's 1994 Interpretive Bulletin also included a discussion of shareholder activism generally, providing a list of the types of corporate issues that should be of concern to plan fiduciaries. For the most part, these issues included matters regarding the independence and competence of corporate management, executive compensation, the use of a corporation's assets, its capitalization and debt structure, and other economic and financial matters that any prudent fiduciary would consider. See IB 94-2(3). Also included in the list, however, were matters such as "workplace practices" and "non-financial measures of corporate performance." See id. With regard to this broader corporate governance context, DOL stated that plan fiduciaries must act in accordance with their fiduciary duties and that, as with proxy voting, the appropriate due diligence assessment by plan fiduciaries of whether to engage in shareholder activism is a cost/benefit analysis. See id. Thus, a fiduciary may engage in "activities intended to monitor or communicate with corporate management if the fiduciary expects that such activities are likely to enhance the value of the plan's investment, after taking into account the costs involved." Id.

In the present age of corporate scandal, many avenues of shareholder activism have been identified and pursued by trustees and other plan fiduciaries, including sending letters to corporate directors and officers and holding meetings to express concerns; developing investment responsibility guidelines for advisors and brokers coupled with the threat of divestment; working with SEC to enhance its civil and criminal enforcement capabilities; working with appropriate offices of the U.S. Attorney to seek criminal prosecution of corporate officers in egregious instances; working with insurance companies that underwrite errors and omissions policies on "best practices" procedures that could be followed by a corporation in exchange for reduced insurance premiums; engaging in shareholder litigation; and seeking lead plaintiff status in appropriate shareholder litigation cases. With regard to these last two items, DOL specifically indicated in its 1994 Bulletin that corporate governance activities included participation in shareholder litigation. According to DOL, "[a]ctive monitoring and communication may be carried out . . . by exercising the legal rights of a shareholder." IB 94-2(3).

Seeking Lead Plaintiff Status Can Be Consistent With or Even Required by the Fiduciary Duties of Loyalty and Prudence

Less than a year after DOL issued its 1994 Interpretive Bulletin, Congress passed the federal Private Securities Litigation Reform Act (PSLRA), opening the way for institutional investors to seek lead plaintiff status in securities class action litigation against corporate bad actors. In some of these cases, where an employee benefit plan fiduciary has served as lead plaintiff, defendants have argued that fiduciary rules such as the duties of loyalty and prudence bar these fiduciaries from holding lead plaintiff status. See, e.g., DOL's Amicus Br., *In re Telxon Corporate Securities Litigation,* No. 98 Civ. 2876 (N.D.Ohio) (filed Apr. 23, 1999) (describing defendant's argument); see also *In re Waste Management, Inc. Securities Litigation,* 128 F.Supp. 2d 401 (S.D.Tex. 2000) (describing defendant's argument). This argument is based upon the premise that a fiduciary's duty to act exclusively in the interest of plan participants and beneficiaries would be compromised should the fiduciary become lead plaintiff in a class action, because class action rules require a lead plaintiff to represent the interests of a group other than plan participants and beneficiaries, i.e., the interests of class members. See Fed. R. Civ. P. 23.

This argument has been rejected by both DOL and the courts. In its brief in *In re Telxon Corporate Securities Litigation,* DOL argued that ERISA's prohibitions do not prevent a fiduciary from "taking actions that benefit their charges as well as parties with similar interests." Id. The Department then took the position that not only "is a fiduciary not prohibited from serving as a lead plaintiff, the Secretary believes that a fiduciary has an affirmative duty to determine whether it would be in the interest of the plan participants to do so." Id. The Department grounded this duty in the duty of prudence and that duty's derivation from the common law of trusts that requires a fiduciary to take reasonable steps to realize on claims held in trust. See IIA Scott on Trusts, §177. Noting DOL's position, the court in In re *Waste Management, Inc. Securities Litigation* also rejected the defense theory. See 128 F.Supp. 2d 401.

In determining whether it is in the best interests of plan participants to serve as lead plaintiff, the Department noted that a fiduciary "may have a duty to serve as lead plaintiff where no single individual has sufficient interest or resources to serve in such capacity or where, as a large stakeholder, the fiduciary has an interest in assuring that an alternate class representative with a less substantial stake in the outcome does not unduly compromise the interests of the class in settlement, fail to vigorously prosecute the action, or fail to protect the interests of the class vis a vis its attorneys." DOL's Amicus Br., *In re Telxon Corporate Securities Litigation,* No. 98 Civ. 2876 (N.D.Ohio) (filed Apr. 23, 1999).

Conducting a prudence analysis of whether to seek lead plaintiff status in class action securities litigation is not easy, given that ordinarily an institutional investor will receive the same payment whether or not it serves as lead plaintiff. A good illustration of how to conduct the analysis is the policy developed by the California State Teachers Retirement System (CalSTRS). To aid in its analysis, CalSTERS evaluates whether to seek lead plaintiff status in relation to three objectives: (1) increasing the net monetary value of settlements, (2) increasing the long-term value of CalSTRS shares held in the target company and (3) deterring corporate conduct that undermines the integrity of the financial markets.

Decisions Regarding Shareholder Activism Must Be Consistent With Fiduciary Duties of Loyalty and Prudence

In making shareholder activism decisions, trustees and other plan fiduciaries should keep in mind that ERISA's duty of prudence, by definition, is evaluated in the context of "the circumstances then prevailing." ERISA §404(a)(1)(B). Thus, as circumstances change, the definition of prudence changes, requiring plan fiduciaries to reexamine their role as corporate shareholders and determine whether engaging in shareholder activism is consistent with or required by their fiduciary duties of loyalty and prudence.

Appendix J

AFL-CIO Proxy Voting Guidelines

The following has been excerpted from *AFL-CIO Proxy Voting Guidelines.* This portion of the guidelines is reproduced herein without comment and with the AFL-CIO's permission.

Introduction

The *AFL-CIO Proxy Voting Guidelines* (the Guidelines) have been developed to serve as a guide for Taft-Hartley and union benefit fund trustees in meeting their fiduciary duties as outlined in the Employee Retirement Income Security Act of 1974 (ERISA) and subsequent Department of Labor (DOL) policy statements. Most Taft-Hartley and union benefit fund trustees do not retain proxy voting authority but instead delegate it to another voting fiduciary (whether to an investment manager, custodial bank or other registered investment adviser). Although the Guidelines have been drafted specifically for this circumstance, and thus provide guidance to "the voting fiduciary," plan trustees who decide to vote proxies in-house can also adopt the substance of the Guidelines as their fund's proxy voting policy. In addition, the Guidelines have been created to aid public employee trustees in the review and development of guidelines for their funds.

I. Trustee Policy Statement

This statement sets forth the policy adopted by the plan's fiduciary (hereinafter "the trustees") for the voting of stock proxies. Any investment manager or adviser (hereinafter "the voting fiduciary") who is under contract to acquire, manage or dispose of plan assets, and who is responsible for the voting of common stock, is expected to take these proxy voting guidelines into consideration in making voting decisions. Additionally, the trustees request that the investment manager or adviser provide a copy of the manager's or adviser's own proxy voting guidelines to compare with these Guidelines.

Proxy voting rights have been declared by the Department of Labor to be valuable plan assets and therefore must be exercised in accordance with the fiduciary duties of loyalty and prudence. The Guidelines are intended to reinforce the voting fiduciary's duty to vote proxies loyally and prudently. The Guidelines, therefore, have been carefully crafted to meet the requirements of loyalty and prudence and will be employed by the trustees to monitor the voting fiduciary's proxy voting procedures and decisions.

The duty of loyalty requires that the voting fiduciary exercise proxy voting authority solely in the interests of participants and beneficiaries and for the exclusive purpose of providing plan benefits to participants and beneficiaries. The voting fiduciary is prohibited from subordinating the interest of participants and beneficiaries to unrelated objectives.

The duty of prudence requires that proxy-voting authority be exercised with the care, skill, prudence and diligence that a similarly situated prudent person knowledgeable in such matters would exercise. Thus, in making proxy-voting decisions, issues shall be reviewed case-by-case with final decisions based on the merits of each. The voting fiduciary should seek out information from a variety of sources to determine what is in the long-term economic best interests of plan participants and beneficiaries. A fiduciary who fails to vote without taking reasonable steps under the particular circumstances to ensure that the proxies for which the fiduciary is responsible are received, or casts a vote without considering its impact, or votes arbitrarily with management, would violate this duty.

The duties of loyalty and prudence require the voting fiduciary to make voting decisions consistent with the "economic best interests" of plan participants and beneficiaries; this does not mean that the voting fiduciary is required to maximize short-term gains if such a decision is not consistent with the long-term economic best interest of the participants and beneficiaries.[1] Some issues that may have an impact on the long-term economic best interests of participants and beneficiaries are:

- ◆ Share value and dividend yield.
- ◆ Corporate policies that affect employment security and wage levels of plan participants.
- ◆ Corporate policies that affect local economic development and stability.
- ◆ Corporate policies that affect growth and stability of the overall economy.
- ◆ Corporate responsibility to employees and local communities in which the firm operates.
- ◆ Workplace and environmental safety and health.

The voting fiduciary is expected to weigh certain factors in determining how to vote, consistent with fiduciary obligations and the factors indicated by these Guidelines. When any issue arises in the context of an impending or ongoing change in control of a company, a more rigorous review through a thorough cost/benefit analysis is called for to fulfill the applicable fiduciary standards. In this context, the analysis must consider the long-term impact of the business plans of the competing parties.[2]

II. Reporting Requirements

To demonstrate compliance with fiduciary obligations and so that the trustees may fulfill their fiduciary duty to monitor the voting decisions they have delegated, the voting fiduciary will document and report to the trustees on an annual basis:

A. The proxy voting guidelines considered when casting votes.

B. The action taken on every proxy cast on behalf of the trustees.

C. Written justification for the following votes: (1) Any proxy vote on significant or controversial proposals including, but not limited to, such issues as mergers, restructurings, board of directors issues that may have significant impact on the company; or any proxy vote on controversial or major shareholder proposals; (2) any proxy vote that is not covered by

---

1. Joint Dept. of Labor/Dept. of the Treasury Statement of Pension Investments (January 31, 1989), reprinted in 16 Pens. Rep. (BNA) 215.

2. Ibid.

the Guidelines: or (3) any particular proxy vote that is arguably counter to the Guidelines. In addition, the voting fiduciary should provide, when available, the overall outcome of such votes.

The voting fiduciary shall also fulfill the fiduciary duty to take reasonable steps to ensure that the proxies for all stocks owned as of the record date are actually received and acted upon. The voting fiduciary shall make the procedures used in this regard known to the trustees.

III. Revocation of Voting Authority

At any time whatsoever and without restriction, the trustee or board of trustees may, upon written notice, revoke the voting fiduciary's voting authorization unless the provisions of the plan document prohibit such revocation. Upon the revocation of the voting authorization, unless other arrangements are made, the voting fiduciary will immediately forward proxy material received to the trustee(s) or their designee.

IV. Trustee Positions On Proxy Voting

(For detailed information related to specific positions regarding proxy voting guidelines the reader is referred to AFL-CIO Proxy Voting Guidelines.)

Appendix K

The Asset Allocation Decision

Provided by Bryce Barnes
Quantel Associates, Inc.

Studies have shown that most of the investment return on the assets of a pension fund are determined by the relative portions of the fund allocated to stocks and to bonds. This asset allocation decision is the most important financial decision that the trustees have to make.

Fund assets must be built up to provide for the orderly future payment of the fund liabilities. An important element of the asset allocation decision is the size of the liabilities expected to be payable each year in the future.

Projecting the fund liabilities and the fund assets over a planning horizon of ten years will provide useful insights in the selection of a stock/bond mix.

The fund actuary can develop the year-by-year future contributions, payments and liabilities by making reasonable assumptions for future work patterns and the rates of death, withdrawal and disability. The most important assumption in determining the liabilities (also called the Actuarial Present Value of Accumulated Plan Benefits) each year in the future is the rate of return used to discount benefit payments.

Projecting fund assets also depends on reasonable assumptions about future returns (and the range of returns) for stocks and bonds, as well as the degree to which the stock and bond returns move together. Of these, the rates of return are the most important assumptions.

It is also important that the assumptions for future returns be developed on a *forward-looking* basis. Simply reviewing the returns for the most recent 75, 50 or 25 years and assuming that these long-term averages will hold true for the next ten years is not appropriate.

For the sake of simplicity, we will work through an asset allocation analysis for a pension fund assuming that the only asset classes are stocks and bonds.

Estimating Stock Returns

One formula that can be shown to be useful in explaining the returns on stocks is as follows:

Annual stock return = Capital gains from price changes + Dividend payments

Annual stock return = $(1+g) \times (\text{Original Yield}/\text{Terminal Yield})^{1/N}$
$+ (\text{Original Yield} + \text{Terminal Yield})/2$

g is the dividend growth rate during the period N, Original Yield is the current dividend yield and Terminal Yield is the dividend yield at the end of period N.

Dividend growth rates have shown a fairly steady pattern over the years, staying in a range of 4% to 8% and averaging about 6% per year. The dividend yield on the S&P 500 (as representative of the stock market) was 2% for 2003. Assuming that this dividend yield does not change over the next ten years, the estimated stock return is 8% per year.

The table below shows the estimated stock returns based on various assumptions for dividend growth rates and dividend yields.

Dividend Growth Rate	Original Yield	Terminal Yield	N	Estimated Annual Return
8%	2%	2%	10	10.0%
8	2	6	10	0.8
6	**2**	**2**	**10**	**8.0**
6	2	6	10	−1.0
4	2	2	10	6.0
4	2	6	10	−2.8

Estimating Bond Returns

A large portion (85% or more) of the return on a portfolio of bonds comes from the coupon return. A reasonable estimate of the bond return is the yield on ten-year Treasury Notes as forecasted by the Congressional Budget Office over the next ten years of 5.5%.

Pension Fund Assumptions

ASSET MIX AND RETURN ASSUMPTIONS

Asset Class	Current Asset Allocation	Expected Return	Range of Returns "Low" to "High"
Equities (Stocks)	30%	8.0%	−11.7% to 29.2%
Fixed Income (Bonds)	70%	5.5%	1.8% to 13.0%

High" and "low" were determined such that there is a 10% chance that the returns will be equal to or better than the "high" and a 10% chance that the returns will be equal to or worse than the "low."

CONTRIBUTION, DISBURSEMENT AND ACTUARIAL LIABILITY ASSUMPTIONS

Year	Contributions	Disbursements	Actuarial Present Value of Accumulated Plan Benefits
2004	$5.25	$6.45	$120.00
2005	5.25	6.45	126.00
2006	5.25	6.60	130.50
2007	5.25	6.60	136.50
2008	5.25	6.60	142.50
2009	5.25	6.75	148.50
2010	5.25	6.75	156.00
2011	5.25	6.90	162.00
2012	5.25	6.90	169.50
2013	5.25	7.05	177.00

Provided by the fund actuary. ($ in millions)

Future Fund Growth

Based on these assumptions, the fund may be expected to grow as shown in Exhibit K-1.

If the fund earns the expected rate of return, 6.3%, the Actuarial Present Value of Accumulated Plan Benefits will be 90% funded in 2014, compared to 85% funded in 2004.

Could we improve the funding of our liability by increasing our allocation to stocks?

Based on an asset allocation of 60% stocks and 40% bonds, the fund is expected to grow as shown in Exhibit K-2.

Increasing the allocation to stocks increases the expected fund value after ten years by $12.3 million, from $159.2 million to $171.5 million. This is a desirable benefit. It is expected that the Actuarial Present Value of Accumulated Plan Benefits would be 97% funded in 2014, compared to 85% funded in 2004. At the same time, however, the "Low" fund value decreases by $10.5 million (from $118.6 million to $108.1 million). This decrease represents the additional risk the fund must bear to attempt to achieve the additional return.

The fund's asset allocation should be analyzed once a year in order to provide the trustees with the opportunity to reflect the changing expectations for the capital markets.

Exhibit K-1

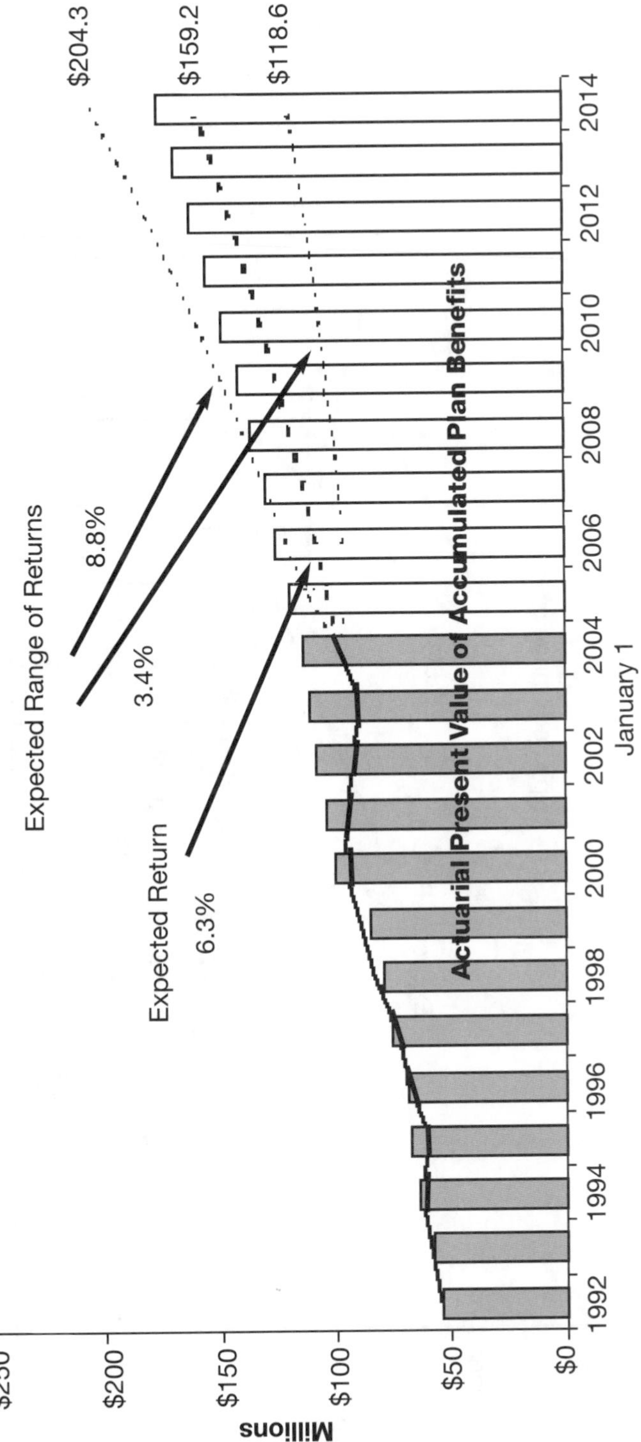
Millions
$250
$200
$150
$100
$50
$0
1992
1994
1996
1998
2000
2002
2004
2006
2008
2010
2012
2014
January 1
Actuarial Present Value of Accumulated Plan Benefits
Expected Range of Returns
8.8%
3.4%
Expected Return
6.3%
$204.3
$159.2
$118.6

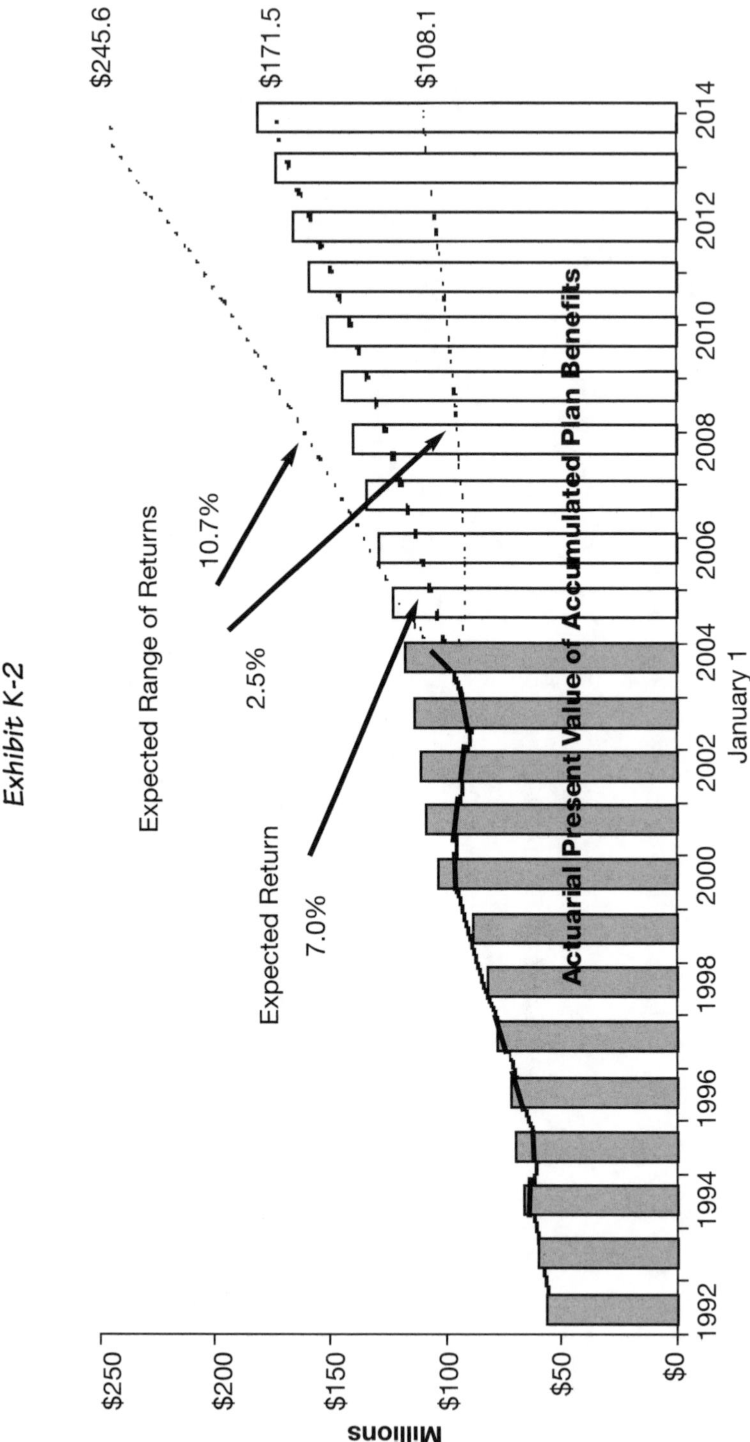

Exhibit K-2
Expected Range of Returns
10.7%
2.5%
Expected Return
7.0%
$245.6
$171.5
$108.1
Actuarial Present Value of Accumulated Plan Benefits
Millions
$250
$200
$150
$100
$50
$0
1992
1994
1996
1998
2000
2002
2004
2006
2008
2010
2012
2014
January 1

Index

A

B

C

D

E

F

G

H

U

W

Y